D0984187

Grattan

Grattan

A Life

R.B. McDOWELL

THE LILLIPUT PRESS
DUBLIN

First published 2001 by
THE LILLIPUT PRESS LTD
62–63 Sitric Road, Arbour Hill,
Dublin 7, Ireland
www.lilliputpress.ie

A CIP record for this title is available from
The British Library.

1 3 5 7 9 10 8 6 4 2

ISBN 1 901866 72 6

Set in Hoefler Text
Printed by MPG Books, Bodmin, Cornwall, England

Contents

Preface

Henry Grattan has been commemorated by half a dozen biographies, three statues (two in Dublin, one in London), a bust in a public garden and a portrait in his old college. He won renown as an early prophet of Irish nationality (more extreme nationalists would place him among the minor prophets) and he is also remembered as a brilliant parliamentary orator in the Irish House of Commons and at Westminster. Parliamentary oratory is an ephemeral genre. Only dryasdusts are enthralled by debates on dead issues. Still it is fair to say that some of Grattan's speeches (or fragments of them) deserve to survive as literature. Infused with fire and drive, imaginative, often tinged with emotion, they are a rhetorical expression of the Romantic movement. But it would be a mistake to dismiss Grattan as *Vox et praeterea nihil*. A man of firm conviction, upright and generous, he brought a strong intellect to bear on a wide range of political and social issues. His opinions reflect the outlook of an ardent, intelligent and independent Whig in an era of vehement controversy, great wars and rapid change.

Acknowledgments

I am most grateful to my sometime colleague Dr David Dickson for his encouragement and valuable advice, based on extensive knowledge of the period, and to Mr Brendan Barrington for his acute and sustained criticism. I must also thank Dr Elizabethanne Boran and Mrs Valerie Jobling for unstinted help, and Ms Mary Clark, the Dublin city archivist, for information about the Chantrey statue of Grattan. I am indebted to the Olive, Countess Fitzwilliam Wentworth settlement trustees and to the Earl of Rosse for permission to use material, and to the staffs of the libraries and repositories in which I have worked for their ready assistance.

Grattan

I

Family Background and Education

Henry Grattan was born in 1746 of Irish Protestant professional and landed stock. Irish Protestants, especially those who belonged to the established church, believed that the social and political framework in which they were so satisfactorily placed, holding most of the land and almost monopolizing professional life, was securely riveted and that their political predominance was unchallengeable. In retrospect, fatal weaknesses can be detected in their position. Ireland included some of the poorer regions in the British Isles and poverty could breed social tensions. The bulk of the population (perhaps three quarters) were Catholic and almost half the Protestants were Presbyterian dissenters; fortunately, from the establishment point of view, the latter were concentrated in the north, well away from Dublin which on the surface seemed an Anglican city. Although the Catholics were severely penalized and the Presbyterians suffered from some disabilities, neither were debarred from making money and there were many comfortably off Catholic or Presbyterian large farmers and businessmen. Thus there was developing in Ireland what contemporary social philosophy deplored, a serious separation between property and political power. Finally, Irish Protestants in general were well aware that they owed their preservation in the seventeenth century to British intervention and that British power continued to be the essential guarantee of their safety and status. Consequently they had to permit Great Britain to exercise a measure of political control over Ireland which might work against the economic interests of the country.

But all these portents of danger and difficulty were discounted by the politically and socially privileged in Ireland, who affirmed their confidence in their country's economic future by conspicuous consumption. The Catholic problem did not seriously disturb them. It was bound to diminish as intelligent, go-ahead Catholics conformed to the established church; the lower orders would probably follow their superiors and in any event their opinions and prejudices were of little significance. A united, prospering Ireland could look forward to an equitable adjustment of Anglo-Irish relations. The outlook of the Irish ruling world was one of robust and unquestioning self-assurance which reflected the sensible confidence of European man in an enlightened age, the landed classes' conviction that they had the right and duty to lead the country, and the Irish Protestants' belief that, sharing the British heritage, they represented in Ireland sound religion, civilization and political liberty.

Both Henry Grattan's parents, his father James Grattan and his mother Mary Marlay, belonged to families whose fortunes had waxed with the advance of Protestantism and English power in Ireland. The first of Henry Grattan's ancestors to play a fairly conspicuous part in Irish history was Sir William Brereton, a Tudor civil servant and soldier. Brereton arrived in Ireland in 1534 in command of a force dispatched to suppress O'Connor, the Cavanaghs and 'the Toles'. He negotiated with O'Neill and for a few months shortly before his death was in charge of the Irish administration as Lord Justice.[1] His grandson, Edward, was in Elizabeth's reign provost-marshal of Connaught; Edward's great-grand-daughter, Grisel Brereton, a County Cavan coheiress, married in 1669 the Rev. Patrick Grattan. Patrick Grattan had entered Trinity College, Dublin, in 1655 during the period of Puritan predominance. In June 1660, along with a number of other members of the College, he signed a loyal Address to the Chancellor of the University, the Duke of Ormonde, recently returned from exile, violently denouncing the provost and fellows intruded during the Commonwealth. In 1661 he was himself elected a fellow and ten years later, presumably anxious to escape from the obligation to remain celibate, which was a condition of holding a fellowship, he left Trinity for one of the better college livings, Cappage in the diocese of Derry, obtaining about the same time a prebend in St Patrick's Cathedral. Head of a close-knit and affectionate family, a squire through his wife as well as a parson, with a rectory in County Fermanagh and a substantial house, Belcamp, in north County Dublin, Patrick Grattan was a successful, and probably happy, professional man. As a comfortably situated Irish Protestant he went through a few dangerous and humiliating years when during the reign of James II the Catholics controlled the Irish administration. The parish church in Cappagh was defaced by the Jacobites[2] but Patrick Grattan seems to have lived quietly in County Dublin, entering a son in Trinity in July 1689 just six months before the fellows and students were expelled and the College turned into a barracks. But after the battles of the Boyne and Aughrim the Jacobite and Catholic cause rapidly declined in Ireland and the Irish Protestants soon found themselves in secure possession of political and social power.

Patrick had seven sons, all of whom had successful if unspectacular careers. The eldest son, Henry of Garryross, inherited the Cavan property. It was not a large estate – it may have amounted to about a thousand acres – but Henry was indubitably a landed gentleman. He married Bridget Fleming, the daughter of another County Cavan landlord, and, a small, spirited man, he was active in county affairs, being a militia captain, Justice of the Peace, and High Sheriff.[3] Three of his brothers, John, Robert and William, became clergymen. William, a sometime fellow of Trinity, succeeded his father in Cappagh, John was well beneficed, and Robert, a prebendary of St Patrick's, was a friend of Swift, who appreciated the large, well-stocked Belcamp cellars. Another brother, Charles, having resigned his Trinity fellowship because he was unwilling to take Orders, read for the Bar and finally became headmaster of one of the royal schools, Enniskillen. His brother James, a medical man, became president of the recently founded King and Queen's College of Physicians in Ireland, and the seventh brother, Richard, who pursued a non-professional career, prospered as a merchant and was elected Lord Mayor of Dublin and knighted.

Henry's son and heir, James Grattan, inspired perhaps by his uncle's achievements, was not content to be an influential County Cavan squire. Having graduated from Trinity in 1731 he was called to the Bar in 1739 and a year later married Mary Marlay, a daughter of Thomas Marlay, a justice of the King's Bench.[4] Thomas Marlay was the most distinguished member of an interesting and successful professional family. In the middle of the seventeenth century Sir John Marlay, a rich hostman and colliery owner, was five times Mayor of Newcastle-on-Tyne. A strong Church of England man and a fervent royalist, he led the defence of the town against the Scots and the parliamentarians. When the royalist cause was defeated, having lost much of his fortune, he went into penurious exile. But while fearless he was not altogether *sans reproche*. Towards the close of the 1650s (most inopportunely as it turned out) he began to supply the Commonwealth Secret Service with information about royalist activities. Charles II, sympathetic to human frailties, forgave his lapse, but his reputation was shadowed; and though in 1660 he put himself at the head of the Newcastle royalists and was returned to the Cavalier Parliament, his fortunes were not restored. (His Whig descendants, unaware of his secret dealings with the Commonwealth authorities, saw his fate as exemplifying royal ingratitude.)[5]

Sir John's son, Anthony, though he probably retained some property in Newcastle, was after the Restoration for about twenty years a captain of foot in Ireland, where he married Elizabeth Morgan of Sligo, whose family had flourished during the Commonwealth.[6] Two of Anthony's sons, Thomas and George, graduated from Trinity. George took Orders, married a sister of Thomas Connoly, the Speaker of the Irish House of Commons, and became Bishop of Dromore. He founded a landed family, the Marlays of Belvedere, and one of his daughters married David La Touche, a member of a great banking and landed family. Thomas went to the Bar and became an MP, Solicitor-General, Attorney-General, a puisne judge and finally in 1741 Chief Justice of the King's Bench. Facets of his character are reflected in two surviving literary fragments, a pungent charge to the Dublin grand jury in which en passant he castigates Dr Charles Lucas, the city demagogue, and a cheerful if clumsy attempt at light verse.[7] Three of the Chief Justice's sons, Anthony, Thomas and

Richard, were professionally successful. Anthony, a barrister, was commissioner of appeals and MP.[8] Thomas joined the army and during the Seven Years War took part in the defence of Minorca and distinguished himself at the Battle of Wilhelmstahl, being commended by Prince Ferdinand of Brunswick who presented him with a snuff-box. He retired shortly after the war ended, as a lieutenant-colonel, leaving his regiment, the 23 Foot, in a highly efficient condition. He settled down in Celbridge and on his death in 1784 he left his property to his five children by Mary Doyle, 'now living in the house with me', appointing his nephew Henry and his brother Richard, by then a bishop, as their guardians.[9] Richard, who took Orders, was an amiable, witty and worldly ecclesiastic, famous for 'the best little dinners and the best company in Dublin'. He was a member of Johnson's Literary Club and Edmund Burke, his college contemporary, had a high opinion of 'his abilities ... his honour and integrity and the wonderful kindness, sociability and pleasureness of his nature'. Shortly after ordination he became rector of Drumballyroney in his uncle's diocese of Dromore, and Lord Townshend, a good-natured if pugnacious Viceroy, made Marlay one of his chaplains and secured for him a valuable preferment. An unfair but not altogether unperceptive anti-Castle satirist wrote:

> Concerning that long-legged, strolling abbé,
> Who oft with his Excellency holds a long parlay,
> The vain, self-sufficient, satirical M–rl–y,
> In whose composition so closely combine,
> The light poetaster and the flimsy divine!
> This famous half-laic we frequently meet
> Linked fast to some Red-coat patrolling the street;
> And oft in the nook of the theatre stuck,
> May see with his glass, the canonical Buck;
> A vagrant renowed for his gibes and his Sneers,
> A friend of low wits, and companion of Peers,
> In public caressed by the great and small,
> But secretly censured and hated by all.[10]

In 1787 he became Bishop of Clonfert in spite of, rather than because of, his nephew's political distinction; and, according to Henry Grattan, 'he enlarged his dinners and lost his fire ... he had lords and ladies to his table – people of fashion – foolish men and foolish women'.[11]

In marrying a daughter of Mr Justice Marlay James Grattan allied himself to a vigorous, successful family, and he himself had abundant ambition and drive. Four years after his marriage he became one of the small band of Irish KCs; in 1756 he was elected Recorder of Dublin and in 1758 he came forward as a parliamentary candidate for the city at a by-election consequent on the death of one of the sitting MPs.

A Dublin city election could be a strenuous contest. The electorate was by eighteenth-century standards large and well informed. It was composed of the freeholders and freemen, the freedom of the city being customarily obtained through admission to the freedom of one of the twenty-five guilds. The result was that while a number of landed gentle-men and professional men were enfranchised, most of the electors were businessmen – merchants, shopkeepers and small manufacturers. Since Dublin was the seat of the viceregal court and parliament, had several newspapers and a number of bookshops and coffee-houses, a Dublin cit-izen could easily pick up scraps of political gossip and glance at newspa-pers and pamphlets. Political awareness was stimulated by the workings of the municipal constitution. Dublin had a bicameral governing body, with an upper house composed of the Lord Mayor and twenty-four alder-men, and a lower house, the Commons, comprising ninety-six represen-tatives of the guilds. Since aldermen were co-opted for life and common-council men elected for a three-year term, disputes between the two assemblies were accentuated by the realization that they represented the classic conflict between oligarchy and democracy.

James Grattan's candidature was almost certainly favoured by a major-ity of the aldermen and he expected an unopposed return. But another candidate came forward, James Dunn, a merchant and alderman, who at the beginning of the contest resigned his alderman's gown. Grattan con-ducted a highly idiosyncratic campaign. It was customary for a parlia-mentary candidate to publish in the newspapers a short address expressing willingness to serve and soliciting support. But Grattan had more to say than would 'fall within the compass' of a conventional address and said it in two short pamphlets (distributed gratis in coffee-houses). He began by declaring he was not going to canvass electors individually, though he was ready to meet them collectively in their guild-halls. A personal approach might, if the elector refused his vote, 'create personal dislikes', or it might end in the candidate making improper promises. Grattan made it clear that he thought it would be unfair to his family to incur heavy election expenses. The Irish public, he believed, was utterly unreasonable, expecting candidates to spend lavishly on entertainment and then professing to be deeply shocked when MPs tried to reimburse themselves by seeking places and pensions. He also had not much time for municipal democracy – he concluded his second address by telling the electors that most of them would be better employed in minding their own business concerns instead of indulging in 'political bustle'. Grattan saw himself as a moderate Whig, his political hero, surprisingly, being Lord Falkland, the hesitant, tolerant royalist, who was killed early in the Civil War. But though he campaigned vigorously he was narrowly defeated, obtaining 1292 votes to Dunn's 1362.[12]

Two years later Grattan, it was rumoured, intervened behind the scenes in municipal politics by helping Sir Charles Burton, who had sat for the city from 1749, to draft the Dublin constitutional reform bill which reached the statute book in 1760. This measure may have been devised with the aim of preserving the aldermen's power by making some concessions to the Commons. It certainly considerably increased the popular assembly's status and role in city government and seems to have stimulated its political awareness, with the result that after 1760 the city (or at least the Commons), following the example of London, from time to time thrust itself into national politics, by emphatically expressing the opinion of the citizens on major issues – a development which was to influence the career of the Recorder's distinguished son.[13]

At the close of 1760 James Grattan had a second opportunity of securing a Dublin seat, the death of George II in October 1760 being followed by a general election. On this occasion Grattan allied himself with Sir Charles Burton and they received the support of a majority of the aldermen, but there were four other candidates – Dunn, fighting to retain his seat, Perceval Hunt and David La Touche, who belonged to well-established Dublin families, and, sensationally at the last moment, Charles Lucas. Lucas had had an extraordinary career. A Dublin apothecary, he had in the forties attacked the aldermen for infringing the rights of the commons, going on to denounce political corruption and the subordination of the Irish Parliament to Westminster. In 1749, threatened with a prosecution for seditious libel, he went into exile. He acquired a medical doctorate at Leyden and took a conspicuous part in an acrimonious scientific controversy over the value of Spa waters. In March 1760, returning to Dublin six weeks before the opening of the poll, he plunged into the fray with zest and skill, canvassing and pamphleteering. As a pamphleteer he was prolix, hyperbolical and excitable. As a speaker he probably displayed the same faults. Henry Grattan, years later presumably re-echoing his father, the Recorder, recalled that when Lucas 'rose to speak in parliament he had not a friend in the house; when he sat down he had spoken so ill that he had not an enemy'.[14] Lucas in fact turned out to be an effective and respected MP, and he certainly knew his way round the Dublin guild-halls. His nose for an abuse, his telling hits at men in power, his pluck, his perseverance, his fervent Protestantism and his reverence for conventional Whig wisdom, made him a hero in the eyes of city liberals and advanced Whigs. He was in some ways an absurd figure, over-vehement and vulgar in style and manner. Strangely enough the statue which his admirers shortly after his death placed in the Royal Exchange suggests his weaknesses. It is that rare phenomenon, a monument to an eighteenth-century politician deficient in dignity. Lucas is shown as slightly theatrical and definitely didactic – a family physician deferentially advising the electors rather than thundering in the senate. But he was a portent. He was the first public man to advocate what struck many contemporaries as radical solutions for a range of problems, to build up a strong middle-class backing and to appreciate the power of the press. Lucas attacked Grattan for defending the aldermen's usurpations, and the vigour with which he campaigned compelled Grattan, who did not relish giving pledges to the electorate, to promise to support a bill limiting the duration of the Irish Parliament. However, Grattan had the satisfaction of being on this occasion victorious, the successful candidates after thirteen days polling being Grattan with 1569 votes and Lucas with 1302. James Grattan soon settled down to being a hard-working MP, but his membership of the House was to be tragically short.

James Grattan, though professionally and politically ambitious, was a man of strong family feeling. By his wife, Mary Marlay, he had five children, four daughters and a son, Henry, the subject of this biography.[15] Henry, the only son and the future head of the family, was given a very good education by contemporary standards. To start with he was sent to the grammar school in Ship Street, conducted by the Rev. Thomas Ball, which was reputedly the best school in Dublin – there was at this time no outstanding Irish public school and only a few Irish boys were sent to school in England. Thomas Ball, from the number of his pupils who went on to the university, seems to have been a very able headmaster. But great headmasters rarely arouse universal admiration. About this time Jeremy Bentham, a Westminster boy, decided that his headmaster, the majestic and learned Dr Markham, was a pompous and complacent snob, and Henry Grattan soon clashed with the awesome Dr Ball. Ball contemptuously dismissed Grattan's translation of a well-known passage in Lucian and had him whipped for producing it. Grattan resented the punishment and appealed to his father. Father and son had been reading Lucian together and the translation was in fact the father's work. The Recorder was a quick-tempered man and Henry was at once withdrawn from the Ship Street school and sent to a school in Abbey Street conducted by the Rev. John Campbell, an ecclesiastical lawyer, who was later to become vicar-general of Tuam.[16] It may be added that the new school was more conveniently situated, the Grattan family having moved in 1756 from Fishamble Street to Stafford Street.

By a fortunate chance we know the curriculum which Henry Grattan would have followed as a schoolboy. In 1759, five years before he entered Trinity, the College indicated to Irish headmasters its admission requirements. Candidates for entrance were expected to have read St Luke's Gospel and the Acts in Greek, selected works of a dozen Latin and half-a-dozen Greek authors, selected colloquia of Erasmus and Castalio's 'Dialogues' (a seventeenth-century work in Latin dealing with faith, free will and predestination – daunting, it may be thought, to the most precocious schoolboy). It was recommended that schoolmasters should impress on their pupils the importance of quantity and measure and should exercise them continuously in rhetoric, Latin verse composition and translation (literal translations – what a later generation would call keys – being strictly forbidden). Attention was to be paid to classical mythology, history and antiquities and to English composition and punctuation. The 'young gentlemen' should be taught the use of globes and learn to draw maps, and their parents should make sure they knew the common rules of arithmetic.[17] This course, it is fair to say, illustrates the airy way in which university dons may expect schools to attain unrealistic standards (incidentally the use of literal translations was not unknown amongst undergraduates), and the weaker candidates for entrance probably relied on intelligent anticipation rather than intensive study of all the recommended books. But Henry Grattan's undergraduate performance showed that he was diligent and well grounded, so it may be presumed that when he left school he was acquainted with a fairly wide range of Latin and Greek authors, and possessed a knowledge of classical history and a sense of style.

On leaving school Grattan entered Trinity as a fellow-commoner, a category of undergraduate which fell in academic rank and social status between the *fili nobili* and the pensioners who comprised the majority of the undergraduate body. About a quarter of Grattan's contemporaries were fellow-commoners. They paid double fees, wore a more ornate gown than a pensioner and were able to abbreviate the BA course by half a year. Trinity College when Grattan entered was a compact institution, comprising of three moderate-sized squares, the west front, 'without question the noblest of its kind in Europe ... carrying with it more the appearance of a royal mansion than a number of collegiate cells',[18] having just been completed. Trinity, with a small governing body (the provost and seven senior fellows) functioning in a capital city under the gaze of parliament and parents, was an efficient educational institution. It had a well-planned, comprehensive undergraduate course, comprising mathematics, classics and logic. Arrangements were made to ensure that undergraduates worked steadily and systematically. They were obliged to attend 'morning lectures', held in the Examination Hall, in Greek and

Science (i.e. mathematics or logic), and each tutor regularly assembled his pupils in his chambers for catechetical instruction. At the beginning of each term there was an examination on the work of the previous term. The undergraduates of each year were grouped in divisions of about forty and orally examined by two examiners. A number of these examinations had to be passed before a BA could be obtained, and amongst the better men there was keen competition for the premiums and certificates awarded in each division. Grattan twice won a premium (that is to say was the best man in his division) and secured many 'judgements' of *valde bene*. He seems to have been a hard-working and somewhat intense undergraduate. His contemporaries remembered him as small, angular and sharp-featured with a long chin, and because of his curious walk – his heels never seemed to touch the ground – he was nicknamed 'the elastic body'.[19]

It would be pleasant to believe that Grattan and some of his eminent parliamentary contemporaries benefited from the foundation in 1724 of a chair of oratory and history (later divided into two chairs) with the aim of providing teaching for those of bachelor standing still in residence (and presumably preparing for the Church or the Bar) and for 'young noblemen and others of rank and fortune'. The professor would not only lecture on the rules of eloquence but conduct practical classes in which the scholars would learn to speak 'either from reflection or short notes'. 'All means', it was stated, 'must be used to oblige them to dispose their thoughts into clear and exact method – No Facundia without lucidus ordo'.[20] The Professor of Oratory when Grattan was an undergraduate was Thomas Leland, an authority on Demosthenes who seems to have taken his duties seriously, giving lectures on oratory in which he emphasized that true eloquence was the offspring of 'the most noble, most amiable and virtuous qualities of our nature'.[21] But the lectures were intended for men of BA standing remaining on the books, and it is unlikely that undergraduates, who were bound to consider themselves over-burdened, would attend. Still, the existence of the chair was an official acknowledgement of the importance of rhetoric as a subject deserving systematic study.

From time to time groups of undergraduates anxious to prepare themselves for professional and public life, or revelling in argument, founded small, short-lived debating clubs. In these, it was said, 'Poetry and eloquence court our acquaintance, history discloses its variegated pages to our perusal, improvement is naturally blended with delight'.[22] Grattan may have belonged to one of these clubs but there is no evidence that he did. In a very important respect Grattan was home educated. As the son of an MP who sat for one of the few constituencies with a large electorate, he perforce heard in the family circle plenty of candid talk not only on the major political issues of the day but about the forces which influence public opinion and the practicalities of dealing with demanding constituents. According to Grattan's son and biographer, Henry Grattan, Junior, his father and grandfather squabbled over political issues and Henry, having expressed his admiration for the principles of Charles Lucas, was disinherited by his father insofar as it was in the latter's power to do so.[23] This is probably an over-dramatization by a fervent nineteenth-century liberal of a not unusual family situation. James Grattan, vigorous, ambitious and successful, but depressed by bad health, may well have been irritated by his son's lack of purpose. Henry was undeniably doing well in college, but his only positive aim – and it was not very positive – was 'courting the muse'. He does not seem to have been greatly interested in politics (Irish politics at this time was not enthralling), but when there is tension in the family any remark can spark off an acrimonious argument. In 1787 Grattan named his elder son James, which suggests that in retrospect at least he regarded his father with respect and perhaps affection.

About the time Grattan began his college career his father's health was giving trouble. Richard Marlay, with characteristic optimism, thought that his brother-in-law's ailments were largely imaginary. 'His disorder', he wrote, 'was chiefly in his spirit from which most of his complaints proceed'. But in 1766, the year before Grattan graduated, his father, after a short illness, 'in the greatest agony of body and in the extremist distraction of mind, unexpectantly and impatiently died'.[24] A month before his death he had executed a will in which he bequeathed to each of his daughters a substantial sum and the residue of his property to his wife.[25] Henry was not named in the will, the sole executor being a

Dublin merchant (who, it may be assumed, would be more competent than an undergraduate). Although the absence of his son's name is noticeable, the Recorder's will was very reasonable. Under his mother's marriage settlement Henry was ultimately to inherit his father's real property, so understandably James Grattan used the resources at his disposal to provide for his daughters. After his mother's death in 1768 Henry came into possession of two small estates (one in Cavan, the other in Westmeath) together with some pieces of city property, the Westmeath lands and the city properties having descended to James from Sir Richard, the Lord Mayor. Henry Grattan's income from these sources seems to have amounted to over five hundred pounds per annum (and may have been slightly supplemented by fees after his call to the Bar).[26]

Grattan took his BA in the summer of 1767, and the following eight years, a period which terminated with his election to the Irish House of Commons, formed a useful preparatory stage in his career. At the time he took his degree he does not seem to have made up his mind about his future. But he had inherited a tradition of professional achievement, and with his family background the obvious thing to do was to read for the Bar. As his uncle, Richard Marlay, sensibly told him, the study of the law 'though laborious and disagreeable was not as painful as idleness, which persons of the brightest talents are apt to fall into unless they are stimulated by ambition or prompted by vanity or compelled by poverty to exert their faculties. Since you have not ambition or vanity sufficient to rouse you, the narrowness of your fortune will I hope help you into wealth and eminence.'

To become a member of the Irish Bar it was necessary to spend eight terms at an English Inn of Court, so in the spring of 1767 Grattan entered the Middle Temple as a student and by the end of the year had taken up residence in London. Soon he sustained two shattering blows. His sister Katherine, to whom he was deeply attached, after a short illness, 'languished with resigned patience and expired with the utmost fortitude'[27]; and just about a year later in November 1768 his mother, for whom he had both affection and admiration, suddenly died. These loses intensified the pensive melancholy with which at this time he viewed existence.

While he was an undergraduate and a law student, Grattan, a serious, introspective youth, poured out his opinions and emotions in lengthy, highly mannered letters to intimate friends. He was already a very conscious stylist and every sentence in his ostensibly casual correspondence is pondered and polished. In later days his letters continue to be highly polished and often contain striking idiosyncratic turns of phrase. But they are usually short and pointed: Grattan by then clearly believed in conserving intellectual energy. The long letters of his youth are, as might be expected, the epistles of a man of feeling. Sensibility is strongly in evidence, melancholy predominates. At nineteen he laments that 'a fluctuation of sentiment, a listless indolence and the reflections which arise from it make a chaos of my mind'. At twenty-one he is sure that the best of life is past, 'the rapture of boyhood, the bold ambitions of youth are fled; and the time when he felt intensely 'with every book I read and every line I wrote' was past, only to be remembered with gentle melancholy.

At twenty-five he longed for 'the return of those days of boyhood when hope was more sanguine and the credulity of human happiness not disproved by experience'. 'Relish and opportunity', he reflected, 'never go together, and it is the punishment of man to mourne the want of the latter or to be insensible to it.' 'A contrarity of dispositions and habits', he sighed, 'obliges me often to forfeit society or sacrifice to it.' He brooded over his own weaknesses, 'melancholy and contemplative but not studious', 'now intoxicated with company, now saddening in solitude'. He saw himself as prone to 'despondency, regret, apathy and the rest of the deadly train'.[28] In short, he could be diagnosed as suffering from ennui, that fashionable disease.

It is easy to ridicule a young man's self-portrait. Though Grattan paints himself as depressed, lonely and despairing, he had a wide circle of interesting and attached friends and was actively engaged in sampling the delights of London and Dublin. Indeed when his closest friend, William Broome, reciprocated by dwelling on his own despondency, Grattan brusquely took him to task. 'If your mind languishes,' he wrote, 'apply to reason – if your body, to a physician.'[29] Broome, a young cavalry officer, was the friend to whom Grattan felt he could 'unbosom myself with safety for he will not deride my wayward nature' and on whose 'stability' he relied when unsure of himself.[30] Their passionate friendship was based on intellectual interests – Broome, a good classicist, was keen on literature and Grattan was eager to guide his reading – and on emotional affinities – while Grattan was an unenthusiastic law student, Broome was exasperated by the tedium of military life.[31] In the end his temper snapped, and in 1773, having been 'beyond all question disrespectful to his superior officer in the face of the private men', he was court-martialled. But 'the parties having agreed upon the differences which had arisen between them', the court martial merely administered a reprimand. This decision shocked the Lord Lieutenant. He considered that Broome's conduct constituted a grave breach of discipline and he directed the court to reassemble and reconsider its verdict. Sharply reminded of the standards which should be observed, the court sentenced Broome to be cashiered. But stunned by the Lord Lieutenant's rebuke, it failed to state the sentence in the proper form. The matter having been referred to the King, he decided that, though Broome deserved to be cashiered, in the circumstances he should be simply 'superceded'.[32] For some years Grattan played with the seductive idea of retiring with Broome, 'who possesses an absolute domination over my heart', to a hermitage, 'some country lodging where we may enjoy one anothers society, poverty and independency'.[33] But soon after Broome left the army Grattan started his political career and the friendship lost its intensity. Nevertheless they remained lifelong friends, Broome settling in the country south of Dublin after he married. He shared Grattan's enthusiasm for the Volunteer movement and, in an emergency, his purse.[34]

Once Grattan acquired a *métier* – politics – he threw off his indolence and displayed abundant self-confidence, determination, energy and industry. But his early self-analysis throws into relief enduring characteristics which had a significant influence on his later career. Not very robust and extremely sensitive – nervy, it might be said – for most of his life he needed and craved long spells of solitude. In solitude he could relax, enjoy nature, recharge his intellectual and emotional batteries, meditate and, while strolling, shape a speech, forging apophthegms and epigrams. From his early twenties he had a succession of rural retreats, and from his late thirties his permanent residence, in which he rejoiced, was set in an isolated corner on the fringe of the Wicklow hills. Indeed, Grattan was temperamentally scarcely fitted to be a conventional politician. Intensely concerned with the public weal, he nevertheless cut himself off for long stretches of time from political bustle and gossip. Though he had many friends, he tended to be abstracted and aloof, and while willing to co-operate heartily with those who shared his principles, he always set a high – some would say excessively high – value on independence, consciously distancing himself from the mass of men engaged in public life. His attitude was in many ways that of an artist, with his great orations for his oeuvre, rather than that of a mundane man-of-affairs.

In spite of his pessimism, loneliness and low spirits Grattan found plenty to interest and amuse him during the London years. He had chambers in the Temple, high up, but 'comfortable and cheerful' and spacious enough to accommodate a guest. From time to time he took holidays in the country, staying near Windsor, in the midst of a country 'covered with nature without the least interval of art', and near Southampton where he had to put up with a garrulous landlady.[35] He paid visits to Ireland, and in the autumn of 1771 with John Tydd, later an Irish MP, he went to France, visiting Paris and the Loire valley. In old age he said he met only two Frenchmen, an abbé and a swindler, but his correspondence shows this to have been a conversational exaggeration.[36] He frequented coffee-houses, went to Ranelagh, 'a splendid, tiresome amusement', was a theatre-goer and attended parliamentary debates (which he preferred to the theatre). He had a number of friends, including Robert Day, a future Justice of the King's Bench, with whom he met Oliver Goldsmith; Walter Birmingham from County Roscommon, who years later was to marry Grattan's sister-in-law; John Fitzgibbon, the future Lord Chancellor, whom Grattan thought at this time 'good humoured and sensible' (he was to revise this opinion);[37] and Jonathan Lovett, later 'the father and grand patron of the independent interest in Bucks', who was to be created a baronet.[38] Probably his most stimulating companion at this time was Hugh Boyd, who had been his contemporary at Dr Ball's school and Trinity. Boyd, the son of a well-known Irish MP, after considering joining the army, entered the Middle Temple and in 1776 was called to the English Bar. A man of charm and lively intellect, devoted to chess and claret, 'born to animate, fascinate and delight', Boyd soon built up a large social circle, drawn from the intellectual and the fashionable world. He was also interested in politics and acquired some reputation as a pamphleteer on the popular side – writing with such verve that his admirers believed he might be Junius. He fascinated Grattan, and for a time the young men were said to be inseparable. But Boyd had a weakness: he was a reckless spender on himself and others – 'his extensive sensibility tempted him to acts of benevolence which his scanty and precarious income was ill suited to supply'. He soon ran through his inheritance, and marriage to a Jamaica heiress only temporarily restored his fortunes. The tactics with which he met his difficulties are illustrated by the story of his first (and probably last) meeting with William Pitt. One evening Boyd met the future prime minister, then an inexperienced youth, leaving the House of Commons. His comments on the debate so impressed Pitt that he was delighted to continue the conversation over dinner. When the time came to split the bill Boyd discovered that by an unfortunate mischance he had left his purse at home. Ten years or so earlier Boyd's attitude to his debts exasperated Grattan who, though capable of generosity, was careful. 'I have', he wrote in 1770, 'received a letter from Boyd, he talks of Jamaican remittances, of the difficulty of payment, complains of disappointments and with much coyness unravells his system of imposition. I have not yet answered his letter, and have not sought to impede the natural exertion of the law. To law he may open the stores which have been shut to friendship and must do that justice to the insensibility of the former, which he refused to the disinterested warmth of the latter.' The friendship cooled rapidly and Grattan and Boyd seem to have lost touch long before the latter left England to become editor of the first English newspaper in India.[39]

Grattan's obligations as a law student were not very taxing. The minimum requirements for gaining credit at an Inn of Court were eating dinners and paying fees. A student who was anxious to succeed at the Bar would in addition attend the courts and read hard. About a year after he entered the Temple Grattan announced that he had a plan for 'breaking the neck of the law by a course of sustained reading'. It is doubtful if he persisted. Certainly three years later he declared he had now turned from poetry to law – 'instead of Pope and Milton's numbers I repeat in solitude Coke's distinctions in matters of fee-simple and constructions of perplexing feudal statutes' – and shortly after being called to the Bar he mournfully decided he would have to spend a vacation reading law.[40] But he read widely in other directions. He admitted that he only read enough theology 'to make me singular, not deep'; in poetry he admired Milton, Pope ('correct and sublime'), and Gray ('the first poet of the age'). He attempted poetry himself, but his muse 'proved a slatten and stumbles frequently', though he managed to turn out neat couplets.[41] In history he read Clarendon ('instructive but ill-arranged and partial'), Burnt ('vain'), Hume (the only author who 'deserves the title of an English historian'), and Bolingbroke, whose confident rapidity gave him 'sometimes a real and sometimes a seeming superiority' over his opponents, a useful lesson for a future parliamentary debater. At the end of the sixties he began to study contemporary history by reading the parliamentary debates, 'performances which abound with natural reasoning and easy expression but which cannot pretend to precision or eloquence'.[42]

During his stay in London Grattan's interest in politics was steadily developing. His time at the Temple coincided with a critical and eventful period in British politics. The collapse of Chatham's ministry was rapidly followed by the Middlesex Elections – productive of constitutional argument and rioting – the Boston Tea-Party, and tussles between the House of Commons, striving to prevent the publication of parliamentary debates, and the press. To some it seemed that the constitutional rights of Englishmen were imperilled; to others it was clear that faction and mobs were threatening to render government impossible. What was undeniable was a greatly heightened interest in politics and a rapid growth of the politically-minded public – a public which provided avid readers for Junius' suspicions and sneers.

From 1768 Grattan was assiduously attending the debates in both Houses at Westminster. An intent listener and a keen partisan, if he could not speak he could criticize and in private planned speeches and rehearsed them when strolling in Windsor forest. Of the speakers who attracted his attention he was rather dismissive of North and George

Grenville. The former spoke 'in a manner impetuous not rapid, full of cant not melody, and deserved the eulogium of a fervent speaker not a great one'; the latter was 'peevish and wrangling, and provoked those whom he could not defeat'. Grattan was pleased by his fellow Trinity graduate Isaac Barré, whose 'boldness and fury were engaging and his military character sustained with warmth and sense'. He was full of admiration for Burke, 'boundless in knowledge, instantaneous in his apprehensions and abundant in his language', though Grattan did not fail to notice that Burke suffered from 'the want of energy, the want of grace and the want of elegance in his manner'.[43] But the speaker who fascinated Grattan and who was to be an exemplar throughout his career, was Chatham, 'aloof from the sordid occurrences of life' and 'like the spinning of a cannon ball alive with fatal, unapproachable activity'. 'Great subjects, great empires, great characters, effulgent ideas and classical illustrations formed the materials of his speeches.' A loyal subject but no courtier, a commanding figure in debate, 'superior to the knack of oratory', but 'reaching the point by the flashing of his mind, which like those of his eyes were felt but could not be followed', Chatham was both a great war minister, inspired by a sense of Britain's imperial destiny, and an avowed tribune of the people. 'With one hand', Grattan wrote with admiration, 'he smote the house of Bourbon and wielded in the other the democracy of England.'[44]

Back in Ireland for a vacation Grattan attended the Irish House of Commons and was impressed by Flood ('fine'), and Hussey Burgh ('promising') and less favourably by John Scott, the Attorney-General. Scott, a vigorous debater, quick to employ a rollicking good humour, was dismissed by Grattan as 'indecent, not convivial'. (It was unfortunate he did not get to know Scott, who devoted considerable attention to a technique Grattan never mastered, voice production – try, Scott told himself, to soften and mellow the voice by throwing it back more into the throat.) Comparing the Irish and British Houses of Commons, Grattan pronounced that British MPs were 'not so deficient in language and not so overrun with vulgarity' as their Irish equivalents.[45] At twenty-five he was a political pessimist, very critical of the administration both in Great Britain and Ireland but without much confidence in its opponents.[46] In

Great Britain, a parliament purchased by the Crown together with the army were opposed to 'an undisciplined, a divided and a luxurious nation'. In Ireland the government's critics were divided, the people and parliament lacked perseverance and Irish good nature, 'the social disposition of our country as well as its moderation', ruled out the possibility of a sustained attack on the administration.

Through his brother-in-law Gervais Parker Bushe, who became an MP in 1768, Grattan met a number of Irish politicians including Flood, the most formidable debater in the Irish House of Commons. With a good grasp of constitutional law, polished and precise, Flood aimed at carrying conviction by hard, undecorated argument. Supremely confident in his own intellectual superiority and rectitude, he diffused an intimidating sense of mental and moral supremacy. He was not, he once observed, ashamed to compliment himself, 'for honest fame is the just reward of an upright heart'. To men of his own generation Flood seemed arrogant and overbearing – even a eulogist was constrained to admit that Flood's mind 'was not of the texture to be controlled by inferior spirits'.[47] But to a young and docile admirer Flood, well connected, well informed, an accomplished classicist, a man of the world and an experienced politician, could be an entertaining and stimulating companion. In the early seventies Grattan found him to be 'the most easy and best tempered man in the world, as well as the most sensible' and they collaborated in turning out political squibs against the Irish administration and took part together in amateur theatricals, Grattan playing MacDuff to Flood's Macbeth. It was a relationship which did not survive Grattan's election to the House of Commons.[48]

About the time he met Flood, Grattan was introduced by his uncle Richard to another well-known parliamentary figure, William Gerard Hamilton, the early patron of Burke and a friend of Dr Johnson. Hamilton, as a brilliant young man, made a few striking speeches shortly after he took his seat at Westminster, and some years later, when Chief Secretary, he gave the Irish House a taste of his quality. But proud and diffident, he was quickly discouraged by setbacks and became and remained for thirty years a silent back-bencher at Westminster, reserving much of his energy for conversation. Hamilton had the ambition to produce a

Clausewitzian study of the theory and practice of parliamentary debate, and ten years after his death his *Parliamentary Logic* appeared, a work in which, according to the shocked Jeremy Bentham, 'profligacy can be seen stark naked'. In fact it consists of a series of maxims, many of which are truisms neatly expressed: 'it is candid to allow weight to an objection, but not prudent, unless you can afterwards answer it'; 'take into view not only the measures of the session, but of the same man in other sessions'; 'watch the manner of stating the question at the outset: there is generally the fraud'; 'ff, as is likely, someone makes a ridiculous and unteneable assertion, it is easy to treat this as the argument of all who have spoken'; 'sooth, flatter and alarm' and remember that 'in most arguments people say too much'.[49] According to Richard Marlay, who knew him well, Hamilton when relaxed was lively and pleasant,[50] and Grattan must have found him an instructive if cynical commentator on politics – he resembled Flood in being a frondeur detached from the mainstream of official life. In one respect he may have strongly influenced Grattan's oratorical technique. Hamilton's renowned maiden speech was said to be 'full of antitheses but those antitheses were full of argument'.[51] Grattan certainly employed, indeed over-employed, antitheses, sometimes effectively, sometimes producing a strained, over-violent contrast.

Grattan obviously believed that parliamentary oratory, as both a practical technique and an aesthetic experience, deserved serious critical study. In this he was typical of his age. Eighteenth-century politics comprehended many activities – cabinet councils, closeting, caballing, keeping the administrative machine functioning, balancing interests, attending to personal objectives. But for active politicians and the politically-minded public alike, British political life attained its most concentrated, intense, impressive and dramatic form in a great parliamentary debate. The British Parliament held an unique position in Europe. While in other countries representative assemblies, the estates, had waned in power or ceased to meet, the British Parliament – and to a more limited and less conspicuous extent the Irish Parliament – had waxed ever stronger. It was at Westminster that momentous issues were finally decided, often after a glorious gladiatorial debating contest. To those who attended or read a report of a debate it was not only a matter of

coming to a decision on rational and emotional grounds but of apprais-
ing as connoisseurs the outstanding speeches as works of art to be judged
by long-established standards. Their education had consisted largely of
studying keenly or sullenly a selection of Greek and Roman authors. The
destinies of the ancient world had been swayed by arms and eloquence,
and the rules of rhetoric had received as much attention as the art of war.
It was natural then for British politicians to compare their distinguished
contemporaries to Cicero and Demosthenes and to notice how closely
they conformed to the precepts laid down by Quintilian or in *De oratore*.
'Substitute Tully and Demosthenes in the place of Horace and Vergil',
Chatham wrote to his nephew when he was about to leave Cambridge,
'and arm yourself with all the variety of manner, copiousness and beauty
of diction, nobleness and magnificence of ideas of the Roman consul, and
render the power of eloquence complete by the irresistible torrent of
vehement argumentation, the close and formidable reasoning and depth
and fortitude of mind of the Grecian statesman'.[52] But by the beginning
of the next century a well-known MP wrote with no little complacency
that though 'the great orators of antiquity had given the happiest direction to British genius', British public speaking was much superior to that
of Greece or Rome. In Great Britain to win a reputation for eloquence in
Parliament or at the Bar a man had to combine 'a consummate acquaintance with all that belongs to real life' with a style derived from a careful
study of 'the great models of taste and genius', and above all must be able
to trust 'to the spontaneous or rather accidental effusions of the divine
spirit of man, struck out like fire when its energies are excited by the
great duties which God has imposed upon the few whom he has eminently qualified for the direction and government of mankind'.[53] Of
course only the gifted and audacious could risk embarking on a consciously eloquent and elaborate oration. Failure would be so marked and
absurd. The great majority of peers and MPs, realizing they did not possess 'the gift of the gab',[54] were content to express their opinions in common-sense, matter-of-fact terms, anticipating the almost conversational
style adopted by later generations conditioned by committee work rather
than the classics. But to Grattan and his contemporaries a speech by a
politician of acknowledged oratorical powers was a contribution to liter-

24

ature. Dr Johnson deigned to apply his critical powers to one of Grattan's striking metaphors and the collected speeches of the great masters of parliamentary eloquence found a place on the shelves of many gentlemen's libraries.

II

A Meteoric Rise

At the beginning of 1772 Grattan arrived back in Dublin, after being held up at Holyhead for some days by adverse winds, to begin his career at the Irish Bar, to which he was called in Hilary term. For the next few years he had reasonable grounds for the despondency by which he had been frequently afflicted in the past. A keen versifier, he realized he had not the makings of an outstanding poet; a landed gentleman, he was irritated by tenants and baffled by his agent's accounts. He was depressed by Dublin. 'Its social life', he wrote, 'gives no pleasure and can give no rest'; the theatre was in decline and politics irritating and boring. As for the Bar of which he was now a member, 'the Four Courts', he pronounced, 'are of all places the most disagreeable, the lawyers in general are an ardent rather than an eloquent society", and he sadly realized that if he were going to practise at the Bar he would have to spend his vacations reading law. His quixotic returning of half his fee to a defeated client suggests that he lacked the readiness to ignore past mistakes characteristic of a Stryver, and he appears to have been an almost briefless barrister (or as it was politely put in later days, his merits were overlooked).[2]

Life nevertheless had its compensations. He had a decent income for a young unmarried barrister – and he agreed with Broome that, as Grattan put it, 'marriage is an artificial not a natural institution, and I imagine women too frail a bark for so long and so tempestuous a voyage as that of life'.[3] He could afford a house in Dorset Street, at least two servants, a man and a maid – the man costing about twenty-seven pounds a year – and a horse.[4] An absentee landlord, he enjoyed excursions to the country, visiting his uncle at Celbridge and staying in Enniskerry in Wicklow. He had Broome and other friends available and he was a member of a political club, composed of critics of the government, which met in Granby Row under the presidency of his uncle Richard's close friend the Earl of Charlemont. But between Grattan and many of his political friends and acquaintances there loomed the great gulf which separated MPs from the general public. Without a parliamentary seat Grattan was on approximately the same political level as his quondam friend Boyd, and it would not be easy for him to secure one. His family did not possess county influence or borough patronage and he was not a successful professional man with a reputation and financial resources. Moreover he was a man with principles which he would not sacrifice for a seat (though he may have reflected sadly that he was unlikely to be put to that test for some time). Understandably he was not a candidate at the General Election of 1774 and there seemed little hope of his starting a serious political career in the near future.

Unexpectedly he was suddenly offered a seat on honourable terms by Lord Charlemont. Charlemont combined intense cultural awareness with an acute political conscience. He was a man of letters, a discriminating and extravagant patron of the arts, a venturesome traveller and a pioneer of the Greek revival. In politics he was an austere Whig, concerned to protect the rights of the subject and the rights of Ireland. 'Freedom', he was convinced, 'could only be maintained by constant alertness'. It was essential, he felt, that at least one man of property and rank should keep himself 'wholy independent and as a standard to which upon an emergency men might resort whether actuated by real public principle, or, as is too often the case, by motives of an interested nature, which last species, base as it is, may however often be rendered useful to the public cause'.[5] Very conscious, then, that many men in public life were deficient in moral stamina, Charlemont took his responsibilities as a borough proprietor very seriously. He controlled the parliamentary borough from which he took his title, a small town in County Armagh with an electorate of thirteen, and as a eulogist expressed it, he required from the MPs he returned 'only talents and virtue'.[6] In 1775 the MPs for Charlemont were Francis Caulfeild (a brother of the earl) and Sir Annesley Stewart (a relation), both of whom shared Charlemont's principles (though it was rumoured that Francis Caulfeild, an easygoing army officer who was hard-up, was thinking of offering his support to the administration).[7] In October 1775 at the beginning of the new Irish parliamentary session, Francis Caulfeild left Chester for Dublin in a packet boat which was wrecked in a great storm that swept the Irish Sea. He was among those drowned, and his brother had to find a new member for his borough with the session already under way. Charlemont had met Henry Grattan in Dublin, and, it was said, in London, where the earl was highly impressed by a young law student 'whose conversation was lively without being pert' and who was able to discuss intelligently French and Italian literature.[8] Grattan's personality and principles appealed to Charlemont; he offered him the vacant seat and so Grattan was able in his thirtieth year to enter the Irish House of Commons.

The House of Commons which Grattan entered was composed of 300 members, returned by 150 two-member constituencies. The electoral machinery was complex and, towards the close of the century, was strongly denounced by rationally-minded reformers as anachronistic and absurd. In the counties the franchise was exercised by the forty-shilling freeholders. In many boroughs the MPs were returned by the corporation, in others by the corporation and freemen, in some by the householders, in a few (the manor boroughs) by the freeholders. The great majority of MPs, including Grattan, sat for a borough with a small electorate controlled by one or two patrons. It is impossible to say how many MPs were returned for close boroughs. As has been pointed out, a comparatively large electorate did not necessarily guarantee that the borough would always remain open, and on the other hand an unexpected contest could occur in what seemed to be a securely closed borough. At least 180 and possibly over 200 MPs might be considered as sitting for close constituencies. But however defective the Irish House of Commons was as a representative body, it was 'a high mettled'[9] (Grattan's term) assembly of Irish gentlemen, which reflected the outlook of the dominant classes in Irish society and was not unresponsive to intelligent public opinion.

A proud, historic assembly, the Irish Parliament was subjected to two humiliating restrictions on its powers: British parliamentary supremacy – the British Parliament claimed that it had the right to legislate for Ireland – and Poynings' Law. Unlike British parliamentary supremacy, which was seldom exercised and which for considerable periods could be forgotten, Poynings' Law continuously interfered offensively with the Irish legislative process. It provided that Irish bills were to be initiated by the Irish council and transmitted to England. If the King and his council approved of an Irish bill, it was returned to Ireland to be placed before the Irish Parliament, which could only pass or reject it. During the seventeenth century a procedure was evolved which gave the Irish Parliament an opportunity to exercise legislative initiative. The 'heads of a bill' (i.e. a draft bill), having passed through the normal parliamentary stages in either House, would be presented to the Lord Lieutenant. It was then open to the Irish council either to transmit the heads (perhaps amended) to England as technically a bill originating with itself, or to ignore it. The British council could quash it or return it, unamended or amended, to Ireland to be accepted or rejected by the Irish Parliament. It was exasperating for Irish MPs to see their handiwork 'cushioned' or corrected (sometimes rather pedantically). But it was hard to challenge the legality of the procedure – the heads of a bill after all had no legal status – and so resentment simmered.

The dignity and pride of the Irish Parliament was enhanced by the surroundings in which it met. While the British Parliament was functioning in ramshackle quarters under the shadow of Westminster Abbey, the Irish Parliament was splendidly housed. In 1727 it had decided to replace its undistinguished building in College Green with a new Parliament House designed by Pearce. The new House, with a sweeping, pillared front facing College Green, was graceful, impressive and well planned, having 'an uncommon beauty, order and convenience'. The Commons Chamber was an octennial room, with rows of green cloth-covered seats, rising one above the other, 'so that each member could be seen and heard from every part'. In the centre hung a great gilt-covered chandelier, which, with the candelabra on either side of each of the four entrances to the Chamber, gave a splendid light. Round the room ran a gallery with rows of seats, holding about three hundred spectators. On occasion the front row, being filled with ladies, presented 'a very splendid and agreeable spectacle'.[10] MPs were conscious they were debating under the critical gaze of the public. Sometimes they were annoyed by interruptions; sometimes they were encouraged by the presence of sympathizers – when the galleries were closed for some weeks in 1795 the opposition was definitely discouraged and some years earlier Grattan was accused of trying to introduce a number of his 'admirers' into the gallery (ignoring the rule that an MP could invite only two visitors).[11]

By the time he took his seat in the House Grattan had decided on the principles and developed the prejudices which were, with some slight changes, to determine his attitude to the issues confronting him over the next forty years. His consistency may be commended as reflecting a determination 'to prove all things and hold fast to what is good'; an unfriendly critic might add that Grattan, being for almost the whole of his political career ostentatiously independent, was to a great extent spared the strain of reconciling his ideals with the practicalities of public life. Grattan was emphatically a Whig, a convinced believer in civil and religious liberty who venerated the British Constitution (on which the Irish was modelled) for its success in combining liberty with order, for its fusion of the best elements in monarchy, aristocracy and democracy and for its marvellous system of checks and balances. Of course almost all conventional politicians were by now Whigs. But for Grattan the genuine English Whigs were those active in politics, for instance the Rockinghamites and later the devoted followers of Charles James Fox, who were continually concerned to prevent the constitutional balance being tilted in favour of the executive. In Ireland he sympathized with those MPs who since the beginning of the reign of George III had come to constitute an opposition. This section of the House varied in numbers and was very loosely organized – many critics of the government prided themselves on being independent – but generally speaking it seemed to Grattan that it was endeavouring to apply sound Whig principles to political problems.[12]

30

At the time Grattan became interested in politics it seemed to many opposition Whigs that the ministers of the Crown, operating on a wide front which comprehended both the American Colonies and Ireland, were insidiously endeavouring to extend their powers and were displaying a brusque contempt for the rights of the subject. It was a critical situation, which, according to Chatham, called for a great effort by 'the whole Irish nation, all true English Whigs, the whole nation of America'[13] to check arbitrary action and to destroy the sources of parliamentary corruption. In Ireland the apprehensions of the government's critics were intensified by the realization that the Irish administration was subordinated to that of Great Britain. Irish MPs and their constituents were proud of the ties which linked the two kingdoms, but they were aware that there could be conflicts of interest which might arise between them and that when this occurred the Irish administration would not find it easy to maintain whole-heartedly the Irish point of view. Men in office saw things in a different light. Ministers and civil servants believed they were endeavouring, with inadequate resources and in face of unfair and ill-informed criticism, to keep 'the whole executive government of a vast empire functioning'. It was a mistake, a distinguished Irish office-holder who was a friend of Grattan pointed out, to assume that the supporters of the government were united only by corruption. There must, he declared, always be in public life two types of men – the administrator and the critic.[14]

At this point it may be asked did Grattan ever contemplate becoming a minister, once the influence of the Crown was 'reduced by lawful and quiet measures to its ancient size'.[15] The answer is almost certainly no. Admittedly, during the last quarter of the eighteenth century many of the government's critics saw themselves as offering an alternative administration (though they were disappointed by the exceptional longevity of the administrations headed by North and Pitt). But Grattan, adhering to the old tradition of Court and Country, seems to have regarded himself as destined to be a permanent independent, a constant, alert observer of the administration, delivering commendation and censure as circumstances demanded. No doubt there had to be ministers and some administrative posts had to be filled by MPs. There were too, Grattan acknowledged, placemen who would 'run great risks and make great sac-rifices' for principle.[16] But even if reform deprived the servants of the Crown of many of the fruits of office, there would still be the corrupting pleasure of power, and a strongly principled man who wished to bring an unfettered mind to bear on public issues, would be wise to remain an independent member.

Nevertheless, he had to accept that it was desirable that power should be in the right hands, and after 1782 Grattan was on more than one occa-sion delighted to see men whom he approved of in office and was pre-pared to take part in their councils and to defend them in debate. But he would not take office himself, recoiling sharply from becoming a place-man. This fastidiousness could be condemned as selfish or cranky. To a routine-bound, burdened office-holder Grattan must have appeared inexperienced, irresponsible, elevating fault-finding into a cardinal virtue and urging with magnificent and misleading eloquence ill-considered panaceas. Grattan could have retorted that he was performing his con-stitutional duties as an MP. Temperamentally he would not have adapted easily to the constraints and compromises incident to official life and the enjoyment of power. 'What a slavery is office', he remarked in old age, 'to be subject to the whims of those above you and the persecution of those beneath you'.[17] Though he could on occasion formulate and expound a policy, he was instinctively a critic rather than a constructive administra-tor, and by long habit he became better fitted for attack than defence. Possibly in a later age he would have found his *métier* as the editor of a quality newspaper or a school-masterish magazine, loftily applying severe moral standards, sharply rebuking absurdity and vulgarity and judiciously distributing praise and blame although on the whole unsympathetic to those in a position to take decisive action.

Grattan was able to express his views in the House of Commons vig-orously and vividly. As a prelude to his parliamentary career he had striven by observation, reading and practice to polish and perfect his ora-torical powers. In rhetoric, as in the other arts, the style is the man, and Grattan's style reflected important facets of his personality – his fiery and exhaustible energy, his poetic sensibility, his passionate adherence to his opinions and his high moral fervour. His speeches were not characterized by the 'negligent grandeur' which marked Fox's contributions to debate. His major speeches were carefully prepared. Brooding in solitude, Grattan would seek the apposite word, forge the stinging phrase and hammer phrases into telling sentences, abounding in epigram and aphorism. He excelled in antithesis, with harsh brilliance contrasting performance with promise, past with present, the ideal with its realization; and now and then he would illuminate his argument with a striking simile or metaphor. His speeches are not lacking in form and coherence, but for his total effect he relied less on skilfully deployed argument than on fusillades of pointed phrases. Though he respected reason, his own intense feelings – his pity, indignation, anger, affection – impelled him to play at length on the emotions of his hearers. Elegance, brilliance, sparkle, drive, vehemence were his hallmarks as a speaker. Though Grattan may have escaped being intoxicated by his own verbosity, his attitude to political issues was to some extent conditioned by his oratorical technique. He excelled in denunciation and declamation; in relentless and scarifying attack and glowing and generous eulogy. Balanced exposition was not his forte, and he rarely descended to the systematic explanation of complex detail. His style accentuated his opinions and often camouflaged the moderation and common sense which played a considerable part in dictating his reactions to events. How far his language precisely expressed his thoughts or to what extent his thinking was moulded and coloured by his oratorical technique, it is impossible to say.

As a parliamentary debater he was handicapped rather than helped by his appearance and voice. He was of below-average height, with a crooked, distorted figure. His head, it was said, was placed on the back of his neck and his projecting chin formed 'an obtruse angle with his breast'. His voice was shrill and unharmonious and his gestures awkward and uncouth; his action, it was said, 'was violent to a degree of fury, which is felt because it is genuine enthusiasm'.[18] In compensation for these defects he had the confidence of a man who from the moment he took his seat was bound to be at home in the House. Grattan was one of the many members who were hereditary MPs. His father, grandfather and an uncle had all been members and in 1775 three of his relations were MPs: his brother-in-law, Bushe, and his cousins James Cuffe and David La

Touche. Bushe had begun his political career in opposition, but in 1771 he had crossed the House and been appointed a commissioner of accounts. But it was soon said that 'he seldom opens his mouth and when he does the recollection of his former patriotism choakes him'.[19] Early in the session of 1775–6 he began in debate to criticize the government and as a result at the close of the session he was dismissed. In 1784 he returned to office as a revenue commissioner and shortly before his death published a pioneering essay on Irish demography. James Cuffe, 'a latitudinarian in politics', noted for his affability, managed to be a placeman for many years and to secure a peerage. He was a friend of Grattan and acted as his second when a duel with Flood impended in 1783.[20] David La Touche, a great banker, was a genuine independent who sometimes supported the government. His wife, Grattan's cousin, was an accomplished woman and Grattan greatly enjoyed visiting her house in Stephen's Green, 'always the scene of elegant and refined society'.[21]

Grattan was not only at home in the House but he was very fortunate in the time of his arrival. Eight months before he took his seat the outbreak of the American War of Independence inaugurated a momentous and dramatic era in British and Irish politics. Then two months before he entered the House, Henry Flood, who had for so long dominated debate, tired of opposition, accepted the office of Vice-Treasurer, and, finding himself committed to the defence of decisions he deplored, was condemned to stretches of sullen silence. Finally, Grattan's entry into politics coincided with a development in 'communication' which provided MPs with an opportunity of becoming well known to an audience far beyond the walls of the Parliament House. In Great Britain vigorous battles had been fought between the newspaper and periodical press, which was becoming aware of its power and potentialities, and Parliament, anxious to protect its privacy, over the publication of parliamentary debates. By the early 1770s Parliament had yielded and regular reporting and publication were permitted. In Ireland the press paid little attention to parliamentary proceedings until the beginning of the seventies. Irish editors were either unenterprising or timid, or thought the debates would not interest their readers. However, in 1766 Sir James Caldwell, a Fermanagh country gentleman, published the debates of the

Irish House of Commons for the session 1763–4, dedicating the work to William Pitt, whom he venerated as a statesman and orator. The *Gentleman's Magazine* commended the work, in which a number of topics of interest to both Great Britain and Ireland were discussed with 'great spirit, perspicuity and precision'.[22] Some years later, in 1771, the newly founded *Hibernian Journal* followed suit and soon the reports of debates in the House of Commons became a regular and conspicuous feature in Irish newspapers (very occasionally a House of Lords debate was reported, but the Lords was a less busy and less exciting House).

The debates supplied a growing public demand for political information, and when important debates took place simultaneously at Westminster and College Green almost all other news was squeezed out of the Irish papers. The London papers, it should be said, gave a fair amount of space to Irish parliamentary proceedings. The Irish public was so interested in what was going on in the House of Commons and so appreciative of parliamentary speeches which were 'equal to the most boasted models of Greece and Rome and more proper to be put into the hands of our youth to form them for shining hereafter in any situation in life',[23] that two Dublin publishers were encouraged to produce in 1782 the first volume of a series of seventeen volumes of the *Irish Parliamentary Register*, covering the Commons debates from 1781 to 1797. Irish MPs seem to have been gratified by seeing themselves in print and Parliament did not attempt to prevent the publication of its debates, although from time to time complaints were voiced in the House about misreporting – the impetuous George Ogle on one occasion 'looking at the gallery cautioned gentlemen to be more just in the representation of his words'[24] – and a few editors and proprietors were rebuked at the Bar for printing a misleading report.

The reports have their faults. Caldwell frankly explained that immediately after attending a debate he wrote out the speeches from memory. Other reporters made notes during the debate from which afterwards they tried to reconstruct what had been said. Speeches were published *in oratio obliqua* and are usually much compressed. Even the more distinguished members, while given plenty of space, were rarely reported in full. Flood complained that a person who reported his speeches for the press 'preserved only the flowers but left the roots to wither'.[25] Naturally reporters could lose interest in the proceedings or, if the debate went on late, would go home. It is said that some of the best speeches of Curran, a devastating debater who appreciated the value of having the last word, went unreported, being made at the close of a long debate.[26] If a member after a debate assisted a reporter, he could improve his speech by slipping in a phrase or two he had forgotten to deliver. Still, the reports afforded the assiduous reader a knowledge of issues and arguments, some training in dialectics, intellectual and at times aesthetic stimulus, and an insight into the workings of the political machine. In short, they played an essential part in preparing the middle classes for the responsibilities they were going to assume in the age of reform. Some politicians were bound to benefit disproportionately from the reporting for the general public of parliamentary debates. Those whose approach was bold, broad, vivid, energetic and on occasion amusing were bound to appeal to the reporters and were read throughout the country. Those who were informative but heavy, whose forte lay in presenting a case to their fellow members, or who shone in committee, were likely to be comparatively poorly reported.

Grattan took his seat on 11 November 1775 and within a few days made his maiden speech on a measure which faintly foreshadowed the coming age of administrative reform. Two of the three Vice-Treasurers, Lord Clare and Welbore Ellis, had presented a petition to the House pointing out that owing to the adoption of a new method of paying certain premiums the income they derived from a percentage of all monies issuing from the Treasury was much reduced. The petition asked for compensation. The third Vice-Treasurer, Flood, had not signed the petition (although it was maliciously noted that 'he would receive equal benefit' should his colleagues succeed). When the House took the petition into consideration a couple of public-spirited MPs, Sir Lucius O'Brien and Sir Hercules Langrishe, suggested that the best course would be to pay each Vice-Treasurer £3500 per annum in lieu of all fees, a plan which would ultimately lead to 'a manifest saving'. Grattan opposed this scheme, arguing that the House was being asked at a time of economic distress to vote salaries to absentee sinecurists. Would the Vice-Treasurers resign, he asked, if their petition was ignored? 'All this', he asserted, 'was attempted by an administration which professed candour and preached up management, though now it appears candour is a cheat and management a peculation'. Some members may have thought Grattan's tone presumptuous and priggish for a young man who had just entered the House, but in the opinion of a journalist it created a great impression; being a reply to arguments which had been advanced in the course of the debate 'it could not be a studied speech but was a spontaneous flow of natural eloquence'.[27]

Having found his feet, Grattan did not long remain silent. In the middle of February he severely attacked a government measure legalizing the dispatch of a military force of four thousand men from Ireland as 'delusive' since it omitted to state that the troops were to be paid by Great Britain. A week later he crossed swords with Flood. Flood, defending the embargo imposed on Irish trade with the rebellious colonies, had asserted that 'necessity would often justify what it could not legalize'. 'Necessity', Grattan retorted, 'was the tyrant's plea'; and, not shirking from plunging into legal technicalities, he 'quoted many cases of embargoes and proclamations which plainly showed the illegality of the present one'.[28] On 2 April he supported an address to the King drawing his attention to the great increase in the national debt since 1763 and requesting him to consider 'the reduction of our establishments'.[29] The address was rejected, and immediately after the prorogation Bushe was dismissed from office. On 4 April Grattan revealed his own assessment of the position he had attained in the House within four months of taking his seat, by moving an amendment to the end-of-session address to the Lord Lieutenant. The amendment, which was twice as long as the address, complained that four money bills had been altered in Great Britain ('an insult to the dignity and bounty of this nation'), referred to the increased powers granted to revenue officers, and attacked the embargo and the dispatch of troops to America, 'involving this country in a civil and unnatural war'. Finally, it emphatically dwelt on the deplorable mismanagement of the national finances, 'the pernicious practice of running into debt – the opposition to every project of retrenchment'. It is scarcely necessary to add that this provocative amendment was rejected.[30]

The final, clinching section of Grattan's lengthy amendment drew attention to Ireland's fiscal problems, on which the government's critics concentrated during the next session (1777–8). The eighteenth century was allergic to taxation and neurotic over national indebtedness. In the eighteenth century Irish government expenditure relative to the national income was at a low level. Direct taxation scarcely existed. Most of the indirect taxation (customs and excise duties) fell on luxuries (assuming that beer, wine and spirits are not necessities). Income tax was undreamed of, there was not a land tax nor, it may be added, a poor rate. Irishmen in fact by modern standards were lightly taxed. But from early in the reign of George III the cost of government was creeping up, new taxes had to be imposed, and when the yield of taxation was below what had been forecast, debt increased. The public was alarmed and it was widely believed that the cost of running the governmental machine was grossly swollen by easygoing extravagance combined with the avid desire of the Irish administration to have as much patronage as possible at its disposal for corrupt purposes. Defenders of the administration, especially men in office, argued that in a country with a growing population and an expanding economy, administrative costs were bound to rise; that Ireland had to bear a share of imperial defence; that the value of money had fallen since the seventeenth century; that the pension list included many deserving cases; and finally that for one important and rapidly rising source of expenditure, bounties, the House of Commons was directly responsible. This debate over expenditure and taxation which went on to the close of the century was to some extent conducted on unrealistic lines. The administration's critics tended to dismiss out of hand all the reasons for increased expenditure advanced by the government and to dwell with undue emphasis on the marginal costs of patronage, ignoring the useful functions performed by the administrative machine. Government supporters (averting their eyes from patronage considerations) defended the machinery *in toto* – sinecures, fees, vested interests, all the anomalies which had accumulated while the Irish administration was slowly and haphazardly being built up.

Grattan was not at his happiest in dealing with financial issues. Dry, humdrum detail was not the stuff of high oratory, complex variables did not lend themselves to antithesis, and while attacks on taxation would win the applause of the out-of-doors public, financial debates could baffle and dismay the newspaper reporters. However, Grattan was determined to do his duty or (as a harsh critic would say) could not abstain from debate. He managed to amass a fair amount of information on financial and commercial questions, persuading John Forbes, whom he characterized as 'enlightened, sensible, laborious and useful', to supply him with material.[31] From time to time he made an effective enough speech on an economic issue, but the reports show that when he came up against John Foster, who was continually studying Irish economic problems, or Parnell, Foster's successor as Chancellor of the Exchequer, or Monck Mason or Beresford, experienced administrators familiar with the intricacies of the revenue laws, he frequently was beaten on points. But viewing retrenchment as part of the great battle for 'pure' government, he often infused dry financial detail with high moral fervour and wit. During the session of 1777–8 the administration's opponents in the House of Commons initiated a series of financial debates with the aim of forcing or shaming the government into committing itself to retrenchment. As a rich country gentleman put it, 'whoever governs this country cheapest is the best Lord Lieutenant for it'.[32] Grattan played a conspicuous part in these debates, his theme being that the 'prodigality' of the government, 'not extravagance but riot', 'not plunder but insatiability', was leading to national bankruptcy and ruin, 'without the sword, plague, pestilance or famine'.[33] At the beginning of the session he proposed three resolutions which he thought 'should unite all men and give offence to no man', affirming that expenditure had risen fast between 1773 and 1777, and shortly afterwards he proposed that the expenses of the government should be drastically reduced. In mid-session he moved an address to the Crown calling for economy, painting a grim picture of conditions in Ireland, 'a country with so great a part of it uninhabited, without a market and with a perpetual interdict on her trade'. The minister who is 'confined to the metropolis will be apt to think everything is opulent because in private life most things are extravagant, but look to the extremities of the nation and there contemplate the poverty, the wretchedness, the despondancy of a plundered nation'. Hussey Burgh, replying for the government, regretted that Grattan, owing to 'his splendid imagination', could not discuss the country's economic circumstances 'without colouring them a little too highly', and the Address was rejected. A month later Grattan mounted an attack on the pension list, 'a public prostitution' employed to influence Parliament and 'composed of men who have no interest in any one community under Heaven or of men superannuated in the trade of public servility'.[34] At the end of the session, when the government was compelled to ask permission to improve the terms of the loan it was endeavouring to raise, Grattan enthusiastically supported the suggestion (which the House rejected) that part of the interest should be met by a tax on places and pensions. 'Those ought to refund who have grown rich while their riches have beggared the state, and caused those wants which they called exigencies but he called crimes.'[35] In spite of these hard words, however, he supported the government's proposal to offer a higher rate of interest.

When attacking the Irish administration for fiscal misconduct Grattan did not fail to point out that it was under the control of a British ministry which from 'phrenzy' had involved the whole empire in a general calamity; which 'had conquered the constitution and lost the empire'.[36] When on 27 March following the outbreak of war with France, an Address to the Crown pledging Ireland's support was being debated, Grattan tried to insert an amendment requesting the King to choose 'wiser' advisers. 'As I love England', he declared, 'I do not wish to sacrifice England either to a foreign enemy or a domestic ministry.'[37] But even Barry Yelverton thought the amendment 'improper' and it was rejected. A few days later, when a vote of £300,000 towards the expenses of the war was being discussed, Grattan suggested it should be halved. 'Give me leave', he declared 'to say somewhat confidentially the servants of government are criminal to expect we should not hesitate a little about making such grants which are necessary by the crimes of the English ministry.' He considered that the other half of the grant could be voted if circumstances demanded it. This suggestion laid him open to an ironical counter-attack by Hussey Burgh – 'our men are slaughtered, our fields laid waste, our agriculture ruined, our country desolate but we have saved £150,000'.

At the very end of the session Grattan issued a polite but ominous warning to the British and Irish administrations. At the beginning of August he seconded an address of thanks to the Crown, proposed by Denis Daly, for the very modest commercial concessions recently made to Ireland by Great Britain. Having expressed Ireland's gratitude in measured terms, the Address proceeded to dwell on 'the hope that what had already been granted was but an earnest of future effectual extensions of our commerce.

During the session of 1778 Grattan was a consistent and formidable critic of the administration along conventional lines. But when, towards the end of the session, a novel and, it might be said, 'non-party 'question arose, he was unwontedly hesitant. In the early years of George III's reign the Catholic question, which was to loom so very large throughout most of his political life, was attracting little parliamentary attention. The creation of new disabilities, outworks for the defence of Irish Protestantism, had ceased a quarter of a century back. Protestant gentlemen, secure and fairly tolerant, believed in *quieta non movere*; and the Catholic leadership, though it was beginning to look forward to a relaxation of the laws, was deferential and cautious. By 1778, however, the time seemed ripe for the introduction of a Catholic Relief Bill, and Grattan spoke on this measure when the House in committee was debating whether Catholics should be allowed to purchase freeholds or should be restricted to taking 999-year leases. He was hesitant even when it came to nomenclature, referring to papists or Roman Catholics, 'call them as you will'. Listening to the debate, he said, 'with the most unbiased veneration for every argument that fell from either side, I formed an opinion. I altered that opinion.' He favoured the relaxation of the penal laws – 'I disapprove', he declared, 'of every part that extends humiliation'. He drew attention to the fact that the Catholics had won Magna Charta (a point he was frequently to make in the future), and he thought that the way to dissipate the gloom of superstition was 'to make the Catholic body as rich as possible'. But all the same he was afraid that if the Catholics were permitted to purchase freeholds they would soon possess the bulk of the land, and 'a popish interest would be set up against the Protestant interest'. His intention, then, in so far as it can be discerned from a balancing speech, was to support the more limited form of concession. However, six weeks later when the Bill was being debated on its return from England, Grattan called on the House to reject it because the clause repealing the test debarring Protestant dissenters from office had been deleted in England.[38] When considering the 1778 Relief Bill Grattan may have been influenced by Charlemont, whose liberalism when he approached the Catholic question was strongly diluted with caution,[39] and he seems to have believed that the government wanted 'to make the papists a balance against the Protestants'.

During the session of 1777–8 – only his second in the House – Grattan was generally accepted as being in the front rank of MPs. Hussey Burgh generously remarked that he would be a vain man who wished to speak after Grattan, and John Scott, paying a double-edged compliment, declared that Grattan's gifts were 'never more brilliantly displayed than on the worse side of a case'.[40] In the following session (1779–80) Grattan was not only to acquire fresh parliamentary laurels, he was to become a national hero.

The recess which stretched from August 1778 to October 1779 was marked by a widespread, well-publicized surge of national self-consciousness. The dispute with America had highlighted the constitutional grievances which Ireland shared with the colonies. The dislocation inflicted by the war on the Irish economy had accentuated Irish resentment against the galling restrictions imposed by Great Britain on Irish trade. Another consequence of the war was the withdrawal of a considerable number of troops from Ireland for overseas service. Ireland, Grattan grumbled, was being treated 'as a barrack which the army shall leave in time of danger'.[41] The reduction of the force stationed in Ireland not only left Ireland exposed to invasion but removed one of the main props of law and order throughout the Irish countryside. Protestant Ireland responded to the emergency with alacrity. All over Ireland 'Volunteer' corps were formed. 'Scarlet fever'[42] swept through the country and thousands of Irishmen acquired that 'dignity of danger', which, according to Dr Johnson, was enjoyed by the soldier. Drilling and discipline did not dull their political instincts. A Volunteer corps was a dining and debating club and an embryonic political association. The Volunteers, parading with public spirit and panache, were a vivid embodiment of the community's unity, strength and sense of purpose.

With respectable public opinion (what in other circumstances was termed the *pays légal*) arrayed in armed military associations, whose members far outnumbered the regulars stationed in Ireland, it was obvious that the coming parliamentary session (1779–80) would be highly contentious and unpredictable. The Irish administration hoped to begin it on an amicable note by announcing that the British government intended to make considerable commercial concessions to Ireland. But a fragmented cabinet was unable to formulate an Irish policy before the Irish Parliament met and the Lord Lieutenant could only offer optimistic platitudes in place of a policy. Meanwhile the administration's critics, buoyed up by the belief that they would be speaking for thousands of active, intelligent Irishmen, planned a vigorous offensive. Shortly before the opening of the session, Grattan, Denis Daly and Hussey Burgh met at Bray near Dublin to settle their tactics. Grattan and Daly had drafted an amendment to the address in answer to the Speech from the Throne, and after some discussion it was agreed to adopt Daly's draft, which had been corrected by Pery, the Speaker, an adroit politician. Grattan managed to have a phrase omitted which he thought would annoy quondam supporters of the government.

When Parliament met on 12 October Grattan moved an amendment to the address calling for a free export trade. In 'a most pathetic strain of language' he 'enumerated the distresses of the country' with thousands of manufacturers lingering 'in a state of starving despondance'. Passing from pathos to indignation, he asked was 'a faithful, brave and loyal people' to be sacrificed by the British ministry to 'a few insignificant, paltry manufacturing towns'. The debate then followed an extraordinary course, with a number of prominent office-holders competing in their denunciation of the commercial restraints. Hussey Burgh, on the brink of resignation, rejoiced that he had a place to lose; Flood (who was to stay in office for another two years) contributed his 'mite to the attack like the Roman ladies who cast their jewels into the public fund'. Hely Hutchinson (who clung tenaciously to office until the end of a long life) 'recapitulated the black catalogue of our grievances'.[43] Supported on all sides, Grattan's amendment with the word 'export' omitted was carried *nem con*. Six weeks later, on 24 November, he won another victory, persuading the House to resolve by a large majority (170 to 47) that it was inexpedient to grant new taxes. Later he explained that if money was needed 'we must cut the pension list to the bone and strike to the bowels of the revenue establishment for no man that wishes well to his country but wishes to destroy the vermin of the civil list'.[44] On 29 November he heartily agreed with the decision of the House to use the power of the purse to obtain commercial concessions by voting supplies not for the customary two years but for only six months.

With influence at a discount, with the government's critics holding the parliamentary initiative, with the House of Commons defying Great Britain on a major issue in imperial politics, with the Volunteers demonstrating and Dublin artisans rioting round the Parliament House, the situation was tense enough to suggest that Ireland was set on the path taken five years before by the American colonies. But within a few weeks the crisis was resolved. By the middle of December the British government had announced its intention of abolishing the restrictions on Irish trade and admitting Ireland to a full participation in the colonial trade. Concessions, which Grattan immediately declared, fully met Ireland's desires, the colonial trade, he added, being 'in the nature of a gift'. But at the same time he reminded the Commons that the concessions had been gained by Ireland's 'virtue, her spirit, her pride', and that it was 'to the people we owe that Ireland has changed her place, no longer a corner of the earth but a medium between the old world and the new'.[45]

With this swelling of national pride which he sensed, expressed and inspired, Grattan was sure that 'the people of Ireland should not be satisfied with trade but should go on to liberty'.[46] Other MPs shared this view, and several measures which would contribute to bringing the Irish Constitution into line with the British were introduced early in 1780: the heads of a bill amending Poynings' Law, which failed to obtain the support of the House, and the heads of a Mutiny Bill, a Habeas Corpus Bill and a bill securing judges' tenure *quamdiu se bene gesserint*, all of which were presented to the Lord Lieutenant for transmission to England. But Grattan was not satisfied with this piecemeal approach. Early in the year he decided to raise the fundamental constitutional issue: had Great Britain the right to legislate for Ireland? Had Ireland a sovereign or a subordinate legislature?

The Irish Parliament, of medieval origin, with its hereditary peerage, precedent-based privileges, elaborate procedure, and historic and decorative ceremonial was outwardly very different from the simple, recently created colonial assemblies on the other side of the Atlantic. But it shared with those assemblies the status of a subordinate legislature. Admittedly it had at times been asserted that the Irish Parliament was a sovereign assembly. But the question, so far as Westminster was concerned, had been decisively settled early in the century by a declaratory act, the famous 6 Geo.I., which declared that the British Parliament had the right to make laws binding Ireland and that the Irish House of Lords did not possess an appellant jurisdiction. This resounding declaration, though it satisfied British parliamentary pride, had little practical effect. Ireland was rarely referred to in British legislation and the statutes in which Ireland was mentioned were minor, uncontroversial measures which often indeed purported to confer economic benefits on Ireland. It was through the Irish executive and the workings of Poynings' Act and by legislation concerning the British home market and colonial trade (legally unchallengeable by the most zealous supporter of Ireland's parliamentary rights) that Great Britain exercised a considerable degree of control over Irish affairs.

Nevertheless, the British claim to legislative supremacy was bound to grate on politically conscious Irishmen. What they must have felt was well expressed by Benjamin Franklin when he complained that 'every man in England seems to consider himself as a piece of the sovereignty over America'.[47] When the colonists challenged this claim, Parliament reacted vigorously by passing a second declaratory act (6 Geo.III.c.12) affirming that it had the right to legislate for the American colonies. A great Anglo-American debate began in which modifications to the doctrine of legislative supremacy were suggested. Some colonial politicians distinguished between external and internal legislation. They denied that Great Britain had the right to tax the colonies but admitted a right to regulate through imperial trade. Whig politicians, such as Fox, while con-

45

tending that Parliament should not tax the colonists, thought it desirable that there should be 'a superintending power' in the empire, regulating imperial trade, foreign policy and defence, and that this power must rest at Westminster. Even Lord North, under the pressure of war, agreed in 1778 that, putting aside the question of 'right', Parliament should renounce the intention of taxing the colonies or altering their charters. The whole debate opened up what was to be a fundamental problem in imperial relations for nearly two centuries: how to combine colonial or dominion autonomy with imperial co-operation. For Grattan in 1780 the immediate issue was a simple one. Every effort must be made to secure the repeal of the statutory assertion of an unconstitutional and, historically and morally, unjustifiable claim.

He soon found that some of his political associates thought he was going too fast. His brother-in-law Bushe, with whom he was co-operating over the Mutiny Bill, argued that to challenge Westminster's claim to legislative supremacy immediately after Great Britain had behaved so generously over commercial matters would 'extirpate every idea of conciliation'. However, encouraged by his soldierly uncle, Thomas Marlay, Grattan persisted in his chosen course and on 24 April moved that only the King, Lords and Commons of Ireland had power to bind Ireland. His speech, which in later years he thought was the best he ever made, was staccato, sparkling and vibrant, exhortatory rather than persuasive. He did not dwell heavily on constitutional law and history, wisely enough, for according to two constitutional experts in the House, Hely-Hutchinson and Flood, the British claim was strongly supported by precedent. Instead Grattan appealed to 'the laws of God, the laws of nature, and the laws of nations'. His main theme was that national honour demanded that Parliament should assert its rights. 'A nation infringed on as Ireland, and armed as Ireland, must have equal freedom, anything less is an insult.' Ireland might have obtained a free trade, 'but liberty, the consummation of all trade, is lacking'. Parliament, he insisted, must be inspired by an awareness that there was 'an ardent combination amongst the people, a fire which animates a nation to its own redemption, a sacred enthusiasm which only belongs to the national confidence of freedom'. The time too was ripe for action. The doctrine of British parliamentary supremacy, which had involved the empire in a crippling and inglorious war, was discredited. 'The opportunity prompts, the spirit of the people prompts', and he would never be satisfied 'so long as a link of the British chain is clanking to the heels of the meanest peasant'. But though he was convinced that 'we live too near the British nation to be less than equal to her', towards the conclusion of his speech Grattan emphasized that once Ireland's constitutional claims were met 'common trade, and common liberty will give strength to constitution and incline both nations to immortality'.

Grattan's speech was bound to evoke a sympathetic response from most Irish MPs. Legislative independence would immeasurably raise the status of their House and consequently increase the prestige of its members. But, it was urged, was it wise to pronounce on the question in a time of storm and stress when the British mind was slowly adjusting itself to new conceptions of empire? It was highly unlikely that the British Parliament would pass legislation binding Ireland; and if it were rash enough to do so, Irish judges and Irish juries would refuse to enforce its measures. There were a number of gentlemen Grattan contemptuously noticed 'who lamented the introduction of constitutional questions though they declared their principles were in favour of them'. 'I despise', he added, 'such timid, weak and wavering declarations.'[48] The government skilfully adapted its parliamentary tactics to attract the hesitant. The Attorney-General, instead of meeting Grattan's motion with a defiant negative, moved a resolution implying the indefinite postponement of the issue, and this after a debate which lasted until 6.30 a.m. on 20 April was carried by 136 to 97.[49]

This was not a discouraging result for Grattan, and during the remainder of the session he flung himself into harassing the administration. He strongly supported the heads of an Irish Mutiny Bill which would make the forces maintained by Ireland a parliamentary army not an 'imperial army' – after all 'there never was an allied camp that was governed by the same legislature'.[50] He was disturbed when the administration succeeded in having the heads remodeled so that the measure supplemented rather than duplicated the British act, and he asked Foster, the administration's spokesman, why were they not prepared to copy literally the British

Mutiny Act (the unspoken answer was that to do so would be to challenge openly the authority of Westminster). Afraid the bill would not be returned from England, he badgered the ineffectual Chief Secretary and dramatically apostrophized the administration's leading supporters – 'Let Irishmen on the treasury bench say, will they support the cause of their country [no answer given]'. When the bill was returned he was dismayed to find that it had been changed from a biannual to a permanent measure. A perpetual Mutiny Bill, 'the boldest attempt ever made against the liberties of the subject', he declared, violated Magna Charta, repealed the common law and made the King a dictator. It permitted the British Minister, he argued, to send over 40,000 troops, to disperse the Volunteers and cut their throats (retreating abruptly from melodrama, he added that he did not say this would happen, only that it could). He warned the House that if the bill reached the statute book he would 'secede and associated in drawing up an appeal to the people against a measure which made the king absolute in regard to the army'; in the event he published during the long recess a fiery pamphlet, *Observations on the Mutiny Bill*.[51]

The perpetual Mutiny Bill was in Grattan's opinion 'one of the two instruments of humiliation' passed at the close of the session 1779–80 which together reduced Ireland to 'abject slavery'.[52] The other, at first glance an unlikely instrument for this purpose, was a sugar bill, apparently a routine fiscal measure affecting a luxury trade. But this sugar bill was significant as an attempt under the new commercial dispensation to reconcile British and Irish economic interests. When dealing with refined sugar the administration's policy was to fix the import duty at a level which, while giving a decided preference to the Irish refiner, would not completely rule out British competition and therefore would protect the Irish consumer from the dangers of monopoly. But an influential section of Irish MPs, among whom Grattan was prominent, was eager to encourage the Irish 'refinery by imposing prohibitive duties on imported refined sugar'. Having warned the House to avoid 'a nice, puzzled and tedious examination' of the question, Grattan discussed what he saw as the broad issues. The House should, he emphasized, 'be grateful to the British nation and in our regulations show nothing that is an alienation from that country' but – and in an economic debate a 'but' frequently follows the sort of sentiments he had just expressed – if they allowed the interests of a British industry to regulate their trade, 'your free trade is over'. The Irish sugar refining industry depended on protective duties, the plantation trade depended on the refinery. He brushed aside the danger of creating a monopoly by pointing out that if the sugar bakers managed to keep prices high by forming a combination, other men would enter the industry and 'the consumption of our own manufactures is a public blessing'.[53] When the bill was being considered in England, the Board of Trade decided on a duty approximately midway between that proposed by the Irish administration and that demanded by Irish protectionists, and the House accepted this compromise. Grattan was disgusted. The perpetual Mutiny Act and a duty of nine shillings and two pence on British refined sugar marked a sad decline in parliamentary spirit from the beginning of the session, when the House of Commons 'sojourned with the people' and went to the Castle 'upon the crest of its own army'. Now 'the Nation's crest falls, her plumage fades, the fife faulters, the drum will not beat'. But Grattan was not unduly depressed by 'the ignominious sequel of this session'. He believed that the debates 'had opened the eyes of men from the sleep of a century' and he hoped that when Parliament reassembled he would be able 'to secure to the house of commons the best and dearest privilege, the confidence of the Nation' and to see Ireland 'restored to the respectable rank which it ought to hold amongst the nations of Europe'.[54]

Grattan's own parliamentary status at this time is reflected in the part he played in resolving a controversy which was spreading 'much confusion and distress' among the more substantial Irish tenantry and which cut across the line dividing opposition from administration. Many Irish tenants held their land on a lease for three lives, perpetually renewable on payment of a fine within a stipulated period. It had come to be accepted by the Irish courts that the lease should be regarded as renewed even though the fine was tendered late, but in 1779 the British House of Lords ruled that if the fine was not paid in time the lease lapsed. The Attorney-General, Scott, sympathized with the tenants and probably drafted and certainly supported the heads of a bill, introduced by Grattan, which provided that a tenant should not lose his lease by neglecting to pay a fine in time, 'upon adequate compensation being made'. Two powerful property interests, landlords and long leaseholders, many of them men of substance, were in conflict – the latter, Grattan reminded the House, being 'those who send you to parliament'. There was also involved in debate the interesting political and legal question, how far should the terms of a contract, as defined by the final Court of Appeal, be varied retrospectively by legislation. Grattan handled this question breezily by remarking that 'a most celebrated lawyer told me there was a fashion in equity as in everything else'. The heads were passed by the House of Commons, transmitted to England, returned and enacted at the close of the session. Some years later it was asserted that the provisions of the Act were being used by dishonest heirs to defraud their father's creditors.[55]

In the summer of 1780 Grattan must have been elated by the feeling that he was undoubtedly the most popular Irish MP, admired and supported by the Volunteers, who were fast developing into a new political elite. As early as the middle of October 1779 he was presented with the freedom of Dublin for his efforts to obtain a free trade, and after the debate of 19 April a number of Volunteer corps and other bodies thanked him for his parliamentary services. The Lawyers Corps elected him an honorary member, and when a majority of the Dublin Volunteers (the first corps to be formed in Dublin) refused to address him on the grounds that the corps should not intervene in politics, the minority seceded, formed a new corps, the Dublin Independents, which elected Grattan ('one of the real ornaments of society') to be their colonel.[56] In July 1780 he attended a great review at Belfast, as ADC to Charlemont, the reviewing General; in March 1781 he reviewed three Dublin corps, the Lawyers, the Merchants and the Independents, when they held a field day on Marlborough Green; and in May he reviewed all the corps, horse and foot of the city and county of Dublin, who went through their exercises with 'their usual adroitness'. His ADC on this occasion was Sir Edward Crosbie, who was to be hanged in 1798. A few days later, on receiving news of a victory in the West Indies, he marched at the head of his corps to Phoenix Park, where they fired three volleys and gave three cheers.[57] In his replies to the addresses he received, Grattan was able to practise a

simple form of political journalism. His carefully phrased, pithy state-
ments reiterated the main articles of his political creed: the British connection, free trade, liberty and national pride, a free, brave people, united
in defence of liberty – 'we become a nation and acquire a national character'.[58] Active in arms he did not eschew the law. Although he had given
up any intention of building up a legal practice, he twice during the recess
appeared in court. In May he was one of the council for Lord Tracton, the
Chief Baron of the Exchequer, in an action for libel against a newspaper;
in July, with half-a-dozen other barristers, all opposition Whigs, he
appeared for the plaintiff when a hairdresser sued several naval officers
for illegal impressment and obtained £250 in damages.[59]

When the new session began in October 1781, political Ireland was
restless and expectant. Many middle-class Irishmen enrolled in the Volunteers and, arrayed in all the panoply of war, believed that they were
upholding the ideals for which the Americans were fighting. Though fortunately they had avoided breaking with Great Britain, they were determined that in a remodelled and reformed imperial system Ireland's
rightful place in the scheme of things would be acknowledged. This current of feeling must have encouraged the parliamentary critics of the
administration when bracing themselves to resume the struggle for constitutional rights. On the other hand the Lord Lieutenant, Carlisle, and
the Chief Secretary, Eden, a strong team having worked hard during the
recess to cement a majority, were confident that by an assiduous attention to private claims and some flexibility in policy, they would get
through the parliamentary campaign successfully.

At the opening of the session the opposition was reinforced by Flood,
who after a period of sullen isolation had at length been compelled to
resign his office. Commanding, severely logical, with a wealth of experience and knowledge, Flood was a formidable foe. He was also an exact-
ing friend and uncertain ally. While he had been sitting in silence, bright
young men on the other side of the House had taken up the questions
which Flood in earlier days had handled with eloquent expertise. Flood
resented the rivalry of men who he openly regarded as his inferiors,
short-sighted 'little men' who substituted rhetoric for hard common
sense. He was soon wrangling with Yelverton over the best way in which

to amend the procedure for enacting Irish legislation. When in November Grattan (unsuccessfully) moved for leave to introduce a Mutiny Bill, limited in duration, 'one of the great hinges of the constitution', Flood supported and clearly strove to surpass him by a powerful speech, replete with questions which 'went back to the Roman Commonwealth'. He and Grattan also co-operated and competed in attacking the government's financial policy. Early in November Flood, pointing to taxes accumulating on the one hand and debt on the other, asked, How are we to go on? A few weeks later Grattan attempted to demonstrate from the public accounts 'the accelerated velocity with which they advanced to ruin'. On this occasion Grattan, having admitted that 'calculation is a dull subject', exposed himself to a vigorous and convincing counterattack by John Foster, who accused him of comparing unfairly a period of peace with a period of war and explained that there were unpredictable factors when dealing with the balance of trade and that Grattan had confined himself to linen (which had had an exceptionally bad year), cotton and wool, leaving out the provision trade which was rapidly expanding.

On 2 February Grattan again raised the fundamental question, the legislative supremacy of Great Britain, by moving an address to the Crown, declaring that the Kingdom of Ireland was a distinct kingdom with its parliament the sole legislature thereof, and that Great Britain would be greatly strengthened by renouncing the claim to legislate for Ireland. Grattan devoted much of his speech to examining the legal material bearing on Anglo-Irish constitutional relations, referring to 'pacts, charters, laws innumerable'. But, although confident that precedent was on the whole in his favour, he wisely grounded his case on the law of nature. He replied on 'Locke, Burlamaqui and Hooker – independent philosophers – better authority than dependent judges' when it came to defending the birthrights of Irishmen (which were those of Englishmen). He concluded by emphasizing that Ireland, 'a community of different religions but one political faith', was expressing itself through the Volunteer movement: 'it is the property – it is the soul of the country armed'. Grattan's respect for the Volunteers is understandable. A week before he moved his address a convention of the Ulster Volunteer Corps, meeting at Dungannon, in a series of resolutions had strongly asserted Ireland's right to parliamentary independence.[60] For the moment, however, the government was able to dispose of Grattan's address by a procedural motion postponing a decision on the question.

Realizing unity was strength, Grattan during February was also exerting himself in support of a Catholic Relief Bill. He admitted that his attitude to the disabilities had been changed by the Catholics' behaviour during the free trade agitation. They had thrown themselves 'frankly and freely into the cause of their country' and had eagerly sought to join 'the glorious Volunteers'. He now called on Parliament to grant the Catholics 'natural liberty and the common rights of men'. To reassure apprehensive Protestants he dwelt on 'the enlightening and softening of men's minds by toleration' and prophesized that 'as the Catholics increase in wealth they will increase in learning and politeness'. He would not, he said, 'have a vestige of pain or penalty remaining against my loyal fellow subjects', who should be granted 'every privilege compatible with the Protestant ascendant'.[61]

Having failed in a direct assault on the claim of the British Parliament to supreme legislative power, Grattan joined Yelverton in making a flank attack. On 1 March Yelverton informed the House of Commons that he proposed to deal with what might at any moment become an awkward problem: the validity of an English or British act purporting to bind Ireland. A few hours later Flood declared that he was going to introduce the heads of a bill 'quieting possessions held under English acts of parliament' – a measure characterized by the Lord Lieutenant as 'selfish in its purpose, coarse in its intent and unqualified by any civil expression whatever towards the mother country'. The House reacted unfavourably to this attempt to elbow Yelverton aside, and a committee – Grattan, Yelverton, Hussey Burgh and John Fitzgibbon was appointed to prepare a draft bill. In a few days the committee produced the heads of a bill for confirming English and British legislation binding Ireland, including commercial measures which conferred equal benefits on the subjects of both countries, since 'it was the earnest and affectionate desire as well as the interest of His Majesty's subjects of Ireland to promote the navy trade and common interests of Great Britain as well as Ireland and whereas a similarity of laws, manners and custom must naturally conduct to strengthen and perpetuate that harmony which ought to subsist between the people of Great Britain and Ireland'. Flood took a dim view of this measure. It was a mistake to confirm British legislation en bloc; the acts affecting Ireland should be carefully examined; and, dismissing 'trifling palliatives', he declared that his aim was to make it clear that Great Britain had no right to legislate for Ireland. Grattan in reply argued that while it was obviously desirable that the English legislation binding Ireland should be validated by the Irish Parliament, validation 'should be coupled with something to render it palatable to England' and which would show that Irishmen were anxious to preserve the connection 'on terms of perfect equality'. In spite of Flood's strictures the House accepted the committee's bill, which the Lord Lieutenant, who regarded it as Grattan's bill, pronounced 'respectful in its attitude to the mother country'.[62]

But important as the great constitutional debates in the Irish Parliament may have seemed to the enthralled participants, they were overshadowed by events on a wider stage. The capitulation at Yorktown in October 1781 clearly signified the end of Great Britain's efforts to subdue the American colonies. The immediate reaction of the British and Irish parliaments to Yorktown was to encourage the Crown to show a bold face to Britain's enemies. On the news of the defeat reaching Ireland, the House of Commons at once passed a loyal address, proposed by Yelverton. Grattan was one of the minority which voted against it, on the grounds that it might be interpreted as pledging the country to continue the American War, though 'he had as much regard for England as any man could have that loved Ireland better'. At Westminster the power and prestige of the government rapidly declined. By February North felt he could go on no longer, and at the end of March Rockingham, the Whig leader, became Prime Minister. The new ministers had for years been vehemently denouncing North's American policy and his obstinate and insensitive assertion of parliamentary supremacy and the rights of the Crown, and they were anxious to show by their handling of Anglo-Irish relations that they had a more liberal and understanding approach to imperial problems. What they had in mind was an Anglo-Irish settlement which would both recognize Ireland's constitutional rights and provide for co-operation between the two countries on matters of common interest. Obviously it would require some little time to shape a satisfactory settlement, and naturally the British ministers expected that their fellow Whigs in Ireland, for instance Charlemont and Grattan – 'persons like ourselves' as Fox said[63] – would give them credit for good intentions and not make difficulties. They were quickly disillusioned. In early April Rockingham and Fox wrote to Charlemont suggesting that when the Irish Parliament reassembled on 16 April there should be a further adjournment. Charlemont in his reply, though he expressed passionate pleasure at seeing 'true Whigs and genuine lovers of liberty' in office, explained that he and Grattan, whom he had consulted, agreed that it was impossible to extend the adjournment: the people were impatiently expecting a declaration of parliamentary independence.

When on 12 April Fitzpatrick, the new Chief Secretary, arrived in Dublin he immediately tried to arrange a meeting with Grattan, who 'with great civility' refused to see him until after the 16th of April.[64] The new Lord Lieutenant, Portland, was installed on 14 April so that the Irish administration had just about forty-eight hours in which to find a means of coping with an expectant Parliament and public. It was decided that the best course would be for the Lord Lieutenant on 16 April to send to the House of Commons a short message stating that the King hoped the House would take into consideration the causes of discontent with the aim of arriving at a 'final adjustment' of Anglo-Irish relations. It was planned that a very short motion thanking the Lord Lieutenant would be moved and passed and that then there would be an interval during which a solution of the Irish question could be worked out on both sides of the water. But Grattan was not willing to delay the assertion of an essential principle, although he was prepared to make a small concession on a matter of form. Instead of moving a declaration of Irish parliamentary independence he drafted a long amendment to the reply to the Lord Lieutenant's message, asserting Ireland was a distinct kingdom and that it was the birthright of Irishmen that no body of men could legislate for their nation except the King, Lords and Commons of Ireland.

On 16 April, a memorable day in Irish parliamentary history and in his own career, Grattan was not in the best of health, having been recently operated on for a small fistula. But he was exhilarated at seeing himself coming forward at the end of a long uphill struggle as the triumphant champion of his country's rights. He and his audience – the House was full, there were crowds at the Bar and the galleries were packed – were conscious of being present at the inauguration of a new era of pride, prosperity and goodwill for Ireland – an era which would undoubtedly long outlast the century.

Grattan's oratory was electrified by his sense of the occasion, and his speech, carefully planned if not closely argued, was a confession of faith in Ireland and a constitutional battle hymn. He began by an invocation of Ireland's newly found strength and unity. 'I remember', he declared, 'Ireland when she was a child. I have seen her progress from injuries to arms and from arms to liberty.' Ireland was no longer a divided colony but a united nation, 'manifesting ourself to the world in every simple instance of glory'. They were 'as Christians tolerant, as Irishmen united'. Irishmen had 'met at the altar and communicated a national sacrament, juries, cities, counties, commoners, nobles, volunteers, graduations and religions, a vast national league, a solemn covenant, a rapid fire'. With Irishmen united by shared ideals and a sense of common purpose, he spoke of the country as if it was a spiritual and intellectual being. 'It was necessary', he said, 'for Ireland to be her own redeemer, to form her mind as well as her constitution and erect in her soul a vast image of herself and a lofty sense of her own exaltation'. 'What set one nation above another', he asked, 'but the soul that dwells therein; for it is of no avail if the arm is strong if the soul be not great'. Eager 'to pour into the public mind a considerable portion of pride', Grattan emphatically told his fellow-countrymen that they should attribute their imminent success to their own 'virtue', their perseverance and temper. 'They had', he admitted, 'no trophies but the liberty they transmitted to their posterity is more than trophies.' Then, having listed Ireland's constitutional grievances, Grattan dealt in generous terms with Anglo-Irish relations. If England 'wishes well to Ireland she has nothing to fear from her strength. I do believe the people of Ireland would die for England.' Great Britain and Ireland, he fervently believed, were united in spirit by sharing the same political and constitutional ideals. 'We are not united to England by conquest but by compact. This island was planted by British privileges as well as by

British men – both countries are now united in liberty.' But it was 'necessary to give passion to loyalty; not that passion which six-pence a day will inspire in the mind of a soldier, but what British principles will inspire in the mind of every man in this kingdom'. He concluded by expressing his confidence in Rockingham's government and the new Irish administration. He intended to give it not 'a milk and water support' but a decided and responsible one. However, he would not take office. 'I will', he said, 'go into the cabinet the friend of the people. I will come out of it unpaid and unpensioned.'[65] The speech had a tremendous reception and Grattan's amendment was carried unanimously. Exhausted, he had to rest for a few days but on 19 April he held 'a splendid levee of independent gentlemen'.[66]

Some faults were detected in the speech by a close observer, Flood, who carefully recorded them in a private memorandum. Grattan, he thought, displayed a very superficial knowledge of history, could not distinguish between cause and effect and took far too much credit for the growth of Irish political self-confidence. A more good-natured critic, Fitzpatrick, the Chief Secretary, described the speech as 'all declamatory, very little, and what there was, weak argument', adding that Grattan's manner was 'affected to the last degree'. But he had to admit that the speech was 'splendid in point of eloquence' and that no attempt was made to answer it.[67]

After the momentous debate and vote of the 16th of April a great wave of exhilaration swept through politically-minded Ireland. Ireland had asserted herself, had claimed her place amongst the nations and by the ardour of her orators and volunteers had achieved almost as much as America, without bloodshed and without weakening the Empire. The question then was, what would be the British response to Ireland's demands? It seemed that the British government had only two options, either unconditional surrender or opening negotiations. Grattan hoped it would adopt the former. Negotiations meant postponement, possibly to a time when Ireland would be in a less favourable position, and in a negotiated settlement Ireland, the weaker party, would probably fare less well than Great Britain. Moreover and more importantly, when Anglo-Irish relations were involved, he relied on the spirit rather than the letter. A generous-minded idealist, Grattan did not want the connection between the two countries to rest on formal agreements, guaranteed by detailed legislation and institutional machinery. He despised 'the little policy of making a bargain'. Rather he believed that the two countries should be linked by allegiance to the Crown, common constitutional principles, and, so far as Ireland was concerned, by 'a native affection to the British Name and Nation'. Such a connection would ensure 'the harmony, the stability and the glory of the empire'.[68]

On 18 April, two days after the great debate, he wrote to Fox, emphasizing that Ireland asked nothing 'but what is essential to the liberty and composure of our country and consistent with the dignity and interest of the other [Great Britain]'. England could yield with dignity, because Ireland's claims were, after all, based on principles asserted by 'the liberal and enlightened part of England' and Ireland has pressed those claims with 'a veneration for the pride, as well as a love for the liberty of England'. On the same day, writing to Lord Mahon, a Whig MP, Grattan pointed out that Ireland had defined her grievances and 'is not progressive in her discontents'.[69]

In his reply to Grattan, Fox was friendly and non-committal.[70] He had definite views on how the Irish question should be handled. Great Britain should make concessions and a permanent settlement should be negotiated between the two countries. However, it was clear that immediate action was called for. Portland was drawing alarming parallels between Ireland and America, and the British government, already involved in critical negotiations with America, France, Spain and Holland, could scarcely contemplate embarking on a far-ranging discussion of the Irish problem. So on 17 May Fox informed the House of Commons that the government agreed to the repeal of 6 Geo.I, to an amendment of Poynings' Law and to an Irish Mutiny Bill limited in duration. He also suggested that 'something should now be done towards establishing on a firm and solid basis the future connection of the two kingdoms' – perhaps by a meeting of commissioners appointed by both parliaments.

A few days after the great debate of 16 April the Irish Parliament had adjourned to await news from England. When it reassembled on 27 May, Portland in a speech from the throne detailed the government's concessions. Grattan immediately rose, and having stated that 'all constitutional questions are at an end and we are now as much pledged to moderation as we were before pledged to a proper exertion',[71] proposed their gratitude and determination 'to stand and fall with Great Britain'. This was carried by 211 votes to none, the tellers for the noes being a couple of able, argumentative lawyers, Samuel Bradshaw and David Walshe. Flood, who advised the House to weight the concessions carefully, did not go into the No lobby. After the address was carried, £100,000 was voted towards raising recruits for the navy, a step strongly supported by Grattan. Portland's coach was drawn to and from the Parliament House by the populace; and when the House of Commons went with their address to the Castle, the Volunteers, 'with a spirit which outstrips the resolution of a Roman and an elegance of appearance which would do honour to the Grecian name', lined the streets. Early in June there was a great Volunteer review, with a mock battle, in Phoenix Park.[72]

Grattan was the hero of the hour, the first generally acclaimed Irishman since the early Middle Ages. His speech of the 16th of April, 'taken by the best shorthand writer in the world', was offered for sale printed on a strong sheet which could be framed.[73] The British Society for Constitutional Information entered the speech in its minutes.[74] His old university granted him an honorary LL D in recognition of 'his public virtues and great abilities' and arranged for his picture, painted by Hone, to be hung in the newly built Public Theatre.[75] He had the more dubious distinction of being included in the scandalous series of tête-à-tête portraits appearing in the *Town and Country Magazine*, under the title 'The Irish orator and Miss O'Brien'. (Miss O'Brien was said to be the daughter of a Cork merchant and to have a substantial fortune.)[76] The Leinster Volunteer delegates, meeting with Colonel Flood in the chair, thanked Colonel Grattan for his exertions on behalf of Ireland's rights. In May the Irish Bar held a meeting to consider erecting a statue of Grattan. At the meeting a letter from Grattan was read: 'A statue', he wrote, 'is an honour reserved for the dead, for those who have died for their country', and he suggested the erection of a national monument 'to immortalise the era, not the man'. The meeting appointed a committee to receive designs for a monument, 'to perpetuate the vindication of our national rights and to

express their gratitude to that illustrious assertor of our laws and constitution'.[77] Designs were to be submitted by the 1st of November, but by
then many members of the Bar were uncertain if Ireland's rights had in
fact been vindicated, and the project lapsed.[78]

The Irish House of Commons expressed its gratitude to Grattan in a
remarkable and tangible form. At the close of May Beauchamp Bagenal,
a high-spirited, venturesome country gentleman and a keen Volunteer, in
a couple of flamboyant speeches called on the House to give £100,000 to
'our great benefactor', who 'has saved this empire from an iron age and
restored an unequivocal golden one'. 'The appearance of such a being on
earth', Bagenal declared, 'was so essential to the establishment of liberty
at this most critical juncture, that without superstition men may record
him amongst the most propitious interpositions of Heaven'. In the ensuing debate Grattan was compared to Marlborough and Chatham, but it
was pointed out that if such a large sum was voted he would not accept
it. It was suggested that instead of the £100,000 he should be granted
the house in Phoenix Park, recently purchased for the Lord Lieutenant,
and £2500 per annum. It was objected, however, that it would be 'indelicate' to tie Grattan 'to a spot that possibly he might not like', and in the
end it was decided that he should receive a grant of £50,000 for the purchase of a mansion and landed property.[79]

By making Grattan a substantial landowner, the grant enabled him to
combine a comfortable and dignified way of life with parliamentary independence. The high-minded Rockingham applauded the action of the
Irish House of Commons. 'Though economy', he wrote, 'may be a necessary virtue in a state, yet when awarding great public merit narrow ideas
on the subject are not good policy.'[80] Grattan himself treated the grant
not only as an award for past achievements but as binding him to the
public service in the future. Some placemen may have wryly reflected
that for once patriotism had paid, and political poetasters found the
grant an attractive subject:

> When Grattan so famous was poor as a church-mouse,
> Like an angel he spoke in the Parliament house,
> A friend to his country and true to his king,

With phrases of Grattan how Ireland did ring.
But when unexpectedly cash filled his purse,
His talents perverted became the Land's curse –

O would some kind daemon assistance impart,
To take from his coffers and give to his heart,
So Grattan once more our regard might attain
And we get our fifty thousand again

or

They say he's honest. How that word resounds
What made him honest? Fifty thousand pounds

Grattan dismissed such jibes with contempt. When in the House of Commons he was reminded that he owed his grant (and implicitly his fortune) to a King's letter, he proudly replied, 'Sir I do not owe my property to a King's letter – I hold my property on the same tenure as the house of Brunswick holds the throne of these realms – the gift of the people and the constitution'.[81]

Following the acknowledgement by Great Britain of Ireland's parliamentary independence several important constitutional measures were enacted: a bill granting judges tenure on good behaviour, a bill confirming Westminster legislation affecting Ireland, an Irish Mutiny Bill limited to two years, and a bill amending Poynings' Law, introduced by Yelverton. These measures rapidly reached the statute book, only Yelverton's bill being debated at any length. It provided that an Irish bill having passed through the customary parliamentary stages would be transmitted to England under the Irish Great Seal, and if it returned under the British Great Seal the Royal Assent would be pronounced in Parliament by the Lord Lieutenant. Flood, soured at being overshadowed by his juniors, was extremely critical of Yelverton's handiwork, and, making great play with his constitutional expertise, he advocated a different approach to the problem – a bill declaring that his own construction of Poynings' Law (a construction which no other lawyer accepted and which was not substantiated by the statute book) was the correct one. He also found another serious flaw in the bill. It was essential, he argued, that the royal dissent should be publicly notified in Parliament. Yelverton was not to be brow-beaten and he successfully repelled Flood's attacks. Grattan, having expressed his admiration for Flood and Yelverton, 'two men of uncommon abilities', came down firmly in favour of the latter, emphasizing 'the efficacy' of Yelverton's Bill.[82] Grattan accepted that the British 'negating of our bills is a right never disputed' and Flood more specifically stated that the employment of the British Great Seal, 'with the knowledge of all the great officers of England', to signify the King of Ireland's consent to Irish bills was a bond of union 'he would never wish to impair'.[83] In 1782 nothing seems to have been said about the implications for Irish parliamentary independence of this use of the British Great Seal, but in 1789 during the regency debates it was painfully clear that with the British Great Seal in the custody of a member of a ministry responsible to the British House of Commons, that body would seem to have a degree of control over the proceedings of the Irish Parliament. Grattan was then obviously unhappy and was reduced to distinguishing sharply between the royal assent to bills which were pronounced by the King of Ireland (or his representative) in the Irish Parliament and the 'stamp of authority', the instrument merely used to authenticate the royal will.[84]

Flood, conscious of constitutional expertise, his twenty years' service and his rectitude – 'the whole earth does not contain a bribe sufficient to make me trifle with the liberties of this land' – not only castigated Yelverton but was also very dissatisfied with what Grattan had obtained. He contended that by the repeal of 6 Geo.I the British Parliament had merely cancelled an assertion of its claim to legislate for Ireland. The claim was not renounced and could be revived. Flood demanded that the British Parliament should pass a renunciation act; 'a positive promise', he argued, 'is in every case in the world more to be relied on than a constructive one'. And he further proposed that the Irish Parliament pass a bill of rights, providing that if the King should ever give his assent to a British act binding Ireland, the act annexing the Crown of Ireland to that of England would ipso facto be repealed. It is not unfair to assume that Flood was to some extent actuated by pique. He was clearly irritated at being outstripped in achievement and popularity by his juniors. But he was also influenced by principle and temperament. A realist who saw politics as a continuous power struggle, he thought it probable that Great Britain, if the opportunity arose, would again assert its legislative supremacy over Ireland. He was not prepared to rely on British generosity, what he wanted was 'solid, legal security' – and with dour determination and ruthless dialectical skill he enunciated his views in Parliament and strove to transform the discussion of a subtle point of constitutional law into a widespread popular agitation.[85]

Grattan was bound to resent the denigration of his great achievement. Also he considered that Flood's demands displayed an offensive disregard of English susceptibilities. As he explained many years later, the repeal of the Declaratory Act 'was not any confession of usurpation, it was a disclaimer of any right. You must suppose what I have said unsaid. A man of spirit may say that but he will hesitate to unsay it word by word.'[86] But Flood's forcible advocacy seems for a moment to have shaken him and in June, admitting that simple repeal might be insufficient, he tried to meet Flood's demands. As he was 'unwilling to force the delicacy or wound the pride of Great Britain', he suggested that instead of a renunciation bill a declaration of Irish rights might be inserted in the preamble of a bill or a declaration of renunciation might be issued under the British Great Seal. In Flood's opinion 'the pride of England is in this case the pride of wrong the pride of Ireland is the pride of right'. On the other hand, the Chief Secretary was at this stage not prepared to make any further concessions. So Grattan stiffened, contending in the House of Commons that repeal was the equivalent in law of renunciation and that it was foolish 'to go in a spirit of insatiety, supposing ideal dangers and finding food for perpetual discontent'.[87] Flood then met with two crushing defeats. On 19 July (a week before the session ended) he attempted to introduce a bill asserting the sole right of the Irish Parliament to make laws for Ireland and was beaten by 99 votes to 13; four days later a long amendment which he moved to the address to the Lord Lieutenant was negatived without a division. After Flood's defeat on the 19th Grattan counter-attacked, proposing a resolution declaring that anyone who in speech or writing propagated the opinion that Ireland had not an independent legislature was 'inimical' to both Great Britain and Ireland. Flood rebuked Grattan for trying to muzzle the press. If the motion was passed 'the tongue must not articulate; the pen must fall from the hand of every writer; the child of the mind must not be delivered'. Grattan retorted, 'the Right honourable gentleman may argue with me – may refute me but he cannot rebuke me, I would not be rebuked'. But Flood with his aloof censoriousness came off the better and Grattan was compelled to substitute for his resolution a motion declaring that Ireland's independence was fully and freely acknowledged by Great Britain. Grattan's 'stab at the liberty of the press' (a phrase coined by an indignant journalist) was also attacked in the Lords by Bellomont, a peer noted for gallantry, 'who entertained the ladies' with a speech directed against Grattan. At the close of the debate Grattan 'came up to his lordship and thanked him for his disapprobation. "You have said it", said Lord B., "entirely, your whole conduct, every action of your life and I give you most fully and sincerely". They then mutually bowed.' It is surprising that this exchange was not followed by a challenge, but presumably mutual contempt prevented an affair of honour.[88] In the following session Grattan vigorously supported Foster's Bill for Securing the Liberty of the Press (a misnomer), arguing that it was desirable that every newspaper should be obliged to print the name of its editor, otherwise the press 'would excite the unthinking to acts of desperation'.[89]

While they were debating in the House, Flood and Grattan strove to secure outside support. When in June the delegates of the Ulster Volunteer Corps met at Dungannon, Flood tried through 'his emissaries' to get them to pronounce in favour of renunciation but Arthur Dobbs, a fertile-minded and eccentric MP, after reading letters from Charlemont and Grattan, managed to persuade the Assembly to agree to an address to the King expressing satisfaction at the repeal of the Declaratory Act.[90] Grattan, about the same time, had to exert himself nearer home. At Flood's instigation some members of Grattan's own Volunteer corps, the Dublin Independents, proposed that an address of thanks should be presented to Flood. Grattan hurried to the meeting and was 'obliged, tho very ill to be three hours upon his legs answering the questions they put to him and proving the great inpropriety of addressing Mr Flood upon the present occasion. His arguments, influence and character at length prevailed' and the consideration of the address was postponed for six months.[91]

At the end of July, at the close of the session in which he had won such a glorious parliamentary triumph, Grattan, 'for the recovery of a constitution broken down in the service of Ireland', departed to Spa where, he said, 'all the great people of Europe met in déshabillé'.[92] Portland, as soon as he heard that Grattan intended to spend a week in London on his way to Spa, wrote to Fitzpatrick, the Chief Secretary, who was visiting England, urging him to contrive 'that Grattan was put into good hands' and not to miss 'the chance of rendering him as much use here as an Irishman can ever be'.[93] In fact it was about this time that Grattan began to form the friendships, firmly based on similar tastes and shared convictions, with Fox and some of the Foxite Whigs which gave him so much pleasure. Years later he remarked with a touch of hyperbole to one of the Fox family that the happiest days of his life were spent with Fitzpatrick, Fox's close friend, and his brother Lord Ossory.[94]

During the later months of 1782 Grattan learned how fickle was public favour. From the close of the session of 1781–2 the demand for renunciation became more widespread and strident. Flood campaigned in Ulster. Influential Volunteer corps, the Lawyers Corps and the Belfast Corps, decided that simple repeal was not an adequate guarantee of Ireland's legislative independence. In December Grattan's own corps, the Dublin Independents, informed their colonel that they agreed with the Lawyers Corps. Grattan replied reaffirming his belief that simple repeal was sufficient and offering to resign his post. The Corps promptly re-elected him as colonel. Less graciously, a commentator in the press remarked that £50,000 was a high price to pay a man who had botched the business he had undertaken.[95]

It may seem strange that the almost metaphysical distinction between simple repeal and renunciation could arouse such a public furore. But political Ireland after a prolonged constitutional struggle was restless, contentious and suspicious of British intentions. The Volunteers, having lost their raison d'être with the end of the war, were very ready to desert the parade ground for political meetings and to replace drill by debate. 'The poison of Flood's insinuation', a bright young Irish peer wrote, 'diffused itself through the country more rapidly than even despondency could imagine, and the country soon began to lose confidence in Grattan, 'the most upright and temperate demagogue that ever appeared in any country'.[96] Fuel was added to the fire by Lord Mansfield hearing and deciding on an Irish appeal brought into the King's Bench on a writ of error. It was argued that as the case had been pending from well before the repeal of the Declaratory Act, the Chief Justice had to pronounce judgement; but Irishmen were alarmed and angered by what seemed to be a reaffirmation of the appellant jurisdiction of the English Courts.

Portland's successor as Lord Lieutenant, Lord Temple, intelligent, high-strung and prone to exaggerate his difficulties and importance, was alarmed by the 'frenzy' which he saw sweeping the country. Consulting a wide range of Irish politicians (which included Grattan and Yelverton but not Flood), he quickly came to the conclusion that the only way to resolve a dangerous crisis was for Great Britain to renounce explicitly all legislative and judicial authority over Ireland, and he pressed the British government to introduce immediately a renunciation bill. When they saw the bill in draft Grattan and Yelverton were both greatly aggrieved. It was not, Grattan said, 'our idea at all'. They were prepared to support a request for a British enactment relinquishing the appellant jurisdiction, but Temple's Bill, they thought, implied that simple repeal was not an adequate recognition of Ireland's rights, and Grattan felt that he and Yelverton should be 'warranted by the parliament of England when we vindicate her sincerity'.

At the beginning of January Grattan had a somewhat acrimonious exchange with the Lord Lieutenant. 'Grattan', Temple reported, 'wishes us to fight his battle more avowedly; and I have as repeatedly declared my intention of advancing to the great outline [the renunciation bill] as the first point and backing him *en second*. This does not please but he cannot help himself.' In the end Grattan yielded to circumstances, telling the Lord Lieutenant 'to consult measures not men do whatever will add to the public security or your own ease'. However, he greatly appreciated the attitude adopted by Fox and his party when at the beginning of 1783 the Renunciation Bill was being discussed in the House of Commons. Though they did not oppose the bill, Fox and Fitzpatrick made clear that the act repealing the Declaratory Act, which they had framed in accordance with the views of the gentlemen in Ireland who interested themselves in the business, 'was a sufficient guarantee of Irish rights'.[97]

Shortly after the Renunciation Bill reached the statute book the Shelburne ministry fell, and a coalition government which included Grattan's friends Fox and Fitzpatrick came into office. Temple left Ireland, being succeeded by Lord Northington, who soon after arriving in Ireland asked Charlemont to accept a privy counsellorship. Charlemont, who privately thought that the Council Board 'had been degraded by the admission of a mob', punctiliously explained that as he was so closely connected with Grattan politically he could not accept the Lord Lieutenant's offer unless Grattan was also offered a privy counsellorship. Northington was quite prepared to recommend Grattan, though he could not abstain from remarking that he had noticed Grattan's absence from his first levee (a breach of etiquette which Charlemont deplored). Charlemont immediately wrote to Grattan, who was in the country, urging him to accept the Lord Lieutenant's offer. Grattan replied in a laconic note, saying he would attend the next levee and that 'as to the seat at the council board I have not the least objection to it'.[98] On 12 July he and Charlemont were both sworn of the Irish Privy Council.

Northington, though dismissed by contemporaries as an amiable and dignified nonentity, was by no means deficient in political awareness. He realized that the Irish Parliament, due to meet in October, might be difficult to handle, with MPs conscious of their new status as members of an independent legislature, feeling more self-important than ever but at the same time under increasing pressure from out-of-doors opinion. He therefore decided to form 'a little cabinet' for the management of the House of Commons. This group, which dined together fairly frequently, was composed of Grattan, Yelverton (the Attorney-General), Forbes (the prospective Solicitor-General), Charles Sheridan and John Foster, already an acknowledged fiscal and economic expert. Charlemont was pained at not being invited and mentioned the matter 'jocularily' to Grattan, who promptly secured him an invitation to the next dinner. Charlemont attended, found the discussion too discursive and gossipy, and was surprised at the presence of Sheridan, whom scarcely seemed 'from his rank and situation exactly suited to such company'. In fact Sheridan, who the Chief Secretary thought was too talkative and pushy, had been asked as a friend of Grattan.[99] Though he thought the dinner a waste of time, Charlemont was offended at not receiving further invitations and complained to Grattan. Grattan assured his touchy friend that if he was not asked continuously to future dinners he himself would discontinue his attendance.

By then the friendship and close political alliance between Grattan and Charlemont was in decline. They differed on the Catholic question and Charlemont disapproved of Grattan's collaboration with the Northington administration. He had come to the conclusion that Grattan was actuated by vanity and was lacking in genial warmth – 'he had not a feeling heart'. Charlemont was a man of excessive sensibility and sensitivity, whose friendships were intense and easily strained. Grattan, kindly enough but careless and immersed in family life, neglected the small attentions which meant so much to Charlemont. When in October 1783 Charlemont was confined to the house by 'a tedious illness' he looked forward eagerly to a visit from Grattan, when all would be forgotten and forgiven in an effusive exchange of ideas. Grattan failed to call and two years later Charlemont, speaking respectfully of Grattan's abilities, regretted that 'he was not capable of being a friend'.[100]

Grattan seems for a moment at least to have been greatly exhilarated by his new role; to have enjoyed sitting in council over the dinner table and shaping government policy. Indeed Edward Cooke, an influential civil servant with a waspish pen, commented that Grattan was beginning to talk as reasonably regarding office, reward and majorities 'as if he had been a firm servant of the crown for many years. He has now a stake in the country and his wife is about to lie in.'[101] Characteristically Cooke was over-cynical. Grattan, about the time he was included in the circle of the Viceroy's confidential advisers, told a young friend that although he wished the administration well, he intended 'to pledge them to a set of measures'.[102] But Northington, who was glad to find Grattan disposed to be 'a true and stout supporter of government', thought that his 'patriotic inclines' were of 'little moment'. When Grattan pressed the need for retrenchment the Lord Lieutenant persuaded him to be content for the immediate future with a promise that no sinecurist should receive an increase in salary.[103] The speech from the throne recommended two measures – the creation of an Irish Admiralty Court and of an Irish Post Office – which must have been agreeable to Grattan, and when he secured the appointment of a House of Commons committee to investigate the expenses of collecting the revenue, he was able to announce that the Revenue Board was prepared to co-operate with the committee. He was also pleased by two decisions of the House on fiscal issues. The import duties on English beer and English refined sugar were substantially increased, the administration agreeing that the increase in the beer duty was reasonable.

Early in the session Grattan, when defending the government, clashed with Flood, who was vigorously advocating economy. The subject was a hackneyed one, but Flood had a new suggestion: a reduction in the number of troops maintained by Ireland. When outlining his views on 28 October Flood referred to 'every little man who imagines he is a minister'. Soon Grattan rose and called on Flood to explain 'the propriety' of sending 4000 men 'to butcher our brethren in America'. Flood then launched into a downright attack on Grattan, 'a mendicant patriot' who had decked himself out in a rich wardrobe of words to deceive the people. Grattan replied at some length by describing a politician whose practice it was 'to abuse every man who differed from him and to betray every man who trusted him'. A great egoist, his career might be divided into three stages: 'in the first he was intemperate, in the second corrupt, and in the third seditious'. This philippic, even an admirer of Grattan thought, 'had much more of the broad and coarse ribaldry of the bar than of the pointed, elegant and witty raillery of the senate',[104] and Flood, rising for the third time, assured the House that he knew that all the venom accumulated and discharged by disappointed vanity left his character untainted. After this probably premeditated exchange which thrilled the House – the galleries were said to have been with Flood – both men left the chamber. Prompt steps were taken to prevent a meeting. Flood, on his way to a field near Ballsbridge to exchange shots with Grattan, was arrested by a magistrate, and the Chief Justice of the King's Bench informed the Speaker that he was considering taking both men into custody. On 1 November Flood came down to the House and, rising 'to defend an injured character', delivered a long autobiographical speech. Grattan immediately rose to comment, but the House had had enough and cut him short by adjourning. After their resounding display of invective Grattan and Flood would not sit near one another in the House until in August 1785 they found themselves united in opposition to Orde's Anglo-Irish Trade Bill. Even then Flood remained in his private correspondence a severe critic of Grattan, who, he wrote, 'has arrogance enough to undo a dozen better men'. Grattan, Flood thought, was rated to mishandle any question he took and by the close of the eighties had 'assumed the ideas and fastidiousness of an aristocrat. He can't forgive the people for having ever differed from him.'[105]

In the week following their great verbal duel they had an argument which reflected temperamental as well as policy differences. Flood moved for a reduction in the military forces maintained by Ireland. Grattan, who opposed the motion, asked indignantly, 'has success made us niggardly? Shall we become unkind to England, just at the moment she has shown kindness to us?' Flood, who had already referred to 'silly talk of gratitude', was defeated, but in a few weeks his activities forced Grattan to disassociate himself from Northington's administration over an important issue, parliamentary reform. On 29 November Flood presented to the House a reform bill, endorsed by a national Volunteer convention sitting in the Rotunda. Northington welcomed the opportunity of mustering men of property and conservative instincts behind the administration. Grattan had not taken part in the reform agitation and he was not a member of the National Convention, unlike Flood who was the guiding spirit of the assembly. He could have followed the course adopted by those MPs who, reserving their opinion on reform, refused to accept a measure backed by armed men. Instead in a short, sympathetic speech, he declared himself to be a friend to parliamentary reform, recommending a union between Parliament and the Volunteers, and voted for the bill.

Grattan's attitude on reform and the sugar duties showed that though he was one of the Lord Lieutenant's confidential advisers, he was selective in his support of administration. It may be added that by the close of 1783 changes occurred in the group of advisers on whom the Lord Lieutenant relied which must have given Grattan food for thought. Forbes, having come out strongly in favour of Flood's Reform Bill, informed the Chief Secretary that if he were appointed Solicitor-General he would give only 'an independent support' to the government. In these circumstances they both agreed 'he could not be offered or accept' the post. While Forbes, one of Grattan's natural allies, failed to attain office, John Scott, the fluent unflagging spokesman for the Irish administration from 1777 to 1782, came back to office as Prime Sergeant, and on Yelverton being promoted to the Bench John Fitzgibbon was appointed Attorney-General. Scott and Fitzgibbon were in the front rank at the Bar, but Portland, who saw himself as a custodian of true Whig principles, could not help pointing out to Northington that they 'had been brought up in habits of thinking respecting the conduct of government very different to those consistent with our professions and principles'.[106] Both men in fact had a bias in favour of firm government and were quick to defend the actions of the executive. Portland also did not altogether approve of Grattan being treated as a confidential adviser. Grattan, the Duke explained to Northington, was 'a well-intentioned and honestly disposed person and in that country of very superior parliamentary abilities, but I cannot help being alarmed by his speculations for reform and retrenchment which he does not himself approve but thinks necessary to satisfy certain engagements'. Portland when he was in Ireland had discussed with Grattan 'the subject of popularity' and was convinced that Grattan was 'so far infected with the contagious part of that passion as still to sacrifice his own opinions at that shrine'.[107] Portland was not alone in his estimate of Grattan. Carlisle when Lord Lieutenant had referred to Grattan's 'decided attachment (as he called it) to the people'.[108] Fitzpatrick in the spring of 1782, having written of Grattan as an honest and impractical 'enthusiast', added that his situation is enough to 'turn the head of any man fond of popular applause but the brilliancy of it can only subsist by carrying points in opposition to the government'.[109] And Lady Louisa Connolly, a highly intelligent woman in close touch with Irish political life, said with mild irritation that Grattan was 'a thorough well meaning good man. But his hankering after popularity does provoke me."[110] In

71

short, conventional politicians thought that Grattan, by keeping in close accord with public opinion – that growing power which men of affairs now reluctantly realized could not be ignored – had managed to acquire a special position in public life. But as a result they believed he had developed a dangerous weakness, an avid desire for the approbation of a public that was often ill-informed and volatile.

The year 1782, the year of Grattan's great political victory, was also a momentous one in his private life. Almost simultaneously he became a well-off landowner and a married man. With his parliamentary grant invested in land, he had a substantial estate. He had in addition his hereditary property, and in 1802 his uncle, Richard Marlay, left him a share in his landed estate.[111] By the close of his life Grattan's income was about six thousand pounds a year, though, as was not unusual for an Irish landlord, it was charged with a substantial sum (£147,000).[112] Grattan was all the better off because, in a society characterized by conspicuous consumption, he had no extravagant tastes and seems to have measured his expenditure carefully. It was probably malicious gossip to say that when attending Parliament he stayed in lodgings rather than taking a house so as to avoid the expense of having his family in Dublin (Mrs Grattan probably preferred the country). Even so, at a time when Irish country gentlemen were busy building big houses and laying out their grounds, Grattan in 1782 acquired a Co. Wicklow house called Tinnehinch, which had been a large inn, to which he made only plain additions, leaving the fabric unadorned. As for a garden, while he loved fruit, he found gardeners intimidating. Pictures gave him no pleasure, 'fine furniture' he was afraid of damaging. As an elderly man he once said that if he were rich (which he was) he would have bands of music and fine carriage horses. But music is a pleasure which can be indulged in cheaply and Grattan was never noted for his equipage. On one occasion he summed up his outlook by remarking, 'give me a cottage and crust ... plain fare and quiet, small beer and claret'. (His accounts show he meant good claret as well as good port.)[113] Though he did not want to be bothered by multifarious possessions (except acres) and lacked interest in the decorative arts which appealed to the good taste of the age, he lived comfortably enough in a style befitting a landed gentleman of means. He was hospitable to relations and old friends. He gave generously to charity – as a young barrister half a guinea to a distressed attorney, as an older man thirty pounds for the family of Dr Lucas, and twelve pounds towards the publication of the works of a young poet of humble origin – and he was kind to the poor on his estate.[114] His bias towards simplicity probably strengthened his fiscal Puritanism. Private restraint made him highly critical of public prodigality.

Though at thirty-six he felt 'a sheepishness on the subject of marriage',[115] in December 1782 he married an attractive young woman, Henrietta Fitzgerald, the daughter of Nicholas Fitzgerald of Greenlaw, County Kilkenny. Henrietta had a brother Thomas, who was to retire from the Army as a colonel. She also had a sister married to the Rev. William Elliott, who, before being ordained, had served in the Dragoons and who became Vicar of Trim and a justice of the peace. Henrietta's mother was Margaret Stevenson, a County Down coheiress, whose sister was married to Sir John Blackwood, a well-known MP. Her paternal grandfather, Thomas Fitzgerald of Turlogh, had conformed to the Established Church early in the eighteenth century, and his eldest surviving son and heir married Mary, a sister of the Earl-Bishop of Derry. Their son George Robert was the notorious duelist. Grattan's marriage increased his links with the Irish landed, military and clerical worlds, but he must have been somewhat disconcerted when in 1786, shortly after he had been speaking on the maintenance of law and order in Dublin, George Robert Fitzgerald was convicted and hanged for murder.

Grattan's marriage was an extremely happy one. Mrs Grattan was handsome, dignified, amiable, kind and intelligent, an affectionate and capable wife and mother.[116] Unfortunately she suffered intermittently from bad health (and for the last twenty years of her life was confined to her chair). In 1786 Orde, the Chief Secretary, met Mr and Mrs Grattan taking the waters at Spa. Grattan, who was 'full of spirits and good humour', had found the Cheltenham waters satisfactory but had come to Spa for the sake of his wife. Less than a year later Mrs Grattan was dangerously ill and Grattan was 'quite distracted'. But she recovered rapidly and Grattan soon regained 'his eloquence and power of speech'. When in August Orde visited Tinnehinch, Mrs Grattan, rejoicing in her recovery,

73

almost persuaded him to try calomel, but in the end his faith in Bath remained unshaken.[117]

His marriage had a considerable influence on Grattan's political life. It gave him a background of security and affection which cheered and revived him after the stresses and strains of the session. It also intensified his inclination to retreat for as long as possible to rural peace and quiet. In Wicklow, surrounded by his family – his wife and ultimately two sons and two daughters – and a small circle of attached friends, he was not lonely but happily isolated from the comings and goings, the gossip and contacts which were the breath of life to active men of affairs. Tinnehinch was situated near the north end of the Dargle valley in a picturesque countryside of valleys, woods and mountains (in the Irish sense of the term), studded with the villas of well-off Dubliners. The area had all that an eighteenth-century man of feeling could ask for – striking vistas and well-cultivated demesnes contrasting vividly with solitary stretches of rugged nature. Grattan became deeply attached to Tinnehinch; he planted extensively and Mrs Grattan constructed a much-admired 'cabin' or summer house.[118] Grattan also had congenial neighbours – William Broome; John Blachford, a County Wicklow gentleman who married Grattan's daughter Mary; and George Carroll, a sometime High Sheriff of County Wicklow, who had it recorded on his memorial tablet in St George's, Dublin, that 'he was the friend of Henry Grattan'.

III

An Ornament of the Senate

After the high drama of the early eighties, culminating in the achievement of parliamentary independence, Irish politics were for ten years, until the opening of the war with revolutionary France in 1793, comparatively placid. Admittedly the spirit of protest which animated influential sections of Irish society during the great struggle for free trade and parliamentary rights did not immediately evaporate. The renunciation agitation was followed by a widespread, well-organized demand for parliamentary reform, at first backed by the Volunteers, and by a tariff reform agitation, aggressively supported by the Dublin textile workers. But although reform and protection initially aroused great enthusiasm, they both failed to obtain the consistent, long-term popular support which might have overcome parliamentary obduracy. Soon extra-parliamentary activity ceased to attract attention and Irish politics again centred on the parliamentary session, with Parliament continuing to function on customary lines. The administration strove to secure the supplies and the legislation required if government was to be effectively carried on; its critics continued to call for retrenchment and to denounce any measure which they suspected embodied an undue extension of the powers of the Crown.

For Irish peers and MPs it was a halcyon time. The Irish Parliament was theoretically a far more important and powerful body than it had been before 1782. The country seemed to be prospering, rents were certainly rising, the amenities of life were increasing and the position of the Irish landed world seemed to be unshakeable. Indeed an intelligent, if self-interested, commentator declared in 1783, that Ireland's constitutional claims having been met, 'there can never be hereafter in this country any such thing as party connections founded upon political principles'. After all, he wrote, party politics were about power and in Ireland all power was 'lodged solely with the English government'.[1] This theory, which promised a long continuance of political placidity, was plausible, but events at the close of the decade demonstrated that it was only partly correct.

Before discussing Grattan's political activities in this comparatively placid period something must be said about his parliamentary status. He was widely acknowledged to be 'one of the most conspicuous ornaments of the Irish senate'.[2] His parliamentary career had been meteoric. At the beginning of 1775 he was a briefless barrister; by the summer of 1782 his perseverance, intellectual ability, oratorical talents and success in winning parliamentary independence had placed him in the front rank of Irish political life, *primus inter pares*. At the age of thirty-six he could almost claim to be an elder statesman. But he was not made to be a political Nestor or Polonius. He was too full of nervous energy, too uncompromising, at times too shrill and too ready to intervene vehemently in the battle. Rather he saw himself as a tribune of the people, an independent member, standing aloof from the administration and indeed from any political connections and speaking authoritatively and forcibly on a wide range of issues.

By 1782 Grattan's oratorical style had crystallized. It reflected the influence of the great classical orators, the law courts, the pulpit and his own political position and parliamentary strategy. Since he was usually an opponent (or at least a very candid critic) of men in power, his speeches tended to be denunciatory and exhortatory: a compound of passionately sustained criticism and moral fervour. Point after point was driven home by a series of cascading sentences, carefully polished and pared so as to produce an impression of compressed, irresistible force. There is a mechanical touch about many of his speeches – the repetitiveness (perhaps hard to avoid), the verbal tricks, the steady succession of well-moulded sentences, automatically rising to a crescendo. But there was also the logical strength and ingenuity of his arguments, the mastery of language which enabled him to coin the unexpected and memorable phrase, the flashes of humour and epigrammatic wit, the fire, the *saeva indignatio*, the high seriousness and sense of purpose, the consciousness that the Irish Parliament had a mission – 'to increase a growing people, to mature a struggling though hardy community, to mould, to multiply, to consolidate, to inspire and to exalt a young nation'.[3] Grattan continually brought home to his audience his belief that they were discussing momentous questions and that they would certainly occupy no mean place in history. He often referred to the great events in British constitutional history and from time to time he embarked on a survey of contemporary Irish history, designed to show that Ireland had in recent years won great political victories and that it remained for Parliament to reap their fruits in spite of the manoeuvrings of the Irish administration. Such historical disquisitions, even if eloquent, can be wearisome; and on one occasion when Grattan told the House he was going to explain the circumstances 'which gave rise' to Yelverton's act, he was discouraged by cries of 'No doubt, no doubt'.[4] On another occasion Toler, the Solicitor-General, whose down-to-earth common sense savoured with a dash of buffoonery made him an effective debater, pointed out that Grattan as a historian had 'an infinite advantage. He certainly is the happiest of all historians who is for ever the hero of his own tale; he is not indebted even to the Goddess of his idolatry – common fame – for sounding forth his praises, for a trumpeter he need only be indebted to himself.' Toler continued for some time in this strain and Grattan rose in high dudgeon, hinting that the consequence might be a challenge. But Toler (who did not lack courage) laughed the matter off.

As this episode shows, Grattan was quick to respond with contemptuous scorn to personal criticism. When Toler's predecessor as Solicitor-General suggested he was not a sound lawyer, Grattan retorted by telling him that there was a vast difference between the knowledge of the practice of the courts and a knowledge of the constitution. When Sir Henry Cavendish declared that Grattan's 'principle was opposition to every system and every administration', Grattan remarked that unlike Cavendish 'he had not both supported and opposed the same administration and the same measures'. When a young MP, Marcus Beresford, boldly attacked Grattan's conduct during the Regency crisis as 'tricky and uncandid', Grattan replied that given his opinion of Beresford's 'parts and person', nothing he could say would disturb him. About the same time he had an acrimonious rencontre with another young MP, Lawrence Parsons, an admirer of Flood. Parsons denounced Grattan as a well-rewarded, incompetent politician, reciting a list of his blunders: his belief in a simple repeal, his failure to grasp the implications of Yelverton's act, his change of stance on the commercial propositions. Grattan hit back, remarking that Parsons' speeches afforded 'a melancholy proof that a man may be scurrilous who has not the capacity to be severe'. After a fellow MP had expressed regret at 'the biting, strange, odd, sarcastic way' in which Parsons and Grattan had spoken, the former apologized. But Grattan showed himself reluctant to follow suit, so the Speaker summoned both of them up to his Chair and made them promise to drop the matter.[5] Eight years later Grattan had an even more acrimonious clash with John Egan, a burly Whig barrister who, alarmed by the state of the country, had become a government supporter. Egan attacked Grattan as 'a duodecimo incendiary', one of a group which had degraded Fitzwilliam's administration by their low ambitions. Grattan replied by calling Egan a swaggering bully, remarking that when Egan talked of the guillotine it was easy to visualize the executioner. The Speaker promptly intervened. Both gentlemen were placed under arrest and the House spent two hours discussing the affair.[6]

Grattan was rebuked more gently, and perhaps more effectively, by William Eden when he was Chief Secretary. After Grattan had spoken sharply in debate, Eden complained to Sir John Blaquiere, who it might be assumed would tactfully convey the substance of his remarks to Grattan, that Grattan 'honours me with a more earnest attention and more earnest opposition than public and political circumstances require, we must often jar and spar in debate but my temper and habits of public life are such that these jarrings conducted with personal candour will not diminish my love for his private character and will increase my admiration for his public abilities'.[7] Grattan's outbursts of temper reveal the strain under which he laboured when delivering his carefully planned and polished contributions to debate, and reflect his complete acceptance of the contemporary code of honour which demanded that a gentleman must be quick to resent any hostile criticism of his conduct and character and be ready to risk his life in their defence (though Grattan emphasized that, if a good shot, he should not be a bully).[8]

Grattan's speeches, powerful and enthralling, won the admiration of his fellow members who shared his Whiggery and his belief in the British connection and preened themselves on their House possessing a rival to Pitt and Fox. But paradoxically he was usually in a minority when it came to a division. Many MPs disagreed with his policies and felt that he gave too free a rein to his idealism. Ideals had their place in politics but, they felt, it was not unprincipled to give pragmatic considerations due weight. Grattan, though frequently defeated, did not despair. 'I am accustomed', he said, 'to be defeated upon great principles but I know great principles do not die.' Experience taught him that majorities could melt. 'I am not afraid', he declared, 'of occasional majorities.'[9] He must have expected his arguments to make an impression on the House that would have long-term consequences. He knew his speeches were read avidly by the general public and he enjoyed exercising his powers.

From the early eighties Grattan held a special place in public life as the eloquent exponent of Ireland's right as a nation to a high degree of political autonomy within the British Empire. The question may be asked, on what did he base his conviction that Ireland was a nation with an undeniable title to determine its political destiny? Nationalists in the nineteenth century could readily give reasons for the faith that was in them. They asserted confidently that the community for which they demanded political freedom – Germany, Bohemia, Italy, Ireland – was bound together by language, cultural traditions, history, habits and moral and spiritual qualities. Compared to this full-bodied faith, Grattan's nationalism was thin if heady. His literary interests were those of a cultured Englishman of his day, though incidentally there is no evidence that the publication of the poems of Ossian shortly before he entered college attracted his attention. On the one occasion in which he came forward as a defender of the Irish language he was obviously affected by political rather than cultural considerations. When in 1796 he vigorously attacked a provision inserted by the House of Lords in a bill regulating parliamentary elections, obliging freeholders to take the registration oath in English, it was because it would deprive 'by a side wind' many Catholic free-holders in the West of their recently acquired right to the franchise. Some years later, on the ground that 'the diversity of language not the diversity of religion' would be a source of permanent division in Irish life, he wanted primary education to be based on English – though he hoped the Irish language would not be forgotten.[10] Irish history for Grattan seems to have begun in the sixteenth century and to have become of significant interest with the emergence of Swift and Molyneux, the founding fathers of Irish patriotism. Most of his historical references were drawn from British constitutional history and his heroes were the barons of Runnymede, not Brian Boru or Hugh O'Neill. Although he advised his elder son to study Irish history from the beginning of the Tudor period, he also prescribed for him an extensive course of British historical reading with an emphasis on constitutional history. He confessed that Leland's History of Ireland (a pioneering work covering the period 1172 to 1691) had often sent him to sleep. Admittedly he subscribed to James Hely's edition of O'Flaherty's *Ogygia*, but the exceptionally long list of subscribers indicates not only an interest in the Celtic past but Hely's energetic efforts to secure support. Years later when Charles O'Conor, the Irish antiquarian, sent Grattan an advertisement for his enormous *Rerum Hibernicarum Scriptores Veteres*, 300 days and 300 nights elapsed without an answer.[11]

As for religion, he himself belonged to what in later days would have been labeled a minority denomination. A member of that proud body, the Established Church, he was a loyal, if latitudinarian, Anglican. 'I love the mild government of the Church of England', he once said. 'It is a home for piety; it is a cradle for science; so by an early alliance with divinity, you guard the majesty of heaven against the rebellion of wit. I like the arched roof, the cathedral state, the human voice, and all the power of evangelic harmony to give a soul to our duty; the wisest men we know of, Locke and Newton, were Christians and Protestants; it is the minor genius that mutinies against the Gospel; he affords to the universe one glance and has not patience for the second.' His own religious feelings were intense if idiosyncratic. Asked in conversation if he said his prayers in the morning and evening, he replied, 'No never but I have aspirations all day and all night long'.[12] Believing that Anglicanism had reconciled religion and modern thought, and also, as a man of the Enlightenment, certain that many of the more striking and objectionable dogmas and practices associated with Roman Catholicism were rapidly withering away, Grattan was not disposed to see religion as a distinctive component of Irish nationality. Nor, though he continually expressed warm affection for Ireland and Irishmen, he never embarked on a subtle analysis of the national character with the object of proving that Irishmen inherently possessed unique qualities, nor did he suggest that the Irish outlook and way of life differed significantly from the British (he himself thoroughly enjoyed social life in both countries). His nationalism was essentially geographic. Ireland was a distinctive area and its inhabitants, having common interests, were bound to develop strong community feeling and form a competing group. For this community feeling the Irish Parliament provided a focus, and for Grattan national feeling fused with institutional loyalty. He was, in the strictest sense of the term, a parliamentary nationalist, devoted to defending the rights and privileges of the Irish Parliament and by his contributions to its debates increasing the prestige of the Irish House of Commons.

Grattan was so eager to assert Ireland's nationhood and so sensitive to any infringement of her rights that it is easy to forget that one of the fundamental articles of his political creed, which he held with fervent conviction, was that a close and permanent connection should exist between Great Britain and Ireland. 'Ireland', he declared, 'was wedded for ever to that nation – we may sometimes discuss, sometimes argue – but never separate.'[13] He was of course very conscious that there was a danger inherent in the partnership which had to be guarded against. Great Britain, by far the stronger partner, might from selfishness, ignorance or indifference ignore Ireland's rights and interests. He was very quick to denounce any unfairness on the part of Great Britain, not infrequently personifying Ireland as a woman – an injured lady (an Englishman might be tempted to reflect that Grattan's Hibernia at times seemed like a nagging wife) – and when Anglo-Irish issues were being debated he was often highly critical of British policy and of the morality and motives of British ministers.

Accepting, then, that the connection between the two countries should be 'friendly and lasting', how were tensions between them to be resolved and a good working relationship maintained? Grattan belonged to the school which tended to deprecate the value of legal ties and institutional machinery for ensuring imperial co-operation. He had fought and defeated the British claim to legislative and judicial supremacy over Ireland, and once the Declaratory Act was repealed he had not suggested an alternative method of regulating Anglo-Irish relations by formal contractual arrangements. Rather he relied on goodwill. Common interests, common ideals, allegiance to the Crown and mutual respect would bind the countries together and ensure joint action when necessary and desirable. 'As Irish conformity is necessary to the British empire,' he explained, 'so is Irish equality necessary to obtain that conformity, that is the true principle that connects; it is the breath that lifts, and it is the spirit that moves, and the soul that actuates – without it all is eccentricity – with it the two nations gravitate to a common centre and fulfill their stated revolutions in the imperial orbit, by rules regular as the laws of motion, like them infallible, and like them ever-lasting!'[14]

To some extent his reliance on goodwill seemed to be justified. It was taken for granted in Ireland that Great Britain should be responsible for foreign policy and defence planning. Grattan felt that the contribution to imperial defence demanded from Ireland, the maintenance of a certain number of military units, was reasonable and in 1792 he heartily supported an increase in pay for the rank and file – 'everyman', he said, 'must agree with it'.[15] On the one occasion between 1782 and 1793 when the Irish Parliament was called on to back Great Britain in a dispute with a foreign power, Grattan unhesitatingly supported a vote of credit to maintain 'the commercial rights of the empire' on the west coast of North America threatened by Spain.[16]

Grattan's imperial idealism was easily realized in foreign affairs and defence, but when economic relations between Great Britain and Ireland came to be discussed, goodwill was often in short supply. Though the two economies were to a great extent complementary, in some respects they were competitive and the struggle for markets was intensified and brought into politics by the determination of interest groups in both countries to obtain preferential tariffs, bounties, premiums and drawbacks. Grattan was not at his happiest when commercial issues were being debated, though he frequently spoke. Trade statistics and the problems arising from the conflicting demands of Irish manufacturers, importers and consumers were scarcely susceptible of rhetorical treatment, and Grattan must have been pained by the crude confrontations between British and Irish interests frequently thrust on his attention. When discussing British commercial policy towards Ireland he was often suspicious and resentful. Great Britain, he thought, was not only at times selfish and unfair but was endeavouring to maintain an offensive superiority. For Grattan what was at stake when the interpretation of the Navigation Laws or the levy of the beer duties was being debated was not a mere matter of profit and loss but Ireland's constitutional and international status.

The policy which he consistently advocated for harmonizing Anglo-Irish economic relations was for the two countries reciprocally to lower or abolish customs duties on one another's products. Naturally then he did not support the strident call for protective duties directed against imports from Great Britain which arose in Ireland, and more especially in Dublin, a centre of textile industry, immediately legislative independence had been gained. The opinion was expressed that a man who had obtained £50,000 to adorn his 'civic crown' ought to do something more for his much injured country.[17] But to Grattan tariff reform was 'the unhappy question a question whether we should turn a vast number of articles of English manufacture out of the Irish market – a question taken up so improperly, so furiously agitated and so suspiciously deserted'.[18] Grattan's refusal to exert himself in favour of protection made him a target for popular hostility. In November 1783 a mob of angry artisans (probably incited by some of their employers) poured into the passages of the

Parliament House, shouting 'Protecting duties and that they were all starving'. Grattan was one of the MPs whom they were looking for and a few days later, about eight in the evening, a crowd of armed men gathered round his lodgings in Castle Street, 'threatening his life openly'. Fortunately Grattan was out to dinner and by the time he returned the crowd had dispersed.[19]

Early in 1785 he welcomed the commercial propositions, Pitt's great design for promoting goodwill between the two countries and encouraging economic growth by establishing a common market. 'I must', Grattan wrote to his friend Richard Fitzpatrick, 'rejoice at everything which I conceive will benefit Ireland, and will be very satisfied if it produces a final settlement and cuts up the roots of altercation between the two nations which are in fact one people and whose political and personal connections cannot be too intimate and extensive'.[20] But when in February the scheme was laid before the Irish House of Commons he insisted on an important amendment. Discussing the plan with Orde the Chief Secretary he urged that it must include 'a pledge of economy in Irish expences'. You can imagine, Orde wrote to the Prime Minister, the arguments he used, but 'you cannot well judge the peculiar force his peculiar manner would give them among a peculiar people'.[21] Grattan's demand was met. The tenth proposition in its original form provided that if any year the hereditary revenue (about a third of the government's income) rose above £656,000, the excess should be appropriated to the support of the Navy. This was changed, it being laid down that in peacetime the imperial contribution should be paid only in years when there was a balanced budget. In response to this amendment Grattan agreed that the gap which at the beginning of 1785 existed between income and expenditure should be closed by additional taxation. Thus the scheme was, in his opinion, not only 'open, fair and just' but had the added merit of encouraging fiscal economy. If the government wanted to obtain a naval contribution it would have to control its expenditure.

In February the Irish Parliament approved Pitt's scheme, set out in eleven propositions, and these were immediately laid before the British House of Commons where they were strongly criticized. 'The manufacturers of England', Grattan declared in one of his historical digressions, 'trembled at it they contemplated the low price of labour and provisions in Ireland – they mistook the symptoms of poverty for the seeds of wealth – in your raggedness they saw riches in disguise and in destitution itself they discovered a powerful rival to the capital, credit and commerce of Great Britain'. Moreover the businessmen, 'jealous of your poverty', were backed by 'another party jealous of your liberty', the remnant of Lord North's ministry, 'that remnant which had but one idea with respect to Great Britain Ireland and America – coercion – coercion'. In making this point Grattan of course glossed over the fact that the whole British opposition, including Fox and Burke, exploited to the full the advantages they might gain from denouncing Pitt's bold plan.

In July, after long debates and committee hearings, Pitt won approval for his scheme, by then embodied in twenty propositions. Pitt claimed that the plan was in essence unaltered, the additions and changes merely clarifying and elaborating the original propositions. To take an instance which was to produce a violent reaction from Grattan: when in the eleven propositions as they left the Irish House of Commons it had been laid down that it was desirable that the two countries' tariffs and regulations affecting trade should be identical, the bill embodying the propositions which Orde placed before the Irish House of Commons on 12 August 1785 provided that since 'a similarity of laws, manners and customs must naturally conduce to perpetuating the affection and harmony which ought at all times to subsist between the people of Great Britain and Ireland', the Irish Parliament should impose the same duties on colonial produce as were imposed by the British Parliament and should enact the laws for the encouragement of shipping, granting similar benefits to and imposing similar restraints on the natives of both countries, that were passed at Westminster. These provisions were defended by Thurlow, the English Lord Chancellor, a no-nonsense lawyer. 'One country', he explained, 'must take the lead in making regulations relating to trade and navigation; that such regulations could not be made by common consent; though it would be impossible that the common King of both countries would risque their wider separation by suffering anything partial; that any minister would be fool enough to attempt it; or that Ireland should acquiesce in it if any regulations were of that description. Who then should regulate? The country already in possession of that commerce and better acquainted with it by experience.' This is not how Grattan – who according to the Viceroy was 'wild on the business' – saw it. By the bill, he declared, 'Britain takes the stamp of the Irish Parliament; Great Britain is to prescribe and Ireland to obey'.[22] In the debate of 12 August he attacked Orde's bill, in what Mornington described as 'a most eloquent but the most mischievous and inflamatory speech I have ever heard'. Cooke, who expected Grattan would attack the revised propositions, forecast with some satisfaction that 'if he does not take care he will expose himself most egregiously for he is totally ignorant of the detail of the subject and incapable of attaining it'.[23] Grattan did take care.

The main theme of his speech was the threat to Ireland's constitutional liberties. Economic arguments, Grattan made it quite clear, were of secondary importance. Having in a brisk survey demonstrated that the scheme was not founded 'on the only principle which could obtain between two independent nations, equality', and that its terms might hinder Irish development and enable the British Parliament by tariff manipulation to damage Irish industry, he moved on to familiar ground by asserting that 'from this consideration of commerce a question much more high, much more deep, the invaluable question of constitution, arises in which the idea of protecting duties, the idea of reciprocal duties, of countervailing duties, all that detail vanish; the energies of every heart, the energies of every head, are called up to shield this nation'. What was at stake was Ireland's rights. The bill, he said, was a surrender not only of Ireland's constitutional privileges, but of her rights derived from the law of nature and the law of nations. It was 'an incipient and creeping union, it was a virtual union'. The House of Commons that he was addressing were 'limited trustees of the delegated power' and could not give up their rights. Any such surrender would be void, and if it were made, 'another year would see old constitution advance, the honours of his head, and the good institution of parliament shaking off the tomb to reascend in all its pomp and pride and plentitude of privilege As an Irishman I say perish the empire, leave the constitution.' At that point Wesley Pole, a future Chief Secretary, interjected that 'these words went to a direct separation from Great Britain', and Grattan replied 'the honourable gentleman is not entitled to say that'.[24]

Grattan expressed and stimulated the apprehensions of those Irishmen who believed that status was at stake and that in the commercial sphere they might be embarking on a series of bad bargains. Orde had to withdraw his bill and the Irish supporters of the Commercial Propositions were reduced to prophesizing that when Irishmen, the victims of Grattan's pride and vanity, recovered their senses they would 'discover the recollection of Mr Grattan's splendid periods to be but a slender consolation for poverty'.[25]

Another provision in Orde's bill which was bound to arouse Grattan's ire was the clause confirming the East India Company's rights. It was, in his opinion, not only 'an exclusive company' (many Englishmen of course also resented the Company's monopoly) but its rights rested on an English charter and a British Act of Parliament. Acceptance of these rights meant accepting restraints on Irish trade which resembled 'rather a judgement of God than an act of the legislature, whether measured by immensity of space or infinity of duration'.[26] Irish trade would be debarred from markets of immense value which Grattan pictured in glowing terms – the countries within the Ganges, the Indies which lie beyond the Ganges, the Oriental islands, some equal in size to Great Britain and Ireland, and China 'with her 58 000 000 of people', 'countries in space incomprehensible, in population infinite, and in produce indefinite'. How impossible it was for the members of the Irish administration, with their attention fixed on 'the still, the brewing pan, the provision for their numerous off-spring and the trade of parliament', to comprehend the economic potential of this vast region. Irish exports, Grattan believed, would find a market in the Far East and Ireland had the capital to carry on an Eastern trade. Nevertheless, he realistically accepted the compromise of 1793 by which the Irish Parliament confirmed the East India Company's charter on the condition the Company provided shipping for Irish exports – though characteristically he dwelt sharply on the sacrifices Ireland was making for the sake of imperial harmony.

Anglo-Irish commercial contentions helped to bring home to Grattan that he had been optimistic when he had assumed in the summer of 1782 that all constitutional issues that could create bad feeling between the two countries were settled.[27] He saw that the Irish administration, still appointed by the Lord Lieutenant, a member of the British ministry of the day, tended to put British interests first when commercial questions were being debated in the Irish House of Commons. (Men in office would have said that since in the long run British and Irish interests coincided, their aim was to try and prevent clashes on minor matters.) Grattan greatly resented that the Irish administration, to which he found himself opposed on a number of issues, should be under British control – 'trustees for the British government in Ireland'. 'We have no Irish cabinet', he complained in 1786. 'Individuals may deprecate, may dissuade but they cannot enforce their principles – there is no embodied authority in Ireland.' Five years later, when he perceived that there was an Irish cabinet consisting of the confidential advisers of the Lord Lieutenant, he was still dissatisfied. The cabinet, he explained, was composed of two very similar elements, 'the one part dependent on the minister of England the other part principally composed of the old court accustomed to crouch and bend to the brow of power'. Undoubtedly the two Crowns were united, but, he asserted, 'the executive powers emanating therefrom are essentially distinct'.[28]

Nevertheless, Grattan did not boldly urge that Ireland should have responsible as well as representative government. To do so would have reflected a great spring forward in political thinking. Cabinet government might be functioning in Great Britain but constitutional theory had not caught up with political practice. Though the power of Parliament was recognized, the ministers were still conceived to be in more than a formal sense the King's servants. Understandably, then, Grattan did not anticipate the results of the Durham Report, the imperial conferences of 1926 and 1930 and the statute of Westminster. What he hankered after was a lord lieutenant capable of disregarding the interested advice of Irish officeholders and responsive to the right kind of Irish opinion. But he admitted that though the viceroy should be 'the representative of the King, not of the minister', he should keep in close communication with the British government, and that 'if the English cabinet no longer co-operated with the viceroy it is prudent in him to withdraw'.[29]

Accepting, as Grattan theoretically would, the separation of powers, how was the increasing influence of the executive over the legislature to be diminished? Grattan in the summer of 1782 had a simple answer. Diminish the number of placemen and increase the number of representatives.[30] From then on Grattan was a firmly committed if not very enthusiastic supporter of parliamentary reform, which 'if not absolutely necessary would be extremely convenient'. The borough representation, when considered 'arithmetically', obviously required vigorous reorganization; he wanted an increase in the county representation; and he supported the reform bills introduced by Flood in 1783–4 and 1785.[31] But as a distinguished, much admired member of the unreformed House of Commons he was conscious of its merits and anxious that nothing should be done which would weaken the authority of an assembly which 'had acquired more by wisdom and discretion than others have by the sword'.[32] He was sure that the constitution was 'the best existing' and that although it required 'invigoration' it should be treated with respect, and he disapproved of the reformers' tactics during the years 1783–5: their policy of summoning assemblies of delegates which purported to represent the people better than the House of Commons and their efforts to involve the Volunteers in the reform movement, with the vague implication of the possibility of direct action if Parliament was obdurate. Reformers should not, he contended, 'vulgarize popular exertions'. 'An appeal to the latent and summary powers of the people should be reserved for extraordinary exigencies', such as for instance the struggle in 1782 for Ireland's parliamentary rights, when, as Grattan pointed out, the Volunteers had been content to stand behind Parliament. Moreover, he stressed, it was important when talking about the intervention of the people to distinguish between 'the people' and 'the populace'. In January 1785 he regretted that the Volunteers, that great popular movement, from having been 'the armed property of Ireland', was becoming its 'armed beggary' by admitting the lowest classes to its ranks.[33] Grattan's denunciation of the democratic tendencies in the Volunteer movement delighted the Lord Lieutenant, the Duke of Rutland, who characterized his speech of January 1785 as one of 'the finest and most decisive ever delivered within the walls of the Irish Parliament'.[33]

When it was suggested in the summer of 1783 that an Ulster Volunteer Reform Convention should be held at Dungannon, Grattan expressed his distaste for 'repetitions' of the famous Dungannon Convention, although he admitted that parliamentary reform 'might have little chance unless taken up by the people'. He excused himself from going to the Leinster Volunteer Reform Convention on the grounds that as an MP it would be 'premature' for him to attend.[34] He did not sit in the Volunteer Reform Convention held in Dublin at the close of 1783 and he denounced the organizers of the Reform Congress of 1784 as infected with 'the lust of power' and for 'being too fond of an over-weening interference'. Grattan's attitude to reform threw into relief the contrast between his liberal convictions and his inherent conservatism. He accepted that reform was expedient and was demanded by a large section of the responsible public. But he shrank from an aggressive assault on the status quo and he always made it clear that he considered only a relatively small proportion of the population fit for enfranchisement.

During the eighties and early nineties Grattan preferred to dwell on the other method of diminishing the influence exercised by the executive over parliament, the reduction of patronage. 'The trade of parliament', he declared 'is like original sin – it operates through all political creation.'[35] He was confident that if temptation in the form of places and pensions was removed, MPs, most of whom were decent, public-spirited gentlemen, could be safely left to the dictates of honour and common sense.[36] He expected that the ruthless reduction of patronage would not only destroy corruption but would lessen the burden on the taxpayer and so render Irish industry more competitive.[37] In 1783 he opened his economy campaign by selecting the largest Irish department, the revenue, as 'an object of retrenchment'. In November, being on good terms with the administration, he secured the appointment of a House of Commons committee to inquire into the expenses of collecting the revenue. This committee in April 1784 produced a series of recommendations – that collectors should reside in their districts, that posts in the revenue should be filled by promotion from an inferior rank and that superannuation should be limited to officials of forty years' service or who had been disabled in the course of duty. Northington's successor, the Duke of Rutland, was prepared for the sake of 'the settled health and strength' of his administration to gratify Grattan 'in any little instance of vanity or caprice by which he might have a view of displaying for the public eye some testimony of his affection for the economical collection and expenditure of the revenue'. Therefore when Grattan brought the recommendations of the committee before the House, the government did not oppose him and the House approved of them. In return for the administration not opposing the committee's recommendations Grattan agreed not to introduce a bill embodying and enforcing his suggestions for administrative reform. The guidelines laid down in the recommendations of the committee of inquiry were not very strictly observed, and Grattan's proposals for cutting down the number of revenue officers were skillfully disposed of by John Beresford, who argued they reflected a combination of good intentions and ignorance of revenue administration – it was gleefully whispered in official circles that Grattan, having 'made insinuations of extravagance' in the management of the revenue, had 'made no progress in the discovery of it'.[38] It was not until nineteenth-century utilitarian standards were severely applied to the Irish revenue departments that much was achieved in the way of reform.

Between 1786 and 1792 Grattan produced a sustained denunciation of the pension list, 'this incumbrance', and delivered four vivid surveys of the fiscal situation, the last of which was described by the Chancellor of the Exchequer as the recapitulation of the accumulative invectives of many sessions. During these years Grattan's concern was twofold – to strengthen the moral stamina of Parliament – 'parliamentary integrity is your palladium', he declared – and to lighten the burden on the taxpayer. Realizing that 'figures are irksome to the house' (and possibly feeling they were not his forte), he tended when criticizing government expenditure to generalize, dwelling on the steady rise in expenditure, on the growth of the national debt, on the drop in public credit, on the Irish administration's repeated and unfulfilled promises to economize, and on the difficulty of securing consistency in financial policy with viceroys changing every day. He did however signal out some items of expenditure for severe censure – the cost of collecting the revenue, the increase in the pension list, 'the licentious fooleries for Park and Castle', and Gandon's new Dublin custom house, 'a building which is more a proof of profligal-

ity in the directors than of taste in the architect', 'a building of the sixth
rank in architecture and of first rate in extravagance' (apparently Grattan's only reference in debate to the great architectural achievements of
his age).[39] Grattan did not think it necessary to enumerate in exhaustive
detail the economies which should be made because he ardently supported a proposal which would impose an automatic curb on government
expenditure. He wanted what he termed 'a resolution of restraint' to be
adopted which would compel the government to live within its income,
that income being defined as the produce of the taxes in force at the
close of 1785 after the budget was balanced. If the country prospered the
government might enjoy a larger revenue, but it would have to keep in
mind that no new taxes would be granted.[40]

During his first ten years in Parliament Grattan's attention was
absorbed by constitutional questions, public finance and Anglo-Irish
commercial relations, and he glanced only in passing at Irish social conditions. Shortly after Parliament voted him £50,000 to purchase an
estate he received a letter from Charles Hamilton, a large Irish
landowner, urging him to seize the opportunity to lead a crusade for
agrarian reform. If he turned his new property into a model estate, by
making agricultural improvements, establishing useful industries, elimi-
nating oppressive 'land-jobbers' (middlemen) and fixing rents at reasonable levels, other landlords would follow his example: 'few can resist the
force of fashion'.[41] But Grattan was not destined to become the first of a
long line of prominent Irish politicians associated with the land question.
His interest in agricultural improvement seems to have been mainly
planting (for aesthetic as much as economic reasons), and although a
good-natured landlord, he subscribed to the view that low rents were bad
for the tenantry, encouraging them to live like beggars.[42]

His views on social and economic issues were naturally largely
coloured by the prevalent political philosophy which attributed only a
limited range of functions to government and regarded with suspicion
any extension of the administration's activities. Laissez-faire and whiggery agreed in believing that the general good was best promoted by leaving the intelligent, independent individual to his own devices. But the
century ranked benevolence high amongst the virtues and Irish gentle-

men prided themselves with some justification in belonging to a good-natured age. If Europe had its benevolent despots, throughout the British Isles innumerable country gentlemen, bountiful ladies, clergymen and generous businessmen strove to mitigate the sufferings and improve the lot of their humble neighbours, and as the century progressed there were many signs that benevolence was not only on the increase but was becoming better organized. Religious feeling, humanitarianism, sensibility and a sense of social duty (strong if at times condescending) impelled the better-off to try to cope with want and wretchedness. Moreover, those who moved in polite, comfortable, intelligent and reasonable society could not but be aware of the large masses which in every European country toiled hard for a poor reward, and outbreaks of social disorder, riots and agrarian disturbances were ominous reminders that the civilized way of life which the cultured and propertied enjoyed might be submerged by barbarism.

In Ireland from the middle eighties the Augustan calm of what was thought to be a stable society was shattered by widespread, well-organized and spectacular agrarian rioting in Munster. The rioters moved in large bands robbing the unpopular and intimidating the timid. Their main target was tithe, but they also resisted the collection of county cess (rates) and tried to fix the price of potatoes and sometimes of farms. In such a large province with very different regions, a growing population pressing on the land and changes of land usage under way, there was bound to be considerable economic and social tension, and pamphleteers and MPs argued vigorously over what were the underlying causes of discontent.[43] One thing, however, was clear. An anti-tithe movement was likely to have a wide appeal, transcending to some extent class and religious divisions. Ecclesiastical lawyers might insist that tithe was an incidence of land tenure, analogous to rent, but to the plain man it was a tax collected by clumsy, irritating methods. In France its abolition was one of the first triumphs of the Revolution; in relatively content and prosperous rural England it was a source of continuous litigation; and in Ireland Presbyterians and Catholics were not so ecumenically minded as to enjoy subsidizing the Anglican establishment: even landlords who strongly believed in Protestantism and property displayed, in Grattan's words, 'a

Grattan: A Life

languid neutrality'[44] when the rights of the clergy were in question and were often unenthusiastic when it came to protecting claims to tithe. Indeed, the Irish House of Commons had in 1736, by a simple, self-interested motion, relieved much of the pasture land from tithe.

The government's reaction to the Munster disturbances was simple. Order must be maintained and property rights protected; and during the session of 1787 legislation strengthening the weak machinery for enforcing the law – a Tumultuous Meetings Bill and a County Police Bill – was rapidly passed. Grattan agreed with these measures in principle. 'If the people or peasantry', he said, 'have thought proper to invade personal security and lay the foundation of undermining their own liberties, if they resort to the exercise of torture as relief for poverty, I lament their savage infatuation and I assent to their punishment'.[45] Nevertheless, imbued with the Whig reverence for civil liberty, he criticized some of the details of the Tumultuous Meetings Bill, and he rather tepidly supported an amendment which would have confined the operation of the act to four counties – 'better perhaps restrain the extent of a measure of coercion', he said, 'but at all events a measure of coercion is necessary'. Fitzgibbon, the Attorney-General, was uncharacteristically conciliatory, and when he accepted an amendment limiting the duration of the bill Grattan was content to let it pass (when in 1791 the Act was about to expire it was extended to 1800 and then made perpetual). He also accepted the County Police Bill though he wanted the head constables, who were to be appointed by the Crown, to be 'more dependent on the country gentlemen' and he urged successfully that the assistant barristers (county court judges) should be made incapable of sitting in Parliament.

Grattan certainly believed that law and order should be enforced. But, benevolent and biased against taxation, he was also convinced that enforcement must be accompanied by a redress of grievances – his Munster policy being summed up in the phrase, 'the Whiteboy should be hanged but I think the tithe farmer should be restrained'. The lower orders of the people, he told the House of Commons, 'claim your attention – the best husbandry is the husbandry of the human creature. What! can you reclaim the tops of your mountains and cannot you improve your people.'[46] Convinced that tithe was 'the great oppression', he brushed

94

aside the suggestion that landlords and middlemen were responsible for much of the Munster distress and discontent. 'The middleman's over-reaching compared to the tithe farmer was mercy'; he explained; and he asserted that if Irish landlords were often 'expensive' (extravagant) they were 'hospitable, humane and affectionate people the gentlemen are not extortioners by nature nor (as the tithe farmer is) by profession. In some cases they do set their land too high, but in many not and on that head they are daily becoming more reasonable.'[47] Grattan was convinced that the resident landlord played an essential role in Irish rural society. By improving his estate he civilized his tenantry; as a magistrate he regulated them, so that 'the poor peasantry may not perish for want of medicine, cordial or care'. The landlord-tenant relations drew the rich and poor together, so that each, contributing to 'the strength, order and beauty of the state, may form that pillar of society, when all below is strong and all above is grace'.[48]

Tithe, he was convinced, was the great rural grievance, and in a series of speeches (including four massive orations) delivered between 1787 and 1789 he attacked the tithe system and expounded an alternative that he hoped 'would unite the clergyman and the farmer'.[49] Tithe, he argued was a tax upon productivity; and while the rich grazier was often exempted from tithe, it was levied on potatoes, 'the lowest, the most general, the most compassionate subsistance of human life'.[50] In many Munster parishes the customary rates were steadily being raised and tithe was often charged illegally on articles that were not chargeable. Its assess-ment and collection turned the clergyman into 'a spy upon the husband-man', while he himself was frequently cheated by the squire and involved in litigation by his proctor. The tithe proctor was often an oppressive extortionist. Far worse was the tithe farmer, 'whose rank in society is gen-erally the lowest' and whose 'occupation is to pounce on the poor in the name of the Lord'. A wolf 'who calls in aid of Christianity the arts of the synagogue', he fleeced both the flock and the shepherd.[51]

Grattan fortified his case by collecting through correspondence and from the records of the ecclesiastical courts and chancery a formidable amount of detailed information on the tithe demands made in Munster parishes, and he illuminated his expositions of the amounts involved with flashes of sardonic humour. He also appears to have done some field work, since the Attorney-General in 1788 referred with scorn to the few weeks Grattan had spent in Munster. The conclusions which he drew from the mass of evidence he collected were of course challenged by the defenders of ecclesiastical rights.[52] It was argued that he was selective in the instances he cited and that diocesan averages presented a very different picture – to which Grattan retorted that averages were resorted to 'from an indifference about the real state of the peasantry'. An ecclesiastical lawyer emphasized that the figures Grattan quoted represented the payment due to a clergyman (which was what he would sue for), not what he actually received from the parishioner. Grattan replied to his critics by demanding an inquiry. He suggested in 1788 that a House of Commons committee should inquire into tithe; and in 1789 that a statutory commission to investigate the tithe system should be constituted. Both proposals were defeated, an intelligent, liberal-minded MP declaring, 'I will never consent to have the established church of the kingdom dragged like a delinquent to your bar and arraigned and evidences brought to asperse, perhaps to defame and to caluminate the ministers of the gospel – that would be an unseemly thing'.[53]

Grattan was not merely a devastating critic of the tithe system; he also outlined and urged Parliament to adopt a scheme providing for the financial maintenance of the parochial clergy which, he hoped, would take from tithe 'its deadly sting'. The income of each incumbent was to be settled by taking the average of his annual receipts over the past ten years (some incumbents who had been extortionate to be exempted). But to guard the parson against 'the fluctuation of the currency', this income was to be indexed in relation to the price of wheat.[54] The source of the income so settled was to be a parish rate which might be collected by the county cess collector. If churchmen were strongly opposed to the substitution of a parish rate for tithe, Grattan was prepared to support an alternative scheme: a modus, varying with the price of wheat, should be fixed for all tithable articles. In both schemes the peasant's potato plot was to be exempted and all pasture land was to be taxable or tithable. Grattan also proposed that barren land, flax and rape should all be exempt from tithe, that a quick, simple procedure should be provided by which tithe owners could recover arrears, and that a moderate tax should be imposed on non-resident incumbents, 'because our lower people want more instruction'. Grattan explained that he preferred a tax falling on all non-residents to granting increased powers to the bishop to enforce residence. 'I would not put into his hands', he said, 'the talents and suffrages of the parochial clergy, I would not enable him to say, "Sir you have written too freely on constitutional subjects".'[55] Grattan was well aware 'that everything bold and radical in the shape of public redress is termed impracticable', so he was careful to emphasize that his tithe reform schemes were not only equitable and moderate but practicable. Also, he pointed out they accorded with the Anglican tradition. When 'our Elizabeth established the Protestant religion', he declared, 'she was called an innovator', and, he asked, 'what is the Protestant religion but the interposition of parliament, rescueing Christianity from abuses introduced by its own priesthood?'.[56]

Grattan when handling the tithe problem in parliamentary debate was eloquent, informative, combative and sparkling. His major speech on the issue, a three-hour effort, which appeared in pamphlet form in Dublin and London, was pronounced by the Attorney-General to have been 'the most splendid display of eloquence that the house has ever heard'. Especially admired was the peroration, which began: 'let bigotry and schism, the zealot's fire, the high priest's intolerance, through all their discordancy tremble, while an enlightened parliament with arms of general protection, overeaches the whole community, and roots the Protestant ascendancy in the sovereign mercy of its nature'. The Chief Secretary characterized this as 'brilliant'. Even Lawrence Parsons, the friend and disciple of Flood, reluctantly admitted the speech was effective. It was, he wrote, 'the worst rhapsody I have ever heard from him. It was illustrated with a variety of quotations from the Old and New testament, introduced I thought inaptly and irreverently. The house was thin, and he was not able to excite himself or anybody else, which occasioned his prepared strains of enthusiasm to go off very ill. However he persisted, and the whole was rendered palatable by the sarcasms that were springled through it against the bishops and which by the way were very indiscreet and many of them unfair and indecent. The clergy all foam against him.'[57]

The speech made such an impression that Thomas Campbell, a well-beneficed clergyman with a good mind and a wide knowledge of Irish life, suggested to the Bishop of Dromore that it might be wise for the Church 'to make decent terms while the country is quiet'. Grattan, he remarked, 'has perseverance, and that perseverance has never failed of success in questions where there was less prospect of success than in this, where every man's interest and prejudice are in his favour'.[58]

Campbell's apprehensions, though reasonable, were premature. For all his tremendous exertions, Grattan accomplished little. His schemes which foreshadowed nineteenth-century legislation were not accepted by the House, and of three minor tithe reform bills which he sponsored, bills dealing with the tithe of flax and rape and a barren lands bill exempting newly reclaimed land from tithe for seven years, only the last reached the statute book. The reasons for his failure are painfully obvious. A number of MPs, although they might have been ready to consider plans for tithe reform, were reluctant to impose a solution on the Church. Therefore reform required the backing of a substantial section of clerical opinion. But the Church of Ireland was well endowed with caution and conservatism, and its leaders, conscious that their Church had many hostile critics, Catholic and Presbyterian pamphleteers as well as Erastian-minded MPs, were reluctant to surrender acknowledged property rights for a new statutory tithe. The princely Archbishop of Armagh, whom Grattan in a burst of admiration described as 'a mere instrument in the hand of Providence, making the best possible distribution of the fruits of the earth', was convinced that 'the clergy have no wish for change and that the laws at present in force would do very well if the country was established in peace and subordination to the laws'. If anything is done, he added, 'except a decisive vindication of the laws the clergy are ruined because fresh attacks will be induced by any appearance of having succumbed to this'.[59]

Unfortunately, Grattan's advocacy was scarcely calculated to win the support of zealous churchmen. Shocked by instances of extortion, moved by the plight of the poor and exasperated by the defects of a cumbersome, archaic system and the obstinate inertia of its defenders, he yielded to the temptation to prove by lavish quotation from scriptures and the fathers that tithe was not of divine origin and to denounce in a series of purple passages shot through with biting phrases the worldliness of the Establishment. He made great play of how he was striving to defend true Christianity against certain bishops, 'occupied by the riches, engaged in the amusements and fettered somewhat in the politics of the world'. He sneered at the Munster clergy: 'when their God, their Redeemer and their country are in question, they are silent; but when a twelve-penny point in their tithe is brought forward, then they are vivacious; then the press groans with clerical Billingsgate'. Inevitably too he made a highly rhetorical contrast between the Establishment and the Primitive Church. 'The apostles had no tithe, they did not demand it; they and He whose mission they preached, protested against the principle on which tithe is founded – carry neither script nor purse nor shoes; into whatever house you go, say peace. Here is concord and contempt of riches, not tithe.' The peasant, he asserted, 'may set up against the tithe's proctor's valuation the New Testament – the precepts of Christ against the clergyman's arithmetic'. There may have been some truth in all this but it was hardly relevant. Grattan (of clerical ancestry with an uncle on the bench and a well-beneficed brother-in-law) was not striving to reduce the clergy to apostolic poverty; instead he aimed at providing them with decent, well guaranteed incomes. He was not at heart Voltairian. He professed to have 'the utmost veneration, love and respect' for the Establishment and he regarded many of its clergy, 'a mild order of men with morality enlightened by letters and exalted by religion', with affection.[60] But the overpowering indignation which expressed itself so easily in scathing phrases and epigrammatic invective obscured his goodwill towards the Church and deprived him of useful allies in his campaign to revitalize a great national institution by pruning abuses.

In addition to striving for tithe reform, Grattan also supported another scheme for relieving the Irish poor: the exemption of poor households from the hearth tax.[61] 'Men who received no benefit from the state', he declared, 'ought not to share in its burdens, the peasantry of Ireland when they are quiet, ought to be nursed not taxed'. At first Grattan had opposed the proposal that one-hearth houses should be exempted from the hearth tax, simply because he was afraid that this

would encourage the government to look round for new sources of taxation. But from the later eighties he steadily urged that the poor should
be relieved from the tax. At the beginning of the nineties he urged still
another plan for improving the condition of the people. In 1791 he fervently advocated measures to check the consumption of whiskey, 'the
destructive poison of the people'. He demanded heavy duties on spirits,
'high enough to put them out of the reach of the mechanic and the
labourer', and he proposed that the justices of the peace should be
empowered to control stringently spirit retailers (he was eager to enroll
the country gentry in the temperance crusade).[62] At the same time he
wanted beer duties abolished (though he agreed the malt duty should be
retained). The 'brewery', he once declared, was 'the natural nurse of the
people entitled to every encouragement'.[63]

The House of Commons was a body eager to reform the drinking
habits of the lower orders of the people. Grattan and Robert Hobart, the
Chief Secretary, competed for the honour of supporting David La
Touche, the well-known philanthropist, when he moved that the House
should go into committee to consider the immoderate use of spirits. But
several financial experts dwelt on the complex nature of the question. It
involved not only the distillers and brewers but agriculture, the West
Indian trade and fiscal considerations. Grattan, who was convinced that
'whatever is done to promote sobriety in this country must be done by
parliament', was prepared to sacrifice 'corn and revenue to the human
species' and he was bitterly disappointed by the measures taken in 1791,
an increase in the spirit duties and a reduction in the beer duties. He
regarded the alterations footling. 'Revenue not reform', he suspected,
'was the evident object of administration.'[64] One social-economic issue
baffled him: unemployment, which was extensive in Dublin in 1793.
When the House was debating a measure empowering the government
to take steps to sustain commercial credit, Grattan urged that a sum
should be earmarked for the payment of bounties on the export of manufactured goods. But after Foster had pointed out that the problem was
to find markets for Irish manufacturers, Grattan 'allowed that it was difficult to determine how the house should act on this occasion'.[65]

For ten years or so following the great victory of 1782, Grattan, determinedly independent, although he tended to be a critic of those in power, was not automatically against the government. As has been seen, he had consultations with Temple and was in close touch with Northington. Although he clashed violently with Rutland's administration over the Commercial Proposition, Rutland and Orde were conciliatory and Grattan in 1786 referred in debate to the Duke as 'a young man of very noble, unsuspecting nature', an honest man even if misled on the subject of the pension list.[66] Rutland died unexpectedly at the end of 1787 and the touchy Temple, now Marquis of Buckingham, returned to Ireland as his successor. During Buckingham's first parliamentary session (1788) Grattan's fire was largely concentrated on ecclesiastical abuses. The following session opened on 5 February 1789 in the middle of a major constitutional crisis. Early in November it was realized that the King was suffering from a severe attack of insanity and that provision must be made for the exercise of the royal functions. How was this to be done? There was no statutory authority for the creation of a regency and the precedents for parliamentary action, mainly drawn from the tumultuous fifteenth century, offered uncertain guidance. Pitt's government decided that a British regent, who naturally would be the Prince of Wales, should be appointed by bill (a procedure which incidentally was time-consuming and which permitted limitations to be imposed on the regent's prerogatives); the Whig opposition considered that both houses should address the Prince (who was expected to appoint a Whig ministry), requesting him to assume the regency. Opportunism may have been a factor in deciding the choice of procedure, but both government and opposition agreed in asserting that the course it recommended was from the constitutional standpoint the only proper one, and from late November until the beginning of February the regency question in all its complexity was being debated at Westminster.

The British cabinet of course considered that Ireland should adopt the correct constitutional procedure and appoint its regent by bill, the bill being returned from England according to the terms of Yelverton's act under the British great seal. If the Irish Parliament were to appoint a regent by address it would both flout the arguments advanced by the government at Westminster and suggest that centrifugal forces were dan-

gerously influential in determining Ireland's attitude to imperial relations. But when the Irish Parliament assembled it was very doubtful if
the administration's solution to the regency problem would be accepted.
Buckingham, priggish and self-important even by viceregal standards,
was not a popular lord lieutenant, and it seemed highly probable that Pitt
would soon be out of office. A few days after the start of the session,
Grattan, who had about eight weeks in which to ponder the question and
who had been over in England listening to the debates at Westminster,[67]
pronounced that the Irish Parliament should immediately address the
Prince of Wales requesting him to assume the regency of Ireland 'in plentitude of royal power'. This method of meeting the emergency was, in
Grattan's opinion, constitutionally sound. It also demonstrated that the
Irish Parliament was free and independent and was fortunately the procedure favoured by Grattan's friends at Westminster. Although Grattan
did not fail to emphasize that in following the course he recommended,
Ireland would concur with England in 'the great object, the Regent', his
proposal was attacked by the Irish Attorney-General, Fitzgibbon, who
contended that the Irish Parliament should adopt the plan which was on
the point of being accepted in Great Britain: the appointment of a regent
by bill. Fitzgibbon appealed to both statute law and political expediency,
citing Yelverton's act and the Tudor act annexing the crown of Ireland to
that of England, and argued that the procedure he supported would
ensure imperial unity. He put his case formidably and Grattan was
reduced to dismissing his closely woven argument as mere pedantry and
quibbling.

To what extent Irish peers and MPs were influenced by fine points in
constitutional law or by the probability that the Prince of Wales in the
near future would be able to install his friends in power, is impossible to
say. However it was obvious from the beginning of the session that the
Irish administration's parliamentary influence had evaporated. By the
middle of February both houses had voted addresses to the Prince of
Wales requesting him 'to take upon himself the government of this
realm', and when the Lord Lieutenant, Buckingham, refused to transmit
them, a parliamentary delegation was appointed to present the addresses
to the Prince. Grattan, acting as the effective leader of the House, pro-

posed the names of the Commons delegates; he laid down how the financial business of the session should be conducted and the House accepted his motion of censure on the Lord Lieutenant, whom Grattan had already attacked for combining priggish professions of economy with obtaining a lucrative sinecure for his brother. In the middle of February, the anti-administration majority was, Fitzgibbon admitted, 'the governing power of the country'[68] – a dizzy position for many MPs. At the same time Grattan must have begun to realize the constraints that went with the possession of power. Already Francis Hardy, a keen opponent of Buckingham's administration, writing to a friend had pointed out that Grattan 'must be prepared to give up his tithe business for the session, it can do no good now and to have the clergy join in a cry against us would be very bad'.[69]

The Irish parliamentary situation rapidly changed after it was announced at Westminster on 19 February that the King was steadily convalescing. The Irish administration recovered much of its prestige and soon had again the steady backing of a majority in each House. But one result of the Regency episode was the emergence in the Irish Parliament of a new party, the Irish Whig party, composed of those who had been constant critics of the government and some of those who had withdrawn their support from the administration at the beginning of 1789 and who from pride, principle or dislike of Buckingham were not prepared to rejoin its ranks. The party produced a programme which appealed to Grattan, and he contrasted 'a party united on public principle by the bonds of certain specific measures' with, on the other side of the House, 'an imprudent phalanx of political mercenaries who have neither the principles of patriotism nor ambition nor party, nor honour – who govern not by deliberation but by discipline and who lick the hands that feed and worship the patron who bribes them'. During the years 1790–2 Grattan's moral indignation and partisan fervour were intensified by his conviction that Buckingham and his successor Westmorland were engaged in a conspiracy to establish by the systematic employment of patronage 'in the place of a limited monarchy a corrupt despotism'.[70]

The new party was organized, albeit rather loosely, but Grattan does not seem to have played much part in running it. He disdained managerial skills. But from 1789 he worked in close association with William Ponsonby and his younger brother George, leaders of a powerful Irish connection, who defiantly broke with the administration during the Regency dispute. William and George Ponsonby, the sons of John Ponsonby, the Speaker (who had ended his career in opposition and was closely tied to the Dukes of Devonshire and Portland), were keen Whigs. Admittedly for some years after Pitt came into power they had been rather sulky office-holders, but from 1789 they were happily aligned with their English friends Portland and Fox. The two brothers formed a strong political combination. William, who represented a great county, Kilkenny, lived on a grand and generous scale, maintaining the best hunting establishment in Ireland. Forthright, good-tempered and broad-minded, he was to his friends the embodiment of decent Whiggery. George, though he too was devoted to field sports, being a younger son went to the Bar and soon developed into a very able advocate if not an outstandingly learned lawyer. He was also a powerful parliamentary debater, not a 'quibbling pleader or an ostentatious rhetorician' but a clear, shrewd and fluent speaker, who – it was observed when he was at Westminster – never forgot he was addressing an assembly of gentlemen. After the Union he had an unusual career. Having served as Lord Chancellor of Ireland in the short-lived ministry of All the Talents, he was chosen as the Whig party leader at Westminster and his tact, good humour and good manners contributed to holding a contentious party together during a dreary period in its history.[71]

At the close of the eighties, with a general election in the offing, Grattan was considering changing his constituency. He had represented Charlemont for fifteen years but his friendship with its patron had cooled and Grattan 'could never consent', he wrote, 'to sit for any gentleman's borough and vote against him'.[72] However, until 1793 an Irish MP could not resign his seat. Grattan solved the problem in 1784 by purchasing a borough seat for one of Charlemont's friends. In any case it was highly anomalous that a tribune of the people should sit for a pocket borough. Understandably enough Grattan, a Wicklow resident, thought of coming forward for the county and in December 1789, when visiting England, he approached Fitzwilliam, a great Wicklow landowner, asking for his support. 'The encouragement I have already received from others', Grattan wrote to him, 'gives me with your interest the certainty of success'. Fitzwilliam at first was willing to back Grattan but he was warned by his Irish agent that to do so would antagonize the other Wicklow interests and jeopardize the Fitzwilliam position in the county. The agent's opinion was confirmed by a letter from another large Wicklow landowner, the ambitious and eccentric Lord Aldborough, who arrogantly reminded Fitzwilliam that 'abilities are not the only necessities to carry a county or make the leading men of property and connection immolate their dearest interests at the shrine of presumption'. In the event the MPs returned for Wicklow in 1790 both belonged to well-established county families.

Grattan at this time, it was rumoured, also had his eye on one of the university seats. It was said that he 'was working under cover with some of the young men with whom he is popular' but that his chances were poor because he had deeply offended the fellows by his attack on the tithe system. He also considered standing for County Dublin – 'I should very much like to be returned for a county', he wrote, 'but will go to no expense'. As for the city of Dublin, he felt that it 'should be represented by a merchant not by me'.[73] But at the beginning of 1790 he was asked to contest the city, the most important constituency in Ireland and one with which he had family ties. (The vacancy in the representation of Dublin created by James Grattan's death in 1767 had been filled by Lord Kildare, who six years later succeeded his father as second Duke of Leinster).[74] From then until 1783 the city MPs, two barristers, two medical men and a merchant, Travers Hartley, who had the support of both Flood and Grattan, were all in varying degrees opposed to the Irish administration. But when in 1783 Bradshaw, the Recorder, became a King's Bench Judge, he was replaced by Thomas Warren, a popular Lord Mayor, who both had government backing and managed to give the impression that he shared the views of the city liberals.

In the middle eighties the city liberals were presented with a marvellous opportunity for mobilizing public opinion against the Irish administration. Dublin, the rapidly growing second city of the Empire, was suffering from many of the problems associated with urban growth, including increasing and more sophisticated crime and, what would impress MPs, sporadic outbursts of mob violence. The Irish administration's response to this problem was the creation of a centralized city police force under government control. The Police Act of 1786 empowered the Lord Lieutenant to appoint three police commissioners and four divisional magistrates (all seven in practice aldermen), controlling a force of about two hundred constables and four hundred night-watchmen. Grattan denounced the measure as 'the most obnoxious and alarming that perhaps ever arrested the attention of an Irish senate': 'A bill of patronage not police.' It infringed the City Charter, threatened Dublin independence, and might, he hinted, be a sinister foreshadowing of military rule. 'It approaches near to arbitrary government', Grattan declared, 'to have an armed rabble under the influence of the crown.' In five successive sessions (1788–92) he attacked the new force, alleging it was useless, insulted respectable citizens and abused its powers of arrest. What he wanted was a police force directly under public control.[76]

Within Dublin a well-orchestrated and sustained campaign against the Act, which secured the support both of those concerned for civil liberty and those who deplored a rise in the rates, was mounted. While this stimulating struggle was in full swing, the city liberals had to decide what steps they should take at the General Election of 1790, in view of the fact that the two sitting MPs were not going to stand – the elderly Travers Hartley feeling the time had come to retire, and Warren, who had become a police commissioner, thinking it advisable to retreat to a pocket borough in County Kilkenny. The liberals vigorously exerted themselves, and when the delegates from twenty-three guilds in January 1790 met at the Exchange to select candidates they decided to recommend Henry Grattan and Lord Henry Fitzgerald, the brother of the Duke of Leinster, at the moment in opposition. Their decision was ratified a few days later by a meeting of freemen and freeholders, which promised to return Grattan and Fitzgerald free of expense – a promise which Warren publicly warned Grattan not to rely on. The aldermen, probably encouraged by Warren's election in 1783, put forward two of their own body, John Exshaw and Henry Gore Sankey, who stood as experienced businessmen. But the liberals had undoubtedly the more glamorous candidates and Napper Tandy and other liberals canvassed the guilds before Exshaw and Sankey 'made good any number of friends to support them'; and when on 9 May Grattan and Fitzgerald marched to the hustings, their procession included the bands of eighteen out of the twenty-one guilds.[77]

The procession was observed by William Drennan, a northern radical, a perceptive and acerbic commentator on events. Grattan, 'a little man with a triangular phiz, genteely ugly advanced on his light fantastic toe, hope elevating and joy brightening his crest, his eyes rolling with that fine enthusiasm without which it is impossible to be a great man; Fitzgerald, a fine, tall looking young fellow bending low to hear what Grattan was saying; both bare headed and at times bowing popularly low – each of them holding an arm of the much respected Hartley, while at some distance behind walks Napper Tandy in all the surliness of republicanism, grinning most ghastly smiles and as he lifts his hat from his head the many headed monster raises a shout that reverberates to very corner of the Castle.' There were many banners with suitable mottos – 'Man of the People', 'A Place bill', 'A responsibility bill', and, according to a government newspaper, 'Damn the Police'. Drennan noticed a Negro boy 'well dressed and holding on high the cap of Liberty' but he looked in vain for a reference to parliamentary reform.[78]

Though the nomination of Grattan and Fitzgerald sealed an alliance between the Dublin city liberals and the Whig parliamentary opposition, this did not mean that their views were identical. Some of the city politicians were soon to join the Dublin United Irishmen, the best-known Irish radical society, and the gap between Whig and radical was neatly illustrated in a short conversation between Grattan and Dr Robert Emmet, a physician, the father of Thomas Addis Emmet, who was to become a leading United Irishman. Emmet asked Grattan, was he a friend to parliamentary reform? Grattan replied he was by no means 'averse'. Emmet retorted, 'the people then are enlisted under you as a party, that people who were the principals, and the nation has become a Ponsonby party'. Years later Grattan characterized 'old Dr. Emmet' as 'wild and chimical'.[79] For the moment, however, the coalition could rejoice in a great victory. Grattan and Fitzgerald having by 12 May polled two thirds of the votes, the other two candidates withdrew. The victors were drawn in a triumphal car through the streets and that night the Dublin mob with showers of stones smashed the windows of houses, including the Lord Chancellor's, which were not illuminated.[80]

In old age, addressing a deputation from the Dublin Corporation, Grattan declared: 'To this city I owe my birth, from this city I received my honours, in this city I have passed the best of my days and in this city I hope to conclude them.'[81] But he did not want to live in Dublin. He loved the country, and once he acquired Tinnehinch he seems to have spent as much time as he possibly could in Wicklow. Thus he was less intimately acquainted with Dublin problems than an MP who was continuously living and working in the city. And, immersed in major issues, he must at times have found it hard to switch his attention to municipal matters.

Nevertheless, he did not neglect the interests of his constituents. He presented petitions from Dublin bodies ranging from the Corporation to a number of 'superior servants' (complaining of competition from foreigners). He protested indignantly when Sir John Blaquiere, who was anxious to reform the Foundling Hospital, notorious for its infant mortality rates, proposed to replace the negligent ex-officio governors, who included the Lord Mayor and Corporation, by directors appointed by the Lord Lieutenant. Grattan presented a petition from the Corporation of Dublin against Blaquiere's scheme and suggested that those who professed to be concerned about the condition of the hospital were only eager to secure control of some patronage.[82] Grattan's suspicion that an extension of administrative power probably implied jobbery was again expressed when in 1797 he opposed a bill for regulating building and preventing fires in Dublin introduced by his *bête noire*, Dr Patrick Duigenan. The bill, based on legislation in force in London, provided that builders must use sound methods of construction and good materials. Grattan presented a petition from the carpenters and bricklayers' guild (the master builders) stating that the bill was unnecessary since the Dublin builders maintained higher standards than those observed in London and would 'totally destroy what remains of business'. A week later Grattan successfully opposed the bill, arguing that under its provisions an official would be appointed at a high salary for the purpose of 'teasing the public' and that fires were infrequent in Dublin.[83]

Some years before being elected MP for Dublin he had, as has been mentioned, condemned on Whig principles the Dublin Police Bill. In 1793 he proposed an alternative scheme, introducing a bill which provided for a police guard under the control of the Corporation and watchmen in each parish directed by the parishioners. The bill failed to pass, but in 1795 he presented a police bill on the same lines which reached the statute book.[84] By this act aldermen appointed by the Corporation were to control fifty 'fit and able men' as 'ministerial officers of police', and each parish was to elect nine directors of the watch who were to employ parish constables and watchmen. Duigenan denounced Grattan's scheme for creating 'a democratical army' under the control of 'republican directors', many of whom were United Irishmen. Apparently the House did not take Duigenan seriously, and Grattan remarked that a bill which respected chartered rights could scarcely be termed democratic. But Colonel Blaquiere put his finger on the real weakness of the scheme, arguing that it was better fitted for 'the regulation of a pitiful village than this great metropolis'.[85] Within a decade it was clear the new system of community policing was not working well, and in 1808 the Chief Secretary, Arthur Wellesley, dwelling on the increase in crime, introduced a new Dublin Police Bill which vested the control of the police in eighteen divisional magistrates, two thirds of whom were to be appointed by the Lord Lieutenant and one third by the Corporation; and the Lord Lieutenant was empowered to appoint one of the magistrates Chief Police Magistrate. Grattan and three more conservatively minded MPs, Beresford, Shaw and Duigenan, opposed the bill as infringing the City Charter and Grattan objected to the government being granted additional patronage.[86] But the bill passed and as time went on the civic authorities ceased to have any power over the Dublin police.

Another matter over which Grattan took considerable trouble was the Dublin coal trade. From the beginning of the century Dubliners were greatly concerned about what they regarded as 'the excessive price of coal' which, it was regretted, inflicted great distress on the poor and also of course increased the cost of living for the more prosperous. Middlemen were blamed for keeping prices at an unreasonable level and attempts were made to limit their profits. These proved ineffective and in the early nineties Grattan attacked the question by securing in 1791 and 1793 House of Commons committees of inquiry; and he introduced three bills based on the reports of these committees. The first bill, passed in 1791, proved 'insufficient'; the second, introduced in 1792 after consultations with merchants and coal factors, failed to pass owing to a procedural dispute between Lords and Commons; the third reached the statute book in 1793. Grattan's measures included a number of well-tried methods for holding down coal prices. Factors were to be penalized for forming combinations; captains of coal ships were forbidden to linger in the bay but were to come up promptly to the quays and were to display the price of their coals; the Lord Mayor and aldermen were empowered to fix the wages of coal porters and carmen; and public coal yards were established. In addition it was enacted on Grattan's suggestion that the owners of private coalyards should be encouraged by subsidization to extend their premises and bounties should be granted on coals stored and on the construction of lighters to carry coals from ships to the quays. These elaborate efforts to correct the laws of supply and demand do not seem to have been successful – within a few years it was alleged that the price of coal was being unduly raised by the malpractices of factors and the extortions of coal porters, and early in the nineteenth century the legislation regulating the Dublin coal trade was swept away.

While he was MP for Dublin Grattan also took steps to strengthen the regulations governing another industry, the tannery. Shoemakers complained that tanners were offering for sale hides which were 'in a wet, untanned state, loaded with lips, ears, dew-claws, beech-pieces and other useless parts', and in 1791 he introduced and carried a bill increasing the penalties, imposed by an earlier act, on persons who brought to market badly cured leather or who violated the rule that hides should be offered for sale only in an authorized public market. Again these regulations were abolished in the early nineteenth century. Finally in 1796 he intervened vigorously but unsuccessfully on behalf of a small but influential group of constituents, the printers and publishers. When the budget was being debated the paper manufacturers petitioned in favour of the continuance of an import duty on paper. The printers and publishers petitioned for its abolition. Grattan on behalf of the printers argued that paper should be regarded as a raw material rather than a manufactured product (thus defending his consistency as a moderate protectionist), and he pointed out that because of 'the high price of books in England and the comparatively low price of books in this country', Irish book exports were increasing, large orders being received from America for 'Law books and political discussions'; what he did not touch on was literary piracy, a mainstay of the Irish book trade.

IV

Attainment and Loss of Power

At the time the newly formed Irish Whig party was bracing itself to continue with redoubled force the traditional County versus Court struggle (often employing arguments of respectable antiquity), a period of cataclysmic political change was beginning in western Europe. The fall of the Bastille, the achievements of the constituent and legislative assemblies and the great debate on the implications of the revolution, in which the opening salvos were fired by Burke and Paine, inaugurated a new era of thought and action. Throughout the British Isles radicals were inspired and encouraged; simultaneously men of a conservative cast of mind were convinced the time had come for an unflinching defence of the ramparts protecting the existing order and civilization itself. In Ireland there was a renewal of the agitation for Catholic relief and a revival of the reform movement, with some radicals suggesting a radical reshaping of many Irish institutions. During 1792 Catholic activists and reformers were very busy organizing pressure groups, committees, clubs and Volunteer corps and in producing propaganda. As the year progressed excitement was intensified by events abroad. In August the French monarchy was overthrown, in September Brunswick's army was repulsed at Valmy and in the following months the French overran the Austrian Netherlands and threatened Holland, Great Britain's ally.

Until the beginning of 1793 very little of this was reflected in the proceedings of the Irish Parliament, the debates between 1789 and 1792 following familiar lines. There was, however, one departure from the pattern of business as usual. In 1792 Catholic relief suddenly became a major parliamentary question – and it continued to be an important issue for the next thirty-seven years. After the Relief Act of 1782 there had been a lull in the battle for the abolition of Catholic disabilities, Irish Catholics instinctively realizing that it would be politic to allow Protestants time to accept that further concessions were inevitable and would almost certainly involve a sharing of political power. But in 1790 the Catholics, influenced by the winds of change, started a fresh relief campaign, at the beginning of 1792 petitioning the House of Commons. All they secured was a very meagre Relief Act, but it encouraged them to ask for more and their demands were formulated and backed by an elected committee representing the whole of Ireland, which met in Dublin at the beginning of December 1792. This Convention dispatched a deputation to London. The British government, with war impending, put pressure on the Irish administration to conciliate Irish Catholic opinion, and during the parliamentary session of 1793 a bold Catholic Relief Bill, which swept away a great number of disabilities, was passed.

Grattan's views on the Catholic question kept pace with liberal opinion. By 1792 he considered that Parliament's objective should be 'the progressive adoption of the Catholic body', and a year later he declared that the Catholics should be granted 'the whole now'.[1] From the beginnings of the new drive for relief he was ready to give tactical advice to the Catholic leadership. He was one of the Whigs whom towards the close of 1790 the Catholic Committee tactfully lobbied by asking their advice. Grattan told them they ought to get in touch with the Chief Secretary (a step they had already taken).[2] Early in 1792 Richard Burke, the intelligent and intense son of Edmund Burke, who was acting as agent for the Irish Catholics, showed Grattan the petition to Parliament which he had drafted. Grattan was only too helpful. He ruthlessly cut and toned down Burke's composition and, in the opinion of the affronted author, 'intirely destroyed it'.[3] However, the petition actually presented was on the lines

Grattan suggested. Grattan's relations with Burke's successor, Theobold Wolfe Tone, were happier. During the summer of 1792 Tone paid three visits to Tinnehinch to discuss Catholic affairs. A good stylist, he readily accepted Grattan's rewriting of the Catholic Committee's address to the Defenders (Catholic agrarian rioters) which he had probably himself composed. He enjoyed Grattan's epigrammatical political gossip and appreciated his grasp of political tactics – Grattan explained that there was no point in securing a House of Commons committee on sectarian riots in Ulster as it would misstate the facts, and he was strongly against the Catholic Committee continuing to sit when Parliament was in session: it would give the impression the Catholics were trying to overawe Parliament (the Committee adjourned well before the parliamentary session of 1793 began).[4]

What may have been Grattan's most momentous intervention in Catholic affairs occurred early in 1792, when, after the House of Commons had in February rejected the Catholic petition, a meeting was held at John Forbes's lodgings in Kildare Street between Grattan, George Ponsonby, Forbes and Colonel John Hutchinson, the MP for Cork City, and some Catholics, including John Keogh and Edward Byrne, the chairman of the Catholic Committee. According to Hutchinson, reminiscing some thirty-five years later, the Whigs, especially Grattan and himself, pressed the Catholics to summon a national representative Catholic assembly. The Catholics were at first 'frightened' by this suggestion but, emboldened by the Whigs, they decided to hold a convention at the end of the year.[5] They never said, however, that their great convention of 1792–3 was suggested by the Whigs nor that the stamina of the Catholic leadership had been strengthened by Whig exhortations. Probably Hutchinson, like many raconteurs, was inclined to exaggerate his own role, and the Whigs simply encouraged the Catholics by expressing approval of their plan. Six months later Grattan and Hutchinson, when they met the delegates from the convention in London, were startled to discover that the government had agreed to grant the Catholics the forty-shilling franchise. The two Irish Whigs thought that a much higher qualification was desirable, 'urging again and again the impolicy of so low a franchise'. They had the annoying experience of discovering that a

British cabinet minister when discussing Ireland was prepared to contradict flatly a pair of distinguished Irish liberals, Dundas emphatically stating that the franchise 'must be the same as it was in England'.[6]

Besides offering advice to the Catholics Grattan in the early nineties became what he was to remain for the rest of his career: an outstanding parliamentary advocate of their cause. During the sessions of 1792 and 1793, in four powerful speeches, he expounded his approach to the Catholic question. With wit and zest he refuted what he regarded as the archaic and absurd arguments against emancipation which were current – 'arguments', he remarked, 'of extraordinary weakness, of monopoly, of panic, of prejudice, of anything but religion their tendency is to make freedom a monopoly, which is like an endeavour to make the air and light a monopoly, their tendency is to make God a monopoly'. To the argument that the Catholics now had everything except political power, he retorted that a community 'which has no share in political power has no security for its political or civil liberty'. It was inconsistent for Irish Protestants to advocate liberty and simultaneously to expect the Catholics to submit to taxation without representation.[7] When it was suggested that the Established Church might be endangered by emancipation, he pointed out that the Presbyterians, who 'were the majority of Protestants', had not attacked the Church, and he was sure that the Catholics would not attempt to establish their own church: 'to do so is an object more of their superstition than of their interest; superstition which is transitory and now decayed'.[8] To those who declared that Catholic enfranchisement would imperil the British connection, he replied that this assertion 'teaches the Catholic to argue, that the British connection is incompatible with Catholic liberty'. If the Catholics had 'a supposed, idolatrous veneration towards their spiritual pastors', the reason was that 'we have forbidden their education, we are responsible for their ignorance'. To forbid a Catholic to obtain a medical degree implied that 'if a man's life be attacked by disease we authorize no man to save him but a Protestant'; however, a Protestant gentleman 'who wants to go home late in the evening' was prepared to defy the law by arming his Catholic servant. Finally, the principal causes for the enactment of the penal laws were the Pope and the Pretender – 'the one has expired, the other is expiring'.[9]

More significant than this swift, piercing dialectical fencing is Grattan's exposition of his general approach to the Catholic question. A progressively minded man, he was convinced that doctrinal differences between Catholic and Protestant were diminishing and were of little or no importance in political and social life. 'It is', he thought, 'an error of sects to value themselves upon their differences rather than upon their religion.' 'The Catholic', he declared in debate, 'acknowledge the same God and the same Redeemer and differ from you only in the forms of his worship and the ceremonies of his commemoration.' Naturally, then, it was 'a sad error' to assume that 'theological opinions form mankind into distinct political societies'. If a religious sect was seen to be acting as a political party it was because it was being penalized, and sectarianism as a political force would decline rapidly with the removal of the disabilities – 'the repeal of the disability is the repeal of the passion that grows with it'.[10] It was important, he pointed out, to grasp that the Irish situation, with its contrast between the small Protestant minority monopolizing power and the far more numerous Catholic body, 'was not peculiar to us but common to all nations; the Asiatics and the Greeks, the Greeks and the Italians, the English and the Saxons, English and Normans, the vanquished and the vanquishers, they all at last intermingled; the original tribe was in number superior; and yet that superiority never prevented the incorporation; so that this state of our settlement is not peculiar to Ireland, but the ordinary progress of the population and the circulation of the human species, and as it were the trick of nature, to preserve by intermixture, from dwindling and degeneracy, the animal proportions'. With the abolition of the penal laws assimilation would proceed steadily, encouraged by the education of Protestants and Catholics together in Trinity College, 'at the time in which friendships and sympathies are formed'; by 'the fraternity of the club and the Bar', by the camaraderie of the Army (the mess, he thought, would prove more influential than the chaplain); by 'the pleasure of the table'; and by inter-marriage, 'a policy as old as Alexander the Great'.[11]

Grattan emphatically reminded Irish Protestants, 'trustees to preserve to Great Britain the physical force of the Catholics of Ireland', that a steady flow of Catholic recruits to the forces (at a time when manpower was of vital imperial importance), would be ensured by emancipation. He also strove to convey to the House of Commons his own intense conviction that in the new, post-emancipation Ireland, the Protestants, enlightened and propertied, would retain an ascendancy. The maintenance of this ascendancy, he explained, did not require 'a constituency purely Protestant, but compounded of such men as were civilized, substantial freeholders'. Fusing his traditional Whiggery with his advocacy of emancipation, Grattan with gusto argued that the enfranchised Catholics would reinforce the Protestant people against an encroaching executive and a monopolizing borough oligarchy, and he painted a glowing picture of a united Ireland, 'a growing nation', devoted to civil and religious liberty, with the Protestant gentry 'at the head of the people for ever'.[12]

The Catholic Relief Bill of 1793 was an item in the programme which the government put together to meet a difficult and dangerous situation. When the Irish Parliament met in January 1793 it was likely that the country would soon be involved in the European war, and in fact France declared war on Great Britain at the beginning of February. By then the agitation for Catholic relief and the parliamentary reform movement were gathering strength and becoming more vociferous. The Irish administration's response was remarkably bold and flexible. Under pressure from Downing Street (the British government with a great war impending did not want to be distracted by Irish discontent) and realizing that something must be done to meet criticism and win support, the Irish administration produced an unprecedently long legislative programme which included not only a Catholic Relief Bill but a number of constitutional and economic measures which might be expected to gratify important sections of the Irish public, together with measures for strengthening national defence and internal security. With the government executing a strategic withdrawal Grattan had an opportunity to play a congenial role – that of a very influential independent MP pressing the government relentlessly 'to give every necessary redress to the public complaints', and judiciously (with a touch of condescension) weighing each item in the government's programme. His professed aims were 'to give the government every necessary support and to give the people every constitutional redress'. But he made clear that supporting the government did not mean countenancing abuses, and that the best way of combating French principles was 'by giving Ireland the advantages of the British constitution – by showing the supremacy of that constitution over those of foreign phrenzy'.[13]

Although at the outset of the session he could not resist the temptation to develop a comparison between the Irish administration and the French Levellers – they were both in their different ways undermining popular respect for the constitution – he strongly supported a number of government measures.[14] He naturally approved of the Catholic Relief Bill, the Place Bill, the Pension Bill, the Hearth Money Bill (exempting 'the poorer classes of the people' from the tax) and the Barren Lands Bill. Though when commending this last-named bill, which was introduced by the Chief Secretary, Grattan could not refrain from sardonically expressing his pleasure that it 'had fallen into such illustrious hands'. He also supported the Alien Bill, the Treasonable Correspondence Bill, the Gunpowder Bill (expressing some alarm at the increased powers given to customs officials by this Bill), the Augmentation of the Forces Bill and the Militia Bill. But he wanted to postpone the second reading of the Militia Bill, partly, he stated, because time was needed for the consideration of its sixty-eight pages, and partly because he felt it should be accompanied by a parliamentary reform bill (privately he was anxious to hold up the bill until the Catholic Relief Bill was safely through the Lords). He badly misjudged the temper of the House. To most MPs the Bill was an urgent wartime measure, and the formation of a militia was of course bound to appeal to country gentlemen. A clamorous House called for a division and carried the second reading against Grattan's angry protests. The last of the government's security measures, the Convention Bill, banning assemblies purporting to be representative, was introduced towards the close of the session avowedly to forestall a reform convention which was to be held at Athlone. Grattan denounced the bill for misstating the law and he emphasized the important part conventions – the Convention Parliament of 1688, the Volunteer Convention of 1782 – had played in history. At the same time he attacked the assembly the United Irishmen intended to hold at Athlone as a 'feeble and frivolous' project. It was reasonable enough to disapprove both of the Reform Convention and the bill, but the House, reflecting the attitude of the blunt, practical man, gave the bill a second reading by 128 to 27.[15]

Grattan himself introduced three bills, a Libel Bill modeled on Fox's Act of 1791, a Dublin Police Bill and a bill disenfranchising revenue officers. The Libel Bill passed but the other bills made little progress, which is scarcely surprising as they were introduced late in the session. He also, along with George Ponsonby, persuaded the House to go into committee on the subject of parliamentary reform, hoping that the committee would agree on the broad outlines of a scheme. But the conservatives successfully stonewalled and by the end of the session no progress had been made. In the past Grattan had been a conscientious rather than an enthusiastic reformer, but by the beginning of 1793 he had decided that if public confidence in the constitution and parliament was to be maintained, parliamentary reform was absolutely necessary.

Fortunately for a man to whom 'the principles of the constitution were sacred', the rotten or private boroughs were of comparatively recent origin, being Stuart creations, and their patrons formed 'not an oligarchy of property but an oligarchy of accident'. In Grattan's opinion a rationalization of the constituency pattern was obviously desirable, and he was very anxious to secure a sound electorate. 'It should', he laid down, 'be property that elects, but property in the hands of the many not of the few'. His aim was to 'embody the mass of property which will be generally found to include the mass of talent, in support of the constitution', and he considered the electorate should be composed of landlords, farmers, businessmen and perhaps superior craftsmen. A man who had no property could not complain that he had not a vote – 'a passenger through your field or a labourer on your farm, has no right to make rules for the management of the same' – and it would be wrong to permit the property of the country 'to be ordered and disposed of by a majority who confessedly have neither estate nor farm, nor lease nor trade'. Labourers and non-proprietors, and those exempted from paying the hearth tax (whom he estimated as being more than half the population) should not be enfranchised. While urging the cause of reform in 1793 Grattan did not fail to mention the benefits conferred on the country by Parliament, though he said that a reformed Parliament would have done even better

– for instance it would have checked the growth of government expenditure. He also warned the public that parliamentary reform would achieve little if the administration retained the power to purchase a majority. Taken all in all, the session of 1793 was from Grattan's point of view the most satisfactory Irish parliamentary session since 1782. Measures he had long advocated had been enacted, which seemed to prove that even an unreformed House of Commons would ultimately respond to enlightened opinion, and circumstances had allowed him, a friend wrote, 'to comport himself more like a great patriotic minister than the chief of an opposition'.[16]

When Parliament reassembled in January 1794, Grattan in the debate on the address declared that although he had disapproved of the war at its outset, he now believed that Ireland must stand by Great Britain.[17] His attitude greatly annoyed Lawrence Parsons, who condemned Grattan's famous phrase 'standing or falling by Great Britain' as 'figurative and indistinct', crystallizing a policy which turned Ireland into a satellite nation and which encouraged the British government, assured of automatic Irish co-operation, to neglect Ireland strategically.[18] On 5 February Parsons moved that the treaties relative to the war which had been placed before the British Parliament should also be laid before the Irish House of Commons. Grattan opposed the motion with 'great power'. When Great Britain was at war, Ireland, he declared, was bound to give its support without 'questioning the causes and objects of the war, unless they pointed against Irish liberty and independence'. Parsons' motion, he declared, tended 'to undermine your own proceedings, to retract your plighted sentiments and to raise a mutiny against your own taxes', and it would encourage the enemy to think that 'their principles were not abhorrent to the disposition of the people here and incline them to try the effects of a descent'. Grattan had characteristically not consulted with his political associates before making this onslaught on Parsons, and Cooke wrote with delight that 'I never saw great marks of chagrin painted on countenances than on those of George Ponsonby, Curran, Duquery, Egan and the lawyers in opposition'. The Irish Whigs were certainly in disarray. George Ponsonby and Curran unenthusiastically followed Grattan; Duquery, Egan and Arthur Browne, all leading members

Portrait of Grattan by Martin Shee, oil on canvas (National Gallery of Ireland)

Portrait of Grattan in Hibernian Magazine, *1780 (The Board of Trinity College, Dublin)*

Irish Volunteers meeting in College Green, Dublin, 4 November 1779, by Archibald McGoogan after Francis Wheatley

Grattan 'urging the Declaration of Irish Rights' in the Irish House of Commons, 1780

Cartoon dated 13 June 1782 and entitled 'Irish Gratitude', commenting on the grant by the Irish Parliament to Grattan of a sum of money for the purchase of a landed estate. The figure on the proclamation in the cartoon is £100,000; the sum actually granted was £50,000. (Robinson Collection, The Board of Trinity College, Dublin)

Tinnehinch, Co. Wicklow (The Board of Trinity College, Dublin)

Portrait of Grattan by Gilbert Stuart, oil on canvas (National Gallery of Ireland)

Two 1799 cartoons charging Grattan with complicity with the United Irishmen. Top: 'The Maidstone Whitewasher', aimed primarily at the Whig MP Charles James Fox (left), counts Grattan (third from right) among the major political figures who were witnesses for the defence at the Maidstone trial of the United Irishman Arthur O'Connor in 1798. Bottom: 'A Peep into the Retreat at Tinnehinch' suggests that Grattan (right) is fully in league with the United Irishmen. (Robinson Collection, The Board of Trinity College, Dublin)

A cartoon giving one view of the climate of Irish politics in 1829, the year of Catholic Emancipation (Robinson Collection, The Board of Trainity College Dublin)

Marble bust of Grattan by Peter Turnerelli (National Gallery of Ireland)

Statue of Grattan by Francis Chantrey, City Hall, Dublin (Dublin Corporation)

of the Bar, supported Parsons, whose motion was defeated by 128 to 9.[19] A couple of days later Parsons discussed the question with Curran, Duquery and Egan. Curran, he thought, was opposed to the war but was reluctant to separate himself from Grattan (according to Parsons he wanted people to think he was an intimate friend of Grattan). The next day Duquery, on behalf of Parsons and Egan, tackled Grattan, demanding an explanation of his views on the war and on politics in general. He found Grattan 'close, reserved, not willing to have any meeting of the party, and inflexible on the war'.[20]

When in mid-February Grattan raised the question of the equalization of British and Irish customs duties, his speech seemed to Douglas, the Chief Secretary, as 'far from hostile'. To Parsons the speech was 'that of a lawyer hired to oppose his friend. Popularity was the fee, government the friend.' Grattan, he noted, spoke like 'a gentle, bending, complimentary courtier' and the Chief Secretary responded by pouring 'fulsome adulation' on Grattan. Though Grattan was vigorously, rather too vigorously indeed, supported by Duquery, who asked was Great Britain 'of so haughty a character that she must be fawned and courted to do justice', Grattan withdrew his motion on being assured that action would probably soon be taken along the lines he proposed. Privately he pressed Parnell, he Chancellor of the Exchequer, to take up the question, reminding him 'you will want much, very much next session'.[21]

Shortly before the close of the session he supported against the government a reform bill introduced by George Ponsonby which was defeated by 142 to 44. Grattan attacked borough-mongering and ministerial corruption along familiar lines, but the most striking part of his speech was a fiery denunciation of manhood suffrage, which was the main feature of the plan of reform recently published by that 'blasted Jacobin society', the Dublin United Irishmen. Grattan painted a grim picture of the results of 'establishing a representation of existence, a conceit which is affected and nonsensical'. The non-propertied, the majority of the voters, would monopolize the representation, so that 'those who had nothing in the common stock would make the laws and the men who receive alms would vote the taxes'. 'A revolution of power', he declared, 'would speedily lead to a revolution of property.' It was possible that the government might, by using the army and the treasury, for a short time influence elections, and it was also possible that some rich men might ally themselves with the mob. What was certain was that the middle classes, 'the people', would be politically powerless. Instead of canvassing the farmer, 'the squire would go to the farmer's dung-yard and canvass the boys of his bawn'.[22]

Both the Chief Secretary, Sylvester Douglas, and Cooke appreciated the immense and unique value of Grattan's support. As Cooke shrewdly said, 'the government is strong in numbers. They want not aristocratical addition. They want the chief of the people.' But harnessing this potent and erratic political force was a difficult task. Grattan, in Cooke's opinion, though undoubtedly 'steady and honourable' was 'resentful and suspicious' and naturally reluctant to jeopardize 'his great sway over the public mind'. Moreover it was clear that 'he does not want, perhaps would not take situation; he would stipulate for measures'.[23] Nevertheless the Chief Secretary thought something could be done towards cultivating Grattan's goodwill by conventional methods. When the archbishopric of Tuam fell vacant in August 1794, Richard Marlay, Bishop of Clonfert for twelve years, intimated to the Chief Secretary that the time had come for his promotion, and Douglas mentioned the matter to the Prime Minister, adding that a friend of Grattan had reported 'that Marlay's promotion is much at his heart'. Unfortunately for Marlay he had an irresistible rival, William Beresford, Bishop of Ossory, who was both a brother of the Marquess of Waterford and the brother-in-law of the Lord Chancellor. But just after Tuam was filled, the death of the Primate suggested the possibility of a series of translations, and Marlay (whom, it was rumoured, the Prince of Wales was backing for the Primacy) was quick to renew his claims. The Home Secretary in the new coalition government, the serious-minded Duke of Portland, summed up Marlay's right to promotion succinctly – 'intitled to consideration as uncle to Grattan – as a prelate not at all so'. In the event, Marlay at the beginning of 1795 was moved to Waterford, a less isolated diocese with a larger episcopal income.[24]

Douglas discussed with Grattan both general politics and patronage questions – the problem of finding a seat for Grattan's old friend Tydd (an administration supporter); the possibility of placing Robert Day, Grattan's close companion when he was at the Temple, on the bench; and what could be done to promote the aims of 'our friend Mr Cuffe'. 'May your views for the prosperity and dignity of Ireland be successful', Douglas wrote to Grattan, because 'they are intimately connected with those of this country and of the empire'. And at the beginning of 1795 he pressed Grattan and Mrs Grattan to visit him and his wife in England. Writing candidly to an old friend he remarked that Grattan was 'a genius and an orator but a very bad man of business, full of antipathies and prejudices and pledged to most dangerous measures'.[25]

Events soon drew Grattan into even closer contact with the government and for a short, critical period transformed him from being an independent critic of men in power to being the principal spokesman for the Irish administration in the House of Commons. In the summer of 1794 Pitt and the Portland Whigs at last coalesced. Portland became Home Secretary and, anxious to apply Whig remedies to Ireland, he insisted that there should be a Lord Lieutenant with whom he would be in close agreement. It was therefore decided that Lord Fitzwilliam, who in July 1794 had been appointed President of the Council, should become Lord Lieutenant as soon as an official niche could be found for Westmorland, who had held the office for the previous four years. Fitzwilliam seemed an excellent choice. A great Yorkshire landed magnate, he had extensive estates in County Wicklow and was married to an Irish woman, a cousin of William and George Ponsonby. Moreover, he was high-minded, intelligent, generous and amiable. Admittedly he was inexperienced and, what was less apparent, impressionable, impetuous and subject to bouts of pride and prejudice.

Even before the new ministers took office the Irish Whigs were being encouraged to believe that a coalition would mean changes in Ireland. At the close of June Portland had a talk with his cousin, William Ponsonby, in which he told him that Pitt was convinced that there would have to be a total change of system in Ireland, that the direction of Irish affairs would be handed over to Portland and that this arrangement was 'his principal inducement to agree to Mr Pitt's proposal'. The Duke went on to say that he accepted all the measures advocated by the Irish Whigs together with Catholic emancipation, and he agreed that his friends in Ireland could not be expected to work with Fitzgibbon, Beresford and 'the clerks' (the under-secretaries).[26] Unfortunately, Ponsonby's memorandum recording a conversation, so satisfactory and specific, was prepared nearly a year later when Ponsonby was convinced that Portland had failed the Irish Whigs. It is certainly surprising that Portland should have readily accepted the whole Whig programme, including Catholic emancipation. Loughborough, who knew him well, stated that the Duke regarded the Catholic Relief Act of 1793 as fixing the limits of concession.[27] There is, however, a simple explanation. 'The duke', a fellow of Trinity College, Dublin, observed about this time, 'is not a man of much address. He is too modest, an odd quality in a man of his rank.'[28] Extremely fluent on paper, Portland was diffident in speech, and chatting with his cousin he would have preferred to dwell on what they might together achieve for Ireland rather than to stress the points on which they might differ. It may be added that Grattan in a conversation with Portland towards the end of 1794 also got the impression that the Duke favoured Catholic emancipation, although he admitted that Portland had emphasized there might be 'a difficulty in a certain quarter'.[29] If Portland is to be blamed for sheering away from divisive issues, it is only fair to add that Grattan and the Ponsonbys, eager to see a Whig administration installed in Dublin Castle, did not insist on a clarification of the Duke's views on the Catholic question.

In August Fitzwilliam informed a number of Irish Whigs, including Grattan, that he was coming over as Viceroy. Asking Grattan for his support, he explained that he would 'make the duke of Portland's administration the model of mine'. Grattan replied at once that Fitzwilliam's acceptance of the viceroyalty was regarded as 'our redemption'. He went on to say that he had had 'no intercourse with government' since Portland was Lord Lieutenant. There were times when he had ceased to oppose the administration but he never had been connected with it because 'there were in its cabinet certain men whose principles fundamentally and diametrically differed from mine'.[30] Towards the end of the month George Ponsonby arranged a meeting between himself, Grattan, Yelverton and Thomas Lewis O'Beirne, who had been Portland's chaplain and private secretary when the Duke was in Ireland, to prepare a programme for Fitzwilliam. They agreed that the country should be put into a proper state of defence by the formation of local corps on the lines of English Volunteers; that the Catholics should be conciliated; and that 'a system of government with that character of purity which would take away all pretence of censure' should be pursued. It was also agreed to recommend Fitzgibbon's removal from office – although George Ponsonby from personal friendship was loath to take the initiative in this matter.[31]

In the middle of September Grattan, whom the Duke of Portland had hoped would come over, arrived in London. There he discussed the education of the Irish Catholic clergy with Hussey, the persuasive and politic chaplain to the Spanish Embassy, who was eager to secure government support for the establishment of Catholic seminaries in Ireland.[32] Grattan also energetically intervened in the struggle over the succession to the provostship of Trinity, vacated by the death of Hely-Hutchinson. It was rumoured that the successor might be another political lawyer, Arthur Wolfe, the Attorney-General. Grattan was strongly opposed to this, for the sake of both the College and Wolfe. Hely-Hutchinson, he pointed out, 'had been almost stung to death by obtruding himself into the hive of the Academy'. The fellows, he thought, had 'a natural right to reap their own harvest and to wear their own laurels'.[33] It soon emerged that the Lord Lieutenant was not prepared to accept this natural right, his candidate being William Bennet, the Bishop of Cloyne, a classicist and antiquarian who had been Westmorland's private secretary. The fellows understandably pressed hard for the appointment of one of their own number. They were backed by the Whig leaders, who regarded the appointment as a test case that would indicate whether merit or old-fashioned patronage considerations would be the deciding factor in official appointments. It was rumoured that, if the bishop was made Provost, Grattan and Ponsonby were prepared to attack the appointment in the House of Commons,[34] but in the event one of Fitzwilliam's few appointments was that of Richard Murray, a quiet mathematical don, to the provostship.

The opening of the new era in Irish politics was delayed by the difficulty of finding an acceptable post for Westmorland, whose self-respect required that he should not be demoted, and during the autumn the Whigs chafed at the delay while despondency spread amongst Pitt's Irish supporters. To them the official changes which the Whigs were urging as part of their programme for the purification of public life merely reflected the Whiggish proclivity for place. To Cooke, the key to the Whigs' Irish policy was their determination to turn Ireland into a permanent party power base, and by early October Pitt himself had become concerned over Irish developments. It seemed to him that Portland and Fitzwilliam believed that they could treat Ireland as a private Whig demesne, ruthlessly disregarding the claims of Pitt's Irish supporters – one of whom, the domineering and indomitable Fitzgibbon, was the embodiment of what the Whigs detested in Irish politics. Such an attitude, in Pitt's opinion, illaccorded with collective responsibility and the coalition spirit, and in October he raised with his colleagues the question of how Irish problems were to be handled. This produced an explosion which threatened to destroy the government. Portland and Fitzwilliam, great Whig magnates, deeply attached to their party and still suspicious of Pitt as a power-hungry Prime Minister, were both highly emotional men and they were soon talking and writing about betrayal and resignation.

To those whose minds were fixed on the strategic situation and who saw the fate of Europe trembling in the balance, it was a tragicomedy that a strong British cabinet should fall apart over comparatively trivial Irish issues. As Loughborough, the recently appointed Lord Chancellor, wrote, it was absurd to be arguing over Irish promotions and proscriptions when 'proscription in all the force of the term hangs by a very slender thread over all property and legitimate power'.[35] At the end of October Loughborough, assisted by Burke and Grattan, endeavoured to reconcile Pitt and his Whig colleagues. Concerned about the war and eager to see a Whig Lord Lieutenant in the Castle, Grattan had already, when on 15 October he had an interview with Pitt, tried to arrange a compromise. He expressed some sympathy with the Prime Minister's attitude over Fitzgibbon and seemed to have agreed that Fitzgibbon might continue in office if it was 'clearly understood on both sides of the water' that he was to play no part in politics.[36] This from the Whig point of view was an advantageous compromise. Confined to his chancery work, Fitzgibbon would cease to be formidable. Grattan indeed at this time was so conciliatory that Portland seems to have thought it necessary to exert himself to postpone another meeting between Grattan and Pitt. Grattan, he wrote, was so anxious to avoid a split in the ministry that 'we should have been demolished wholesale and retail'.[37]

At the beginning of November Grattan along with Burke had a long talk with Fitzwilliam, after which they both called on Loughborough and conveyed to him what they had gathered were Fitzwilliam's sentiments. Then, two days later, Grattan and Fitzwilliam had a talk with Loughborough. This exchange of opinions cleared the air. Fitzwilliam accepted that Ireland was not to be treated as 'separate from the general mass of the king's government' and he was assured that Pitt would wholeheartedly support his administration in Ireland.[38] With good relations re-established, it was decided to hold a ministerial meeting to iron out all the difficulties that might arise over Ireland and to provide Fitzwilliam with guidelines. In preparation for this meeting Grattan and the Ponsonbys prepared a memorandum for Fitzwilliam setting out the terms on which 'they and their friends will agree to support Lord Fitzwilliam's administration'. These were 'a regulation of the trade between Great Britain and Ireland' (a commercial settlement), the abolition of the remaining Catholic disabilities, a Place Bill, a Responsibility Bill, the repeal of the Dublin Police Bill, the disenfranchisement of revenue officers, and the abolition of a number of revenue posts created in 1789. The Duke of Leinster, George Ponsonby, John Forbes and Curran were to be admitted to office and the under-secretaries dismissed.[39] In another memorandum prepared for Fitzwilliam, possibly by Grattan, the importance of repealing the Convention Act, as 'being contrary to the bill of rights', and of lowering British duties on Irish imports were stressed.[40]

On 15 November Pitt, Grenville, Fitzwilliam, Spencer and Windham met at 10 Downing Street to settle the details of the Irish policy. It was a preoccupied group. Belgium had been overrun and Holland was in grave danger, and since there were in the room a prospective viceroy, an ex-viceroy and two sometime chief secretaries, the discussion was understandably lengthy and discursive. It was agreed that the provostship should be filled by the appointment of a fellow and that George Ponsonby should be Solicitor-General. Fitzwilliam raised the question of abolishing the revenue posts created in 1789, but since 'it soon appeared that he was by no means acquainted with the subject', it was decided that he should collect information in Ireland and then give his colleagues an opportunity of considering what should be done. The Catholic question was 'considered as one of much delicacy' and 'no decided sentiment as to the line which it might ultimately be right to adopt upon it was expressed by any person present'. Fitzwilliam, it was decided, was to inform his colleagues upon the state of opinion in Ireland, to try to prevent the question being raised during the coming session and 'in all events do nothing in it which might commit the King's government without fresh intructions from hence [England]'. Fitzwilliam himself summarized the decision on this point in the following words – 'that the Roman Catholic question not be brought forward by the government, that the discussion of the propriety be left open'.[41]

When the Irish Whig leaders received from Fitzwilliam a summary of the Downing Street discussion they were very disappointed (and possibly irritated by Fitzwilliam's ineptitude in committee). Having complained that his memorandum 'contains nothing', they commented severely on its implications. The suggestion that a reduction of duties should be postponed until the end of the war was, they thought; tantamount to a refusal. Referring to the proposal that the Whig bills and the abolition of revenue posts should be considered by Fitzwilliam after he arrived in Ireland, they stated that if this meant those subjects were going to be discussed in principle, they rejected the suggestion; but if the discussion would only be on points of detail they would support Fitzwilliam's administration. As for Catholic emancipation, 'a measure necessary to be done either by the government or by us', they were prepared to yield to the government 'the post of honour or bring it forward themselves in their individual capacity'.[42] But having criticized the cabinet's decisions as reported by Fitzwilliam, Grattan and the Ponsonbys told him they wanted him to accept the post of Lord Lieutenant. They were eager to see a sympathetic Lord Lieutenant in office, they were confident that once the Irish Whigs were in power they would obtain considerable parliamentary support and they assumed that the British cabinet, which did not want to be distracted by Irish problems, would accept a policy guaranteed to promote internal peace in Ireland and increase the Irish contribution to the war effort. Fitzwilliam perhaps should have insisted on his colleagues formulating their advice in more precise terms, but he was intensely eager to embark as soon as possible on his crusade to raise the standards of Irish public life and rally Ireland against revolutionary France.

After three months of wearying but fruitful discussions in London, Grattan in the middle of December returned to Ireland. On his arrival in Dublin, according to Fitzgibbon, he sent for the Catholic leaders Edward Byrne and John Keogh and told them that 'he pledged Lord Fitzwilliam to them for the unqualified repeal of all the laws which affected them and directed them to pour in petitions to parliament'.[43] Whatever Grattan may have said – and he may have given information rather than advice – the Catholic leadership was bound to be encouraged by the impending arrival of a Whig lord lieutenant and steps were taken to ensure that at the meeting of Parliament Catholic petitions demanding complete emancipation should be presented simultaneously from all over Ireland.

Fitzwilliam landed at Balbriggan on 4 January 1795,[44] and a few days after his arrival in Dublin he took steps to remove from office the Attorney-General, the Solicitor-General, the First Revenue Commissioner and the two Under-Secretaries. The Irish Whigs who had been urging the removal of a number of office-holders must have been pleased by these dismissals though they do not seem to have been consulted by Fitzwilliam over the timing of the operation. His self-assurance mounted rapidly after he became Lord Lieutenant and he accepted full responsibility and credit for the dismissals. However, he co-operated closely with his Irish allies over parliamentary business and when Parliament met on 22 January Grattan, the two Ponsonbys, Curran and Hardy were on the Treasury Bench with Parnell and the Secretary.[45]

The Irish Whig leaders had apparently wanted Grattan to take office – possibly as Chancellor of the Exchequer. But although he was ready to support the Fitzwilliam administration, he shrank from being a placeman. In October 1794 he told Loughborough that he intended to be 'Minister' [leader] of the House of Commons without taking office because he 'had been purchased as it were by the people'. Loughborough told him his attitude was absurd. A leader of the House had to be a responsible minister and be prepared to sacrifice 'popularity in defence of unpopular measures'.[46] Grattan was unmoved by this argument and acted as the principal parliamentary spokesman of the Fitzwilliam administration in the ambiguous position of adviser without portfolio. Moving the address in answer to the Speech from the Throne in a sparkling speech (incidentally his only major ministerial oration), he emphasized that the new administration's policy was based on two principles: a whole-hearted commitment to the war effort and a determination to promote national harmony. He denounced French aggression and French doctrine with all the fervour of an early admirer of Chatham and a disciple of Burke. The French Revolution was that 'inundation of barbarity, that desolation of infidelity, that dissolution of government'. Besides propagating by intrigue and arms poisonous ideas, France, 'the ancient enemy of these realms and the eternal rival in all shapes, monarchical and republican, of Great Britain', aimed at continental domination – 'the throne of Spain flies before her, the petty princes of the German states disappear, the Prussian retires, the Hollander negotiates', only Great Britain barred her progress and if Ireland hung back from action Great Britain might be driven to make peace on terms that would disgrace her Empire. Therefore they must stand by Great Britain, maintaining the connection, the constitution and 'the high station you now possess in Europe'. 'External energy', he stressed, 'must arise from internal union'; and the administration aimed at uniting 'all the property of the country in support of the laws and all the talents in support of the property'.

Grattan went on to emphasize the administration's interest in education, primary and secondary, and he mentioned two measures it had in mind: the foundation of two great, endowed schools, well provided with scholarships for the sons of the Protestant clergy, and the foundation of two seminaries for the education of the Irish Catholic clergy. He then warned 'the banditti' (agrarian rioters) who were creating trouble in County Meath that the government would not tolerate their activities, and he concluded by referring to an event 'which no Irishman can speak of without emotions of joy and affection': the marriage of the Prince of Wales and Caroline of Brunswick. Grattan was seconded by Robert Stewart, the future Lord Castlereagh, in a sensible speech in which he emphasized that Great Britain possessed far greater resources than France. Duquery, an outstanding lawyer and very independent Whig, spoke of the desirability of opening peace negotiations; and Lord Edward Fitzgerald, who was moving from Whiggery to radicalism, declared that the war was a war of tyranny against liberty and that if Pitt defeated France he would not be surprised if 'we were forced to sing Te Deums for the happy settlement of your Irish constitution'.[47] The Address was carried by 148 to none, Grattan and Stewart telling for the Ayes and Lord Edward and Alexander Montgomery of Donegal for the Noes.

The first few weeks of the parliamentary session was an exhilarating time for Grattan and his fellow Irish Whigs. Triumphant after five years of painstaking opposition and frequent frustration, they were now in a position to place before Parliament a programme endorsed by the Castle. The military forces maintained by Ireland were increased, £200,000 was voted for the navy, and Grattan announced that the government intended to form 'a county armament' – a local defence force. 'The property of the country', he said, 'armed and commissioned shall preserve the peace.' All this, he admitted, would cost money, 'but you will bear it with fortitude'.[48] Although the Chancellor of the Exchequer, Parnell, who had remained in office, was facing a deficit, he made two concessions in the budget. Occupiers of one-hearth houses were exempted unconditionally from the hearth tax, and the beer duties were abolished (although the malt tax was increased). Consequent on the latter change, Grattan introduced and carried a short bill repealing all legislation regulating 'the trade of a brewer'. Thus, Grattan said, the government paid attention to the health and morals of the people.[49] The cost of the war, met partly by increased taxation and largely by borrowing, accentuated the long-dormant demand for retrenchment. In February Robert Graydon, a keen Whig, moved for the appointment of a committee to inquire into the cost of collecting the revenue. Grattan, who was about to move a similar resolution, gracefully gave way and a committee, on which they both sat, was appointed. On the same day Graydon secured the appointment of a committee to inquire into the sale by the Wide Street Commissioners of a large plot of land west of the Custom House. Any one *au fait* with Irish politics could see that there was a common factor behind the appointment of these two committees. John Beresford, a Whig *bête noire*, was both First Revenue Commissioner and a Wide Street Commissioner. The committee on the revenue reported towards the close of the session. It found that during the previous twenty years the cost of collecting the revenue had increased absolutely and relatively in proportion to the amount collected. Two years later, after a change in the political balance, another House of Commons committee with similar terms of reference reported that between 1774 and 1794 the revenue had increased and that from 1784 the relative cost of collection had fallen. Also that much of the increased cost was clearly unavoidable. As for the committee on the Wide Street Commission's property transactions, after hearing much complex and baffling evidence relating to the Commissioners' dealings with developers it was unable to agree on any conclusions.

Turning to legislation – a Juries Bill, which provided that persons accused of libel could claim a special jury (a bill that Duigenan, an ultra-conservative, said would prevent 'libellers being brought to trial as long as the world should last'),[50] received a second reading; House of Commons committees recommended the introduction of a Responsibility Bill, a Dublin Police Bill and a bill strengthening the powers of the Irish Treasury; and on 12 February Grattan obtained leave to introduce a Catholic Relief Bill, its preparation being entrusted to Grattan, George Ponsonby and George Knox. Grattan did not on 12 February outline the measure he intended to present although he made clear it would include the abolition of the remaining disabilities. Fitzwilliam declared himself willing to submit Grattan's bill to the British Cabinet and endeavour to meet its wishes on points of detail.[51]

During the first six weeks of the session the administration certainly had the backing of the House of Commons. An opposition to Catholic relief was mustering, with vocal leaders in Ogle and Duigenan. But it is highly unlikely that it would have succeeded if the bill was known to be a government measure. The administration had also its candid friends. Sir Lawrence Parsons, the quintessence of independence, always ready to intervene in debate from an unexpected angle, asked early in the session if the gentlemen 'in the confidence of the government intended to adhere to the policies they had professed in opposition'. Grattan answered emphatically in the affirmative, adding however that 'the first principle is the defence of the country and to that all others must be postponed'. When Parsons then asked about specific measures – reform, the repeal of the Convention Act, the disfranchisement of revenue officers – Sir Hercules Langrishe, for many years a faithful supporter, was 'put forward to twaddle', until Grattan rose to deliver a well-phrased ministerial statement. In general the gentlemen now in the administration would do all they could to carry their principles into effect, but it would be presumptuous to mention the measures which they expected to pass, as 'it would imply that the ministers possessed over that house an influence which no minister could dare avow'. Another severe critic of the administration, Henry Duquery, though he agreed that Ireland must stand by Great Britain during the war, urged that peace negotiations should be opened as soon as possible and strongly attacked Pitt's record as a war minister, accusing him of displaying strategic incompetence. Grattan at once sprang to Pitt's defence, arguing that 'the reverses of war' were to be attributed to the collapse of Britain's allies and French military power rather than to ministerial ineptitude. Turning to the home front, Duquery took up a cause with which Grattan had been long associated, economy, hinting that the Whig leaders now in office were not showing much enthusiasm for the subject. Duquery also proposed that a tax on pensions and official salaries should be substituted for the leather tax which fell severely on the poor. 'The poor man', Duquery said, 'wears his shoes in a manner truely Irish on his shoulders.' Duquery's suggestion was dismissed with 'uncommon harshness and contempt by Minister Grattan'. Grattan accused Duquery of 'disseminating discontent'. Most pensioners, Grattan explained, were 'objects of compassion' and it was 'boyish' to think of taxing civil servants earning about £40 per annum.[52] Grattan's tone must have sounded exasperatingly ministerial to Parsons and Duquery, and another Whig was to recall a few years later how, during the Fitzwilliam era, Grattan 'strutted in pygmy consequence about the Castle'.[53]

Seven or eight weeks after Fitzwilliam's arrival in Ireland the Irish Whigs could congratulate themselves on the course of events. An alliance had been forged between the Castle and the leaders of progressive and moderate Irish opinion, and although 'the patriots' (to use a hallowed term) were taking the lead in Parliament and had a say in the disposal of patronage, harmonious co-operation with Great Britain was being maintained. But the success of this new departure in Irish politics depended largely on the Lord Lieutenant, the link between the British cabinet and his Irish friends and advisers, and unfortunately by the middle of February Fitzwilliam was rapidly losing the confidence of his colleagues in England. They were already perturbed by his dismissals, which seemed precipitant and partisan, when on 7 February Portland placed before the cabinet a startling dispatch from the Lord Lieutenant. In it Fitzwilliam, after reciting the arguments for immediate emancipation, went on to state that he 'would acquiesce with a good grace' in the introduction of a relief bill unless 'I receive very peremptory directions to the contrary'.

The cabinet must have felt it was being hustled and its reaction was predictable. It postponed a discussion of the Catholic question and asked for more information as to what would be the effect of emancipation on the Established Church and the composition of the House of Commons. Fitzwilliam's response was to emphasize the urgency of the question; the cabinet directed him to use his influence to halt the progress of the Relief Bill; Fitzwilliam made it clear that he would resign rather than reverse his policy; his colleagues decided on his recall. Portland, who had to convey their views to Fitzwilliam, was deeply distressed. He believed that Fitzwilliam had fallen under the domination of Grattan and William Ponsonby. They were both, Portland granted, men of integrity, but Ponsonby and other Irish Whigs were excessively critical of the Established Church and Grattan had a hankering after 'popularity' which inspired him to take up measures such as tithe reform. Fitzwilliam, Portland was convinced, could only recover his balance by escaping to England.[54]

Fitzwilliam had to remain in Ireland until his successor, Camden, arrived at the end of March. Frustrated and embittered, he rapidly produced a justification of his conduct in the form of two letters to his friend Lord Carlisle. He arranged for a wide distribution of these letters and by the beginning of April they had appeared in print. Straightforward in style and even more biased than might have been expected, they offered the public an unusual glimpse into the arcana of government and a simple explanation for Fitzwilliam's failure. Fitzwilliam, upright and self-righteous, could not conceive that the painful imbroglio in which he was involved might have resulted from a misunderstanding. For him, Machiavellianism rather than muddle provided the key. From the time the Whig leaders were enticed into the coalition, Pitt's object had been 'to debase, degrade and disgrace their characters', and although the Catholic question had undoubtedly been left completely to Fitzwilliam's discretion he had been treacherously disavowed, because Pitt 'risques all rather than not extend his protection to his exclusive friends', Beresford and 'the clerks'. Fitzwilliam's account of his viceroyalty was the first in the field and went unchallenged in detail by his cabinet colleagues, who were unanimous in wanting to forget about the episode. When the latter was raised in Parliament, the government's attitude was that the Crown had the right to remove a minister from office and that it was 'indelicate and dangerous to open the secret transactions of government'. Taking this line may have been good debating tactics but it meant that Fitzwilliam's version of the events leading to his recall went for many years almost unchallenged.

To Grattan, Fitzwilliam was a political martyr who had aroused 'the hostility of the most powerful of the English connected with the worst of the Irish'.[55] Both men were easily inflamed by moral indignation, which made them for the moment see and speak of opponents as criminals as well as blunderers. A few days after Ftizwilliam learned that the cabinet would not allow him carte blanche to deal with the Catholic question, Grattan wrote an impassionate letter to Burke, who, he hoped, might be able to influence the Cabinet. Catholic relief, Grattan declared, 'cannot be resisted at this time with any effect short of ruin'. The Irish Parliament had voted 43,000 men for home defence and was prepared to authorize the formation of a yeomanry force, but 'what avails it to give 40,000 men to the government of this Country, if the cabinet of England shall give 3,000,000 of Irishmen to the French'.[56] But allowing for his disappointment and disquiet, Grattan's reaction to Fitzwilliam's recall was more restrained than might have been expected. When on 2 March, shortly after Fitzwilliam's recall, Lawrence Parsons moved that supplies should be granted for only six months, Grattan was not in the minority of twenty-four who supported the motion. When later on the same day the quick-tempered Thomas Connoly announced that he was going to move three resolutions, viz. that the Lord Lieutenant deserved the thanks of the House and the confidence of the people, that a prorogation would be highly injurious to the country and that both these resolutions should be presented to the King, Grattan suggested that for the moment an address to the Lord Lieutenant would suffice, a course the House agreed to *nem con*.[57]

During the long adjournment which followed these debates, Grattan expressed his views on the crisis through the medium of the press. In his reply to an address from the Dublin Catholics he exhorted them to continue their campaign for emancipation: 'it may be the death of one viceroy, it will be the peace offering of another'. The Fitzwilliam administration, he stated, had had 'two great objects, the kingdom and the empire', and Fitzwilliam was entitled to boast that 'he had offered the empire the affection of millions'. Grattan admitted that he trembled at the return to power of 'your old taskmasters', rapacious and tyrannical, and he did not hesitate to prophesy that 'they will extinguish Ireland – or Ireland must remove them'. This phrase angered conservatives. 'A man who cannot govern his own wayward passions', a right-wing London newspaper remarked, 'is clearly very unfit to govern others'. But Grattan made it clear in his answer to another address that the Catholics must reply on constitutional methods, 'the justice of your cause, your attachment to His Majesty, your desire to preserve the connection with Great Britain, the firm but dutiful tone with which you apply for privileges and now the interposition of your Protestant brethren in your favour'. Finally, when he received an address from a group of Trinity students who wanted to disassociate themselves from the official College Address of welcome to Fitzwiliiam's successor, Grattan did nothing to encourage student unrest. Replying to 'ingenuous youth', he took the opportunity of saying to the University, 'Esto perpetua – Thou seat of science and Mother of virtue'.[58]

When Parliament reassembled on 21 April it was not altogether easy for those MPs who had followed the Irish Whig leaders for some years to find their bearings. In Great Britain the coalition remained in place, none of the Portland-whig ministers resigning over Fitzwilliam's recall. The new Lord Lieutenant, Camden, had inherited a title honoured by all lovers of civil liberty, the new Chief Secretary, Pelham, was a Portland Whig, and although Beresford and Cooke returned to office, Pelham relied for assistance on Camden's young relation, Robert Stewart, who had been returned to Parliament as an opposition Whig. There was not a complete reversal of policy. Admittedly a bill for the disfranchisement of revenue officers, introduced by Grattan in April, failed to receive a second reading, and the Juries Bill never emerged from committee; but a Dublin Police Bill, Forbes's Responsibility Bill and a measure establishing a college for the training of the Catholic clergy, for which Grattan had secured a grant of £10,000, received the royal assent at the close of the session. A British cabinet minister, the generous-minded Windham, thought optimistically that it might be possible to induce Grattan to support Camden's administration, and Pelham, the new Chief Secretary, although he thought it would be a mistake 'to court those that show no disposition to coalesce with us', immediately after he arrived in Ireland made an attempt to establish relations with Grattan. He chose an inauspicious moment. Just as Grattan was mounting his carriage to join the procession which escorted Fitzwilliam from the Castle to his embarkation, 'Mr Pelham', Grattan wrote, 'called me back and talked a great deal of indistinct matter'. Although Grattan did not respond to Pelham's approach and remained aloof from the administration, Pelham was impressed by his moderation. This is not surprising. Grattan felt at the time, when the country was disturbed, the opposition must not seem to be actuated by disappointed malice.[59]

However, the Whigs did not allow themselves to be completely paralyzed by self-restraint. On 21 April Grattan moved that the House go into committee to inquire into the causes of Fitzwilliam's recall and on 16 May Curran and Grattan moved an address to the Crown deploring Fitzwilliam's removal. On the first occasion the opposition was defeated by 158 to 48; on the second occasion it did not call for a division –

although Grattan had the consolation that no attempt was made to answer their arguments and he and Curran were left in possession of the field. The Whigs were more successful when on 4 May Grattan moved the second reading of his Catholic Relief Bill. He secured the support of an exceptionally large minority although the bill was rejected by 155 to 84. Grattan was cheered to notice that there was 'less argument on the side of the majority than usual, and that a number of his opponents assumed the inevitability of emancipation.'[60]

In the autumn of 1795 Grattan, who it was rumoured was getting worried about his Dublin seat, made an effort to persuade all the opponents of the government to form a united front, and at the end of August what the Chief Secretary described as 'a curious and interesting meeting' was held over dinner in a Dublin tavern when three prominent Whig parliamentarians, Grattan, William Ponsonby and Curran, met two city liberals, Travers Hartley (sometime MP for Dublin) and Abraham Wilkinson (Governor of the Bank of Ireland), half a dozen leading Catholic activists (including Keogh and Edward Byrne) and a group of 'dissenters' (including Henry Jackson and John Chambers, the bookseller, both prominent United Irishmen). The gathering was 'very convivial' – there were some good conversationalists at the table – but when they started 'sounding one another's sentiments' significant differences of opinion emerged. Grattan began by stressing the growing danger arising from the spread of Defenderism and he suggested that a Dublin aggregated meeting should be held with the aim of pressing for a redress of grievances. Hartley was afraid that such a meeting might lead to disorder and declared that in any event he was too old to attend. Curran, on this occasion a moderate, was against taking any step which might lead to discontent, lest 'pillage and plunder should ensue'. Jackson thought an aggregate meeting would be futile, adding that the Belfast people would prefer 'a more effective plan'. Keogh agreed with Jackson, but adroitly added that the Catholics would support the proposed meeting out of respect for Grattan. He then however vigorously attacked 'the stand or fall maxim', arguing that they 'should hold a language of greater equality with Great Britain than heretofore'. Discouraged by this lack of unanimity, Grattan withdrew his suggestion, ending the evening by calling on those present to exert themselves 'to check the spirit of insurrection'. The French, he said, wanted to 'halloo the lower classes against the higher and make the whole country the scene of massacre'. The Chief Secretary on reading a report of the meeting remarked that he had heard Grattan was frightened by the Defenders and was eager that the Catholic committee should disavow any connection with them but that Ponsonby 'was not disposed to Grattan's plan without making some attack upon the administration and that it was clear that those who attended the dinner would not be able to act together'.[61]

Undaunted by this rebuff, Grattan at the close of the year co-operated with the city liberals at a meeting summoned by the Lord Mayor to vote an address to the King, congratulating him on his escape when his coach was attacked at the opening of Parliament. The liberals, in defiance of the Lord Mayor, took control of the meeting and persuaded it to sanction an address which combined fervent loyalty with the assertion that there was no need for additional legislation for the protection of His Majesty's person. Shortly afterwards Grattan and Curran suggested to a group of city reformers (many of whom were committed radicals) that they might co-operate with the parliamentary Whigs in a great drive for reform. This proposal met with a cold reception. The Dublin radicals, including Thomas Addis Emmet and Oliver Bond, thought that the Whigs simply intended 'to turn once more the wheel of petitioning to parliament, and when it has gone round a great debate and a small minority will be the end of the matter and then the wheel will turn round again'.[62]

V

Defeat and Retirement

The Irish parliamentary sessions of 1796 and 1796–7 were conducted against a grim background which steadily grew more sombre. In April 1795 Prussia pulled out of the war; in May Holland made an alliance with France; in July Spain withdrew from the war; which it re-entered in the following year as an ally of France. At the beginning of 1796 Bonaparte began his Italian campaign, and by April 1797 he was less than a hundred miles from Vienna and Austria was suing for peace. Two months earlier the Bank of England had suspended cash payments and during the spring of 1797 the Channel and North Sea fleets were immobilized by mutiny. Admittedly by then the nadir had been reached. The battle of St Vincent (February 1797) was the first of a series of brilliant naval successes and by the close of 1798 the Second Coalition was being formed. But until the close of 1797 it was not unreasonable to argue that Great Britain could only avoid catastrophic defeat by a humiliating peace. At this critical time there was widespread and dangerous discontent in Ireland, long recognized as being Great Britain's vulnerable flank. During the winter of 1794–5 energetic radicals had been busy building up a close-knit secret organization, the United Irishmen, which soon spread through the country, recruiting business and professional men who sympathized with revolutionary France, and masses of artisans and country people who were either keen radicals or who, if their political views were hazy, had a strong sense of concrete grievances. It was not long before the United Irishmen's leadership was considering direct action in co-operation with France, and soon the rank and file were active in collecting arms, manufacturing pikes and trying to intimidate the more zealous upholders of law and order. The government was from the outset fairly well informed about the aims and progress of the United Irishmen, but it was not until May 1797 that it could publish evidence showing that a powerful organization with revolutionary aims was at work in Ireland. Until then it was possible for liberal-minded men to believe that much of the increasing crime which conservatives thought had a political tinge was in fact the result of endemic agrarian discontent and that it was highly unlikely that the radical leadership would seriously contemplate armed rebellion in alliance with France.

Nevertheless, with militant discontent growing and invasion threatening, Ireland presented a challenge to conventional politicians. The government's reaction was simple – to concentrate on national defence and the preservation of law and order. This policy, if unimaginative and inflexible, was clear, definite and defiant. The Whigs condemned it for confusing the defence of the country and constitution with the maintenance of abuses and anomalies as well as being completely negative. Their own analysis of the situation and the remedies they proposed were, they were sure, more sound and sophisticated. The essence of the Irish problem was the loss of public confidence in the Irish administration, controlled as it obviously was by the British ministry, and a general alienation of the Irish people from the ruling world. At the beginning of 1796, in a letter to Fitzwilliam describing the 'melancholy' state of the country, Grattan wrote that 'a very general discontent has proceeded to treason, in some cases to plunder, in some to a hatred of British government and in all to a total lack of confidence in government'. 'I don't', he immediately added, 'speak of the higher orders or of the gentlemen of the House of Commons.' At the end of the year he wrote that 'as to the people of Ireland my opinion is that they hate the present government, Catholics and Presbyterians and all the Protestants of the lower orders'.[1]

Early in the following year he told the House of Commons that 'if the people perceive this house unanimous or silent upon the subject of their grievances they would consider they were wholly abandoned – that there was a combination of the higher orders against them and therefore when they look for redress they will look to themselves. I wish gentlemen would espouse the cause of the people.'² The term 'the people' was in the Whig political vocabulary a strongly emotive one. Though it had various connotations it usually referred to those who possessed a modicum of property and education. In the later nineties this section of the population was sharply divided, with substantial numbers supporting the government for at least the duration of the emergency. But Grattan, who had become very conscious of social unrest – 'property and poverty' are now at war in Ireland, he wrote in 1796³ – sometimes used the term to designate the masses, and he did not weaken his rhetorical drive by delaying to explain in what sense he was using the term.

The Whigs, therefore, while continuing to perform their primary political duties – the defence of civil liberty, more than ever endangered by the government's emergency measures, and the maintenance of the rights of Ireland – felt that they had another important and urgent task: to bridge the deep gulf which was opening between the governing world and the governed. They had a programme by which, they believed, this could be achieved – Catholic emancipation, parliamentary reform, the promotion of Irish economic development and a severe scrutiny of the details and administration of the emergency legislation. This bold and coherent programme was based on three assumptions – that the measures urged were in themselves desirable, that they were in accordance with constitutional principle, and that they would satisfy a substantial proportion of those who were banded together in bitter hostility to the Irish government and its ultra-conservative supporters. In short stability would be re-established without revolutionary change. To government supporters, which included the great majority of MPs, the programme seemed an unwarranted gamble at a time of crisis. The disaffected, far from being conciliated, would exploit to the full any advantages they would gain from concession and would not cease from striving to obtain a radical re-shaping of Irish institutions.

At the time they were trying to dominate Irish politics by persuading the warring parties to accept a reasoned and reasonable compromise programme, the Whigs were suffering from a great slump in parliamentary strength. A party that in the early nineties had mustered ninety votes in the division lobby, by 1796 numbered about thirty MPs. Perhaps their greatest individual loss was John Forbes, for years the Irish advocate of economic reform, who having become financially embarrassed had accepted a West Indian governorship. (Before accepting the post, Forbes consulted his friends. William Ponsonby felt that as a man of means he was disqualified from giving advice; Grattan was strongly against accepting.[4]) Small in numbers, the Whigs were strong in debating power with Grattan, Curran, William and George Ponsonby and Arthur Browne.

Even in this group Grattan was outstanding. His speeches during 1796 and 1797 were infused with impatience and urgency and closely packed with acerbic antitheses and biting epigrams. Their tone can be explained partly by the fact that Grattan, brooding on Pitt's treatment of Fitzwilliam and exasperated by the obduracy of his parliamentary opponents, felt that he did right to be angry. His irritation must have been intensified by the awareness that he and all his fellow MPs shared common loyalties. It was infuriating that the very men who should have followed his lead and exerted themselves by well-timed reforms to save their country, the constitution and the empire, through bigotry or blindness were clinging to untenable positions. Finally, Grattan's oratory, hardened by twenty years of debate, was ill-adapted to the exposition of consensus policies. He was better at expressing moral indignation than at helping his listeners to find the flat areas of agreement. Attributing the worst intentions to his opponents, he refused to distinguish between ineptitude and evil intent, and during these critical years he would not recognize that a weary pragmatism rather than cunning scheming characterized the British government's Irish policy. Instead he dwelt on an interpretation of recent Irish history which was unlikely to be universally accepted. Since the American War, successive British administrations had systematically aimed at subjecting Ireland to British control by degrading and dividing the Irish. The Irish monarchy had been reduced to 'a clerkship' (that is to say its powers were wielded by a small group of semi-permanent officials); the Viceroy had become a mere agent of the British cabinet; and lords lieutenant such as Buckingham ('the son of the American stamp act') and Westmorland had managed Parliament by 'a blasted, brazen flagitious, unqualified practice of public prostitution'. Grattan arraigned the ministers for corrupting Parliament by the creation of peerages and pensions, for leaving Ireland defenceless by the illegal withdrawal of troops, for the betrayal of Fitzwilliam and for encouraging 'the sects like hell-hounds to hunt one another'.[5]

In his indictment of the British government, the war with France naturally figured largely. Grattan was one of the long line of Whig parliamentary debaters who saw in the conduct of the war (until its victorious conclusion in 1814) a striking confirmation of their poor opinion of Pitt and his political heirs. In 1796 he dwelt scornfully on British strategic ineptitude. The British cabinet had waged war as 'a blind man boxes; they struck they knew not whom or where', with the result that, after three years of what ministers had promised would be 'a brief and brilliant war', Great Britain was 'wasted, scattered, spent and minced in various mangled, murderous expeditions'. At last she saw her resources wasted, her allies dispersed, and 'the funds, that old vanity, drop fathom after fathom like a falling devil'. Incapable of waging war successfully, the cabinet was also incapable of making peace. If in 1796 Pitt and his colleagues were sincere in seeking peace (and Grattan doubted it, he thought more likely that the cabinet intended 'to gamble in politics a little longer') they were stupid, since the terms they offered France could only be proposed to a conquered country. Obviously it was not in Britain's interest for Ireland to 'give her an extraordinary encouragement' in pursuing a ruinous war.[6] Nevertheless Grattan did not suggest that Ireland should cease to stand by Great Britain, and he was careful to distinguish between the British government, which he was attacking so vehemently, and the British people. 'Whatever feelings the country may have of resentment', he declared in 1796, 'let them be directed against the Ministers only, not against the people of England; with whom we have a common constitution and a common empire.' And in the following year he encouraged 'the injured people of Ulster' to rely on the generosity and justice of the British nation.[7]

Turning to domestic affairs, from the beginning of 1796 Grattan and his parliamentary friends were vigorously engaged in the defence of civil liberty. But when they were discussing the government's emergency measures, they were handicapped by the undeniable fact that disorder was spreading fast in a poorly policed country at a time when an invasion might be impending. As George Ponsonby in a burst of exasperation frankly exclaimed, 'who can talk of improvement in the constitution when the dagger of the assassin was at his throat. Or who could talk so eloquently of the faults of an administration to catch attention from him who feared for his life and fortune and clung to the arm of power as alone able to protect him.'[8] When at the beginning of 1796 the government introduced an Indemnity Bill, covering those who had acted over-zealously in the maintenance of law and order, Grattan did not oppose it although he suggested that the assize judges might be summoned to the Bar and examined on the state of the country. Shortly afterwards when the government brought in an Insurrection Bill granting the magistracy extensive powers of search and arrest in districts proclaimed to be in a state of disturbance, Grattan again did not oppose it. He did however propose an amendment providing that it should be mandatory for 'the county' (that is to say the grand jury) to grant compensation to those who had suffered in person or property from mob violence. In County Armagh, he said, the Orange Boys were 'committing massacre in the name of God and exercising despotism in the name of liberty', and he was afraid that although 'gentlemen will indemnify one another ... it is not equally certain they will indemnify inferiors'. The Attorney-General successfully opposed the amendment, pointing out correctly that its purpose was fully met by an act of 1776.[9] A year later when George Ponsonby urged the repeal of the Insurrection Act, Grattan supported him, arguing that 'the penal coercion system had failed for instead of repressing it had increased crimes'.[10] But Ponsonby's motion was defeated by 127 to 14, the majority feeling that it would be unrealistic to deprive the government of its emergency powers when disorder was spreading. When at the opening of the session of 1796–7 the government, following British precedent, asked for the suspension of the Habeas Corpus Act, Grattan declared this measure was unnecessary. The danger of invasion, he pointed out, was 'at present a remote possibility' (within ten weeks a French fleet, carrying a large expeditionary force, was off the south-west coast of Ireland) and there was 'no parliamentary evidence of a conspiracy' (within six months ample evidence was provided by the reports of parliamentary secret committees). Grattan also appealed to national sentiment or prejudice, declaring that the bill gave 'an Englishman, the Chief Secretary, without residence or stake in Ireland and therefore without responsibility, a power to send the Irish to Newgate'. Finally he told the House it had lost the confidence of the great body of the people: 'You must heal, you must harmonize, you must reconcile.'[11]

Along with the suspension of the Habeas Corpus Act the government introduced a bill authorizing the formation of local defence corps, the yeomanry, composed of 'loyal subjects ... voluntarily associated', under the command of officers commissioned by the Lord Lieutenant. The Whigs did not oppose the bill, the need for a local defence force being obvious, but they favoured an alternative solution, corps of Volunteers which would elect their own officers, units which, as Grattan put it, would be 'paid by themselves, honour to honour engaged, freemen bound to freemen'.[12] What Grattan wanted was a revival of the old Volunteer corps, and even before the Yeomanry Bill was on the statute book the question of how local defence corps should be constituted was being debated in Dublin. In September a meeting of the Irish Bar decided by a large majority to form a corps – the Lawyers Corps – under officers commissioned by the Lord Lieutenant. A day or two later the citizens were asked to subscribe to a Declaration, placed in the Royal Exchange, pledging the signatories to associate in defence of the country and the support of the government. Almost simultaneously another Declaration was displayed in the Old Exchange coffeehouse, expressing the readiness of those who signed it to associate in arms in defence of the King, the laws and the people 'in such legal and constitutional manner as may be deemed most effectual'. The first Declaration received a fair number of signatures; the second was signed by Henry Grattan, James Hartley and a very few others ('and those not respectable').[13] In spite of this rebuff Grattan continued to hope for a revival of the Volunteers, who, he believed, 'would infuse a genial spirit and repress the convulsions of the lower orders. The latter would look upon the Volunteers as friends, they consider the yeomanry as enemies.' Characteristically, he offered, if one of the Dublin corps was reformed, to serve in its ranks as a private. In the end, he joined a yeomanry corps, the Powerscourt Troop, commanded by Charles Monck.[14]

The positive aspect of the Whig programme included the two major measures to which they were pledged, Catholic emancipation and parliamentary reform. Grattan on 17 October 1796 proposed a motion stating that the admission of Catholics to Parliament was consistent with 'the safety of the crown' and the British connection. He laid great emphasis on the manpower situation: with 15,000,000 people in these islands facing the 'new France' whose population was more than 30,000,000, it was absurd of the government to discourage recruiting by excluding 3,000,000 Irish Catholics from 'the capacities of citizens' – at a time, incidentally, when the British Minister was in alliance with the Pope. And he warned the House that if 'you force your fellow citizens from under the hospitable roof of the constitution, you will leave them like a weary traveller, at length to repose under the shade of the dreadful tree of liberty'.[15] But most MPs were either opposed to emancipation or thought the motion untimely, and it was rejected by 143 to 19.

Catholic emancipation had profound implications in the realm of Church and State and might have had far-reaching political consequences, but its immediate effects, assuming the political framework remained unaltered, would have been limited: a few Catholic peers in the Lords, a few Catholic MPs in the Commons and some Catholics in the higher levels of the Civil Service. But parliamentary reform would have drastically changed the whole balance of political power. Even some members of the Whig Club felt at the end of 1796 that reform was inopportune and Richard Griffith, a highly intelligent Whig MP, wrote to Grattan arguing that education should precede enfranchisement (anticipating Robert Lowe's 'we must educate our masters'), adding that he was not prepared to examine the plans of an ingenious architect when defending his house against a banditti. Griffith's apprehensions must have been intensified by the Reform Bill which George Ponsonby introduced in May 1797. Anxious to compete with the radicals who were committed to equal electoral districts and universal suffrage, Ponsonby included in his bill equal electoral districts and a variety of qualifications for the suffrage which, taken together, would have enfranchised a considerable proportion of the population. Aware of the strength of the opposition he was facing and presumably conscious that Ponsonby's Bill represented a startling advance on what the Whigs had proposed only three years before, Grattan endeavoured to be as conciliatory as he could. The scheme, he explained, was neither aristocratic nor democratic. A constituency of five thousand houses (that proposed by the bill) could not be turned into 'the borough of an individual'; on the other hand, land and property would continue to have 'their constant and invariable influences'. 'The people', that is to say freeholders, leaseholders, householders, and 'established and resident tradesmen', would be enfranchised, 'the rabble' would be excluded. Grattan admitted that a formidable conspiracy against the established order existed in the country; 'just as your system of coercion advanced', he told the administration, 'the United Irishmen advanced'. But by passing a reform bill, 'you will take from the United Irishmen their proselytes, you will annex these proselytes to parliament – and if you do not annex every man, you will annex the people'. Castlereagh congratulated Grattan on the ability and moderation with which he had urged his views, but the House rejected the bill by 170 to 30.[16]

Parliamentary reform and Catholic emancipation might for a time have stabilized the Irish situation by momentarily satisfying a substantial majority of the 'people', that is to say, of those who would have been enfranchised by Ponsonby's Bill of 1797. But Grattan was acutely aware that on a somewhat lower social level, economic distress and discontent amongst small farmers, cotters, and labourers, constituted a mine 'the extent, the depth and danger of which we don't know'.[17] During 1795, when there was serious agrarian trouble in Ireland, there were food riots in England and British MPs and pamphleteers discussed what should be done to relieve those near the subsistence level. This English debate on social policy may have inspired Curran early in 1796 to draw the attention of the Irish Parliament to the condition of 'the wretched peasantry', lodged in hovels, sleeping upon straw with the families fed (or half-fed) with potatoes. On 28 January he moved for the appointment of a committee 'to inquire into the state of the lower orders of the people and the price of labour'. Always easily irritated by complacency, Curran believed in shock tactics. Dwelling on 'the chaos of the human condition in rural Ireland', he reminded his hearers that the 'labouring orders of the people', four fifths of the population, formed 'the real strength and support of the political fabric'. Grattan supported Curran in a speech which, although it was not lacking in passionate passages, strove to provide a balanced survey of Ireland's social and economic problems and prospects. He accepted that in recent years Ireland had made considerable economic progress, indicated by an increasing taxable capacity, higher rents and an expansion of the linen trade. But, he emphasized, 'the working poor' had not 'participated in your prosperity'. Any observer of the Irish scene would be shocked by the low price of labour and by 'the clothing and housing of the poor'. 'He might', Grattan declared, 'see magnificence but he would lack comfort – he would see the capital enlarged, he would see palaces for the rich, but the habitations of the poor as miserable as ever ... It would appear to him that in this country the proportion of things were broken, vain luxury and horrid poverty – the villa and the hovel, the beggar and the man of fashion.' Grattan also pointed out that middle- and upper-class expectations were unrealistically based on English levels. 'Our luxuries', he explained, 'grew not as in England from the growth of our country, but from the imitation of the wealth of another country, namely England.' Grattan then went on to suggest several measures which would benefit the rural poor: more capital investment in agriculture, greater attention to scientific farming, raising the price of labour, and industrial development. The growth of industry, he admitted, would be 'slow and torpid', though of course it could be encouraged by a reduction of British duties on Irish manufactures. He concluded his speech by an appeal to MPs to exert themselves to check the spread of French principles through a sustained effort to improve the living standards of the lower strata of the population. Don't allow France, he exhorted the House, to 'canvass against you among our people by flattery or bribe them into disaffection by offering wild hopes to inflame poverty. You certainly can relieve that poverty, you have it in your power to amend their condition. Do it.'[18]

Some months later, in July 1796, the Whig Club published a report on Irish social and economic problems, prepared by a committee which was obviously greatly influenced by Grattan. Beginning by pointing out that in some counties the remuneration of the cotter and labourer was not sufficient to maintain a family, given prevailing food prices, the report urged that in any barony where there was marked distress, gentlemen should form a committee. These baronial committees could fix the price of labour, purchase provisions in times of want and sell them to the poor at the customary price, and encourage loan funds, cottage gardens and domestic industries. It was not suggested that the committees should be invested with compulsory powers. The report was confident that there was 'much humanity in the kingdom' and it appealed to self-interest by asserting that 'no doubt the labourer partakes of the nature of every other animal and if well-fed will outwork the labourer who is half starved'. The report having reprobated agrarian disorder – 'the offenders have shown as much weakness and folly as ferocity' – fervently expressed the hope that the schemes it proposed would 'unite all orders of men by the communication of good offices ... so that the rich may manifest their utility and virtue, and extend over the lower orders their influence and ascendancy and establish by good offices a kind of mild and voluntary jurisdiction; thus will the higher orders be familiarized to give and the lower orders to receive and both be endeared to the other'.[19]

Grattan himself continued to advocate a measure which he was confident would in the long run stimulate Irish economic development to the benefit of the whole community: an equalization of duties between Great Britain and Ireland, 'market for market, trade for trade'. Typically, as well as mentioning economic considerations, he made great play with the question of national status – the existing British tariff, he complained, was on 'the true colony principle'.[20] Somewhat inconsistently, perhaps, while pressing for Anglo-Irish economic integration, Grattan supported the proposal put forward by a fellow opposition Whig for an absentee tax (a tax on the landed income of non-residents). He dismissed the idea that such a tax would tend to separate the two countries – 'the old English policy was to have a tax on absentees for the purpose of defending the English interest in Ireland' – and he pointed out that the war taxation had severely hit the poor and that it was unjust 'to burden poverty rather than riches.'[21]

The Irish Whigs not only exerted themselves in Parliament but, realizing that even an unreformed House of Commons was not impervious to public opinion, they tried to mobilize the respectable and intelligent public in support of their programme. Effective mobilization required the co-operation at a local level of all shades of opposition opinion. It is true that while the Whigs wished to preserve the existing constitutional system, modernized by common-sense changes, the radicals were eagerly looking forward to a reconstruction of Irish institutions on rational, egalitarian lines. However, both groups were strongly hostile to the Irish administration and could unite on the highest common denominator of their aims. For the radicals it also involved practising some degree of economy in the theological sense. For instance, Arthur O'Connor, when he provided Charles James Fox with a lucid account of the development of the United Irishmen, pointing out how they were striving to unite all denominations in support of reform, omitted to mention that the leadership had been in touch with France, O'Connor himself having been one of their emissaries.[22] O'Connor's companion on his mission to France was Lord Edward Fitzgerald, who a year later, in May 1797, acted as a fellow steward of Grattan at a Whig Club meeting, and presumably some radicals when discussing joint tactics with the Whigs had to conceal their opinion that there was often 'a strange monstrous conjunction between Grattan in parliament and Giffard in the press' – John Giffard being an ultra-Protestant and conservative journalist and city politician who could express himself with rude force in print and on the platform.[23]

In the spring of 1797 Whigs and radicals co-operated with some success. Early in February a group of Dublin businessmen who belonged to the Irish Whig Club wanted the Club to resolve that a refusal by Parliament to pass a reform bill should be followed by the separation of Ireland from Great Britain. Grattan, Ponsonby and Curran, presumably feeling this was going too far too fast, suggested that the resolution should be withdrawn and that they and the city liberals should together request the sheriffs to summon a meeting of householders for the innocuous-sounding purpose of considering the best means of uniting the country against foreign invasion and for the protection of persons and property.[24] On the sheriffs refusing to take action, a notice summoning a meeting on 3 March at the Royal Exchange, signed by two hundred citizens headed by Grattan, the Ponsonbys and Curran, appeared in the press. The militant radicals supported the meeting enthusiastically and, according to a conservative journalist, a large number of 'the Pill Lane republicans ... and the violent incendaries of the Catholic committee' attended the meeting, many sporting green cravats. A resolution in favour of parliamentary reform and Catholic emancipation was proposed by Hugh Skeys, a wine-merchant, common-council man and member of the Whig Club, who was believed to be Grattan's link with the city radicals, and seconded by Grattan, who declared they were the only measures which would unite the country and enable it to defy its enemies. Beauchamp Bagenal Harvey, a well-known radical, suggested that Parliament should ask 'persons deputed by the people' to assist it in drafting a plan of reform. Richard Griffith, boldly coming forward as the lone voice of moderate Whiggery, declared that although he supported immediate emancipation he was convinced that during the war parliamentary reform implied 'republicanism, anarchy, confusion, bloodshed and slaughter'. Keogh retorted that by now the Catholics would not be satisfied with emancipation unaccompanied by reform. The resolution was carried enthusiastically, and Grattan, the Ponsonbys, Curran and Keogh adjourned to a tavern and dictated an account of the meeting to a journalist with the result that it was fully reported in the press.[25]

Encouraged by this success, the Whigs decided to hold a Dublin aggregate meeting composed of freemen and freeholders. The time seemed propitious. A great wave of anti-ministerial feeling was sweeping England. Towards the end of March the City of London requested the King to dismiss his present advisers; it was rumoured that a number of independent MPs were about to withdraw their support from Pitt; and it was known that the Prince of Wales was willing to come to Ireland as Lord Lieutenant. The sheriffs agreed to summon an aggregate at the beginning of June, and both liberals and conservatives saw the occasion as a trial of strength and planned to attend in force. According to a liberal newspaper, all the government's supporters in Dublin were mustered

– 'the commissioners of the revenue, with all the land-waiters, tide-waiters officers of customs, officers of excise, the post office corps, the paving, lighting and scavenging corps, the different divisions of the ordinance corps, the Castle corps and finally the aldermanic corps down to the pipe-water collectors.' The sheriffs tried to control admission to the meeting but, according to a conservative source, the rabble pushed in and Sir William Worthington ('a citizen of consequence') and Marcus Beresford tried to secure an adjournment on the grounds that the meeting was largely composed of the promiscuous multitude. While Beresford was speaking Grattan entered amidst 'repeated plaudits' ('indecent conduct' which, Beresford remarked, demonstrated that the meeting was not composed only of freemen and freeholders). When a vote was taken on Worthington's motion for the adjournment, the sheriffs declared the Noes had it. The conservatives left the hall. Grattan was moved into the chair, and an address to the King requesting him to remove his present ministers from office was carried unanimously. The sheriffs having refused to sign the address, Grattan as chairman signed it and a committee was chosen to accompany him to the Castle. The next morning John Willis, Henry Jackson and Oliver Bond breakfasting with Grattan 'wanted him to present the petition at once before a counter-petition could be presented'. But there was a hitch. At the meeting only about thirty names had been appended to the petition and Grattan, anxious to show that 'he was sanctioned by the people', wanted further signatures to be procured. The city conservatives meanwhile took prompt steps to produce a declaration with about 350 signatories, which stated, on the authority of the sheriffs, that many of those who had taken part in the meeting were not qualified to do so. On Thursday, several hundred signatures having been obtained, Grattan accompanied by the committee presented the address to the Lord Lieutenant for transmission to England. Camden said he would transmit the Address together with the counter-declaration.[26] The outcome of the aggregate meeting was unsatisfactory to both parties and it must have been discouraging to Grattan to find that the City, which in the past could be relied on to be a useful ally of the parliamentary opposition, was now clearly divided.

In the following month Grattan concluded his speech of the 15th of

May on parliamentary reform with a dramatic flourish. He declared that the supporters of reform, having 'no hopes left to persuade or dissuade', would no longer attend the House of Commons. At the beginning of July he published an address to his constituents, justifying his parliamentary conduct and denouncing the Irish government, which filled seven columns of the *Dublin Evening Post*. Grattan attributed Irish discontent, disorder and disloyalty to two factors: 'the endeavour on the part of the minister to give the monarch a power which the constitution never intended' and a great change in the climate of opinion resulting form the American and French revolutions. 'The progress of the human mind', he wrote, 'has been prodigious in Ireland', and 'the spirit of reform has gone forth cherished, nourished and propagated by the abuses of our government'. Near the close of the address he gratified keen radicals by stating that 'there may be conspiracy, there may be the spirit of republicanism, there may be plunder mixing with the public cause but it is the cause of liberty against tyranny'. Nevertheless he concluded with a declaration of faith in monarchy, the constitution (reformed) and the British connection.[27]

There were classical precedents for a secession, although the Irish Whigs lacked the political clout of the Roman plebs. More recently at Westminster Walpole's opponents, 'the Patriots', had in 1739 withdrawn for some months from the House of Commons (much to the relief of the Prime Minister) and forty years later the Rockingham Whigs had considered demonstrating their deep disapprobation of North's American policy by a parliamentary secession. But secession, it was pointed out by William Smith, an Irish Whig MP who did not follow Grattan in 1797, was 'a mistaken refinement of patriotism' which left the country 'at the mercy of the government – or of rebellion'.[28] Moreover, secession presented a problem. What was to be the next step? Some of the seceding Whigs, including the Ponsonbys, stood at the general election of 1797, which suggests that they intended to return quietly to the House. Fox, when he too in May 1797 announced his withdrawal from the British House of Commons, was careful to say that he had no intention of totally seceding. But Grattan was not the man to qualify a grand gesture and he does not seem to have given any consideration to the tactics of secession. For him it was a vigorous underlining of his moral condemnation of the majority of MPs. Along with righteous anger went disillusionment and depression. It was humiliating to have to accept that rhetorical brilliance was of little account compared with control of the levers of power. Never, since he had attained a prominent position in politics, had Grattan so few supporters in the House of Commons, and never before were the people, whom Grattan always implied were ranged behind him, so clearly divided, with many serving in the yeomanry and many others enrolled in illegal societies.

Another factor which probably inclined Grattan to secession was the danger of losing his Dublin seat and being compelled to find a close borough. Only eighteen months after his triumphant return as MP for Dublin he had found his position in the city seriously menaced. In January 1792 the aldermen and Common Council agreed on an address requesting their MPs to oppose changes which tended to 'subvert the Protestant ascendancy in our happy constitution'. This address reflected a significant shift in opinion. The common council, representing the Dublin Protestant middle class, had been on the whole advanced Whig and anti-administration. Now, with the Catholics claiming political rights, it had to try to reconcile its advanced Whiggery with its abhorrence of popery. As the address showed, it quickly decided that Irish Protestants must not surrender privileges which guaranteed their own safety and the healthy development of the whole country. Grattan's reply to his constituents' address was honest and adroit. He emphasized that the government, as the Police Act revealed, was intent on undermining the political influence of the Protestant community and he declared that he was convinced that Catholic liberty and Protestant ascendancy were compatible.[29] However three years later, after Grattan had given notice that he intended to introduce a Catholic relief bill, a substantial majority of the Common Council (about two thirds of those voting) joined with the aldermen in an address to the King against the bill. After this it is not surprising that Grattan told some leading Catholics that his support of their cause might cost him his seat. The Catholic group promptly offered to pay his expenses (one of them remarking to a conservative journalist, 'Grattan got a large sum before but he is as grasping as Hell').[30] The Catholics were generous, but their help would have proved politically embarrassing.

Would Grattan have been returned for Dublin if he had stood in 1797? It is impossible to say, for when the election was held the government supporters had two strong candidates lined up and the city liberals, discouraged by the withdrawal of both the MPs whom they had returned in 1790 (Lord Henry Fitzgerald having followed Grattan's example), did not put forward candidates. A couple of days before the poll opened a meeting of freemen and freeholders held at the Royal Exchange, with Valentine Lawless (secretly a United Irishman) in the chair, resolved that since the representation of the people should be full, fair and equal they would not take part in the election. Leonard McNally, an embittered barrister and a valuable government informant, strongly criticized the government's use of its emergency powers and Joseph Leeson declared he would resist a union with Great Britain 'as long as he had blood in his veins'. Grattan was present but did not speak.[31] A few days later, however, in a reply to a complimentary resolution passed by the meeting, he assured those who had been present that 'my public duty should not cease with my representative capacity ... My seat in parliament was but part of my situation, my relationship to my country was higher and more permanent – the duty of a citizen is commensurate with his powers of body and mind'.[32]

After the strenuous session of 1796–7 and the preparation of his address, Grattan went for a holiday, going to drink the waters at Castle Connell in County Limerick and visiting two old friends, Sir John Tydd and Lord Pery, the sometime Speaker.[33] Then, about the close of October returning to Tinnehinch without a seat in the new Parliament, he realized that, in Lloyd George's poignant phrase, 'one is never well out of it, one is just out of it'. But, though now on the margin of politics, he could not abstain from trying to influence events. Early in 1798 he seems to have hoped that an invigorated Whig Club might be an effective pressure group. Towards the close of January 1798, at Grattan's suggestion, the Club met and appointed a committee of thirteen (headed by Grattan) to consider a redrafting of the Club's Declaration and the expediency of purging the Club by the expulsion of those members who had 'notoriously adopted a conduct contrary to the original declaration'. The Club met in February to receive the committee's report, but the attendance (Grattan, Hugh Skeys and half a dozen other members) was so poor, that according to Drennan, 'the report was dropped of course and I suppose the club with it'. However, those who had attended enjoyed a good dinner ordered in the expectation of a much larger gathering.[34]

Drennan was over-pessimistic about the Club's future. It met again at the beginning of April and decided that a petition to the King should be prepared. On 14 April with Grattan in the chair the petition was approved, and when Grattan left for England at the end of the month he took the petition with him in the hope it would be presented by Moira and Fox. It is unlikely that George III paid much attention to it, but the public had an opportunity of reading it when it appeared in Dublin in pamphlet form. It was a melodramatic survey of recent Irish history. From 1768 there had been a continuous struggle between the ministers of the Crown and the people, with the former always the aggressors, and from 1789 the government had been engaged in a sustained attempt to undermine political morality in Ireland and destroy the Irish constitution. The petition concluded by declaring that the only way to restore peace in Ireland was by restraining ministerial violence.[35]

By the beginning of 1798 it was becoming clear that the growing Irish crisis would be resolved only by force. Extreme radicals believed the existing order was abominable and that the people (that is to say, those enrolled in the United Irishmen's organization) were justified in employing conspiracy and violence to overthrow it. Conservatives believed that the constitution and civilization itself in Ireland were endangered and that a successful insurrection would lead to a state of anarchy followed by an ill-conceived reshaping of Irish society. With so much at stake, each side when sanctioning or condoning illegal action would not hesitate to plead necessity. Naturally keen partisans, moved by genuine moral indignation, sincerely denounced the crimes of violence attributable to their opponents.

They were also conscious of the propaganda value of atrocities, so allegations and counter-allegations filled the columns of the Dublin newspapers. Early in 1798 the parliamentary Whigs, Moira in the Lords and William Smith in the Commons, condemned the outrages inspired by both political discontent and illegal military action. They seemed, however, to single out for condemnation the Crown forces. This, if unfair, was understandable. Traditionally the Whigs had been the defenders of the subjects' rights against arbitrary executive action, and if military men were guilty of severities beyond the law, they or their unit could be identified and the chain of command was certain. On the other hand, when dealing with the outrages apparently committed by the discontented it was not always easy to distinguish between political and ordinary crime, and with an invisible conspiracy active it was very hard to pin responsibility. Finally, it was natural for the Whigs, who had for ten years or so been vigorously attacking the Irish administration, to continue assailing their accustomed target.

Bringing to book defenders of law and order who displayed excessive zeal was a policy on which Whigs and radicals could co-operate. Humanity and political tactics coincided. At the end of 1797 the radicals set up a committee directed by William Sampson, a barrister (and, according to Drennan, a man of monopolizing egotism), to collect authentic accounts of outrages committed by government supporters. Grattan was interested in the work of this committee and towards the end of February visited Sampson to examine his material.[36] About the same time he went out to a house in Harold's Cross to interview John Bird, an Englishman who for some time had cut a conspicuous figure in Belfast radical circles. Having given evidence to the House of Commons Secret Committee in 1797, he had quarreled with the authorities and provided a radical journal, the *Press*, with sensational revelations about the secret service. Grattan talked with him for five hours, closely questioning him about the treatment of the state prisoners. At the end of the talk he advised Bird to publish his reminiscences as a pamphlet.[37]

Although they might welcome Whig co-operation in denouncing the government's methods of maintaining order, the radicals had a poor opinion of the Whig leaders, whom they dismissed as self-indulgent and politically passé. All they seemed good for was flowery speeches in Parliament and dining and wining together at the Whig Club. Should they at last by some shift of power in England attain office, their policy, 'a flurry of parliamentary reform, which would skim and flutter like a moth round the glaring surface of corruption, a peddling, unnecessary and insignificant profession of economy and the dismissal of flagrant characters who would receive not a gibbet but a pension', would fall far short of what the country demanded. And Grattan's 'stand and fall by England' policy was dismissed as comparable with 'the sentimental nonsense of love-sick girls or boys'.[38]

Grattan's feelings about the radicals were more confused. Exasperated by the government's obduracy, he seems to have been striving to convince himself that the radicals (who, he would have liked to see as advanced Whigs) would be satisfied by the Whig programme, and he remained confident that (in spite of distressing symptoms) they would stop short of treason. During the early months of 1798 he was visited at Tinnehinch by three leading radicals. On a couple of occasions, John Sweetman, the great brewer, Oliver Bond, a wholesale linen draper, and Samuel Neilson, a successful Belfast textile manufacturer who had been editor of the *Northern Star*, drove down to Tinnehinch in Sweetman's carriage and in April Neilson borrowed the carriage (the owner then being in Newgate) and, accompanied by John Hughes, a Belfast bookseller and an active radical, paid a third visit to Grattan. Sweetman, Bond and Neilson may have hoped to sweep Grattan into their movement. More probably they merely aimed at securing his co-operation in holding up to opprobrium military and yeomanry behaviour. Grattan treated the visits as casual calls, and avoided committing himself to anything by the simple technique of asking a string of questions about the state of the country. During Neilson's third visit he was alone with Grattan for half an hour while Hughes was being shown the garden by a servant. Hughes six months later, when giving evidence before the House of Lords Secret Committee, stated that when he and Neilson were driving back to Dublin, he asked Neilson what had passed between him and Grattan. Neilson, according to Hughes, evaded the question but said that he had gone down to ask Grattan 'whether he would come forward and that he had sworn him'. Neilson himself, when he appeared before the Committee, declared that all he had done was to explain the constitution of the United Irishmen to Grattan, adding, 'I do not believe that Mr Grattan was ever a United Irishman'. Presumably Hughes either misunderstood what Neilson told him or was eager to enhance his own importance by sensationalizing his evidence.[39]

At the end of April Grattan responded readily to a request for assistance from a prominent radical, Arthur O'Connor, who had been arrested at Margate when trying to obtain a passage to France and charged with high treason. Grattan was summoned as a defence witness, it being rumoured that he would testify that O'Connor, when speaking in the House of Commons, had not been trying to excite discontent but had simply been explaining that such discontent was a natural response to the government's attitude. Grattan travelled to London with another witness for the defence, William Drennan, who found Grattan 'civil, kind, courteous and accommodating'. They stayed at the same hotel, the White Hart in Holborn, and one evening went together to the opera in Covent Garden. After the performance Grattan, who of course knew London, suggested they should walk back to the White Hart. They soon lost their way and 'for two hours together sought in vain to find it'. Grattan, Drennan wryly remarked, 'would have wandered the whole night without seeming fatigued'.[40]

The trial of O'Connor and four co-defendants opened at Maidstone on 21 May. O'Connor relied largely on evidence as to character, producing half a dozen eminent English Whigs, including Fox and Sheridan, to say that he was a man of integrity whose political opinions coincided with their own. Grattan's testimony was brief but emphatic. He believed that O'Connor, who was 'unreserved' in expressing his opinions, would certainly not favour a French invasion – 'No, rather the contrary'. On 22 May O'Connor was found not guilty. He was promptly re-arrested on an Irish warrant, and a few months later when appearing before Irish parliamentary committees he fully admitted that he had been engaged in treasonable activities since 1796. This placed his Whig friends in an awkward situation, but this does not seem to have troubled O'Connor, a thoroughgoing egotist.

On returning from Maidstone Grattan had an embarrassing experience in London. Valentine Lawless, who had been hustled out of Ireland by his father who was determined to keep him away from dangerous radical acquaintances, had organized in London a small club of Irish law students. Its avowed aim was to assist refugees from Ireland, but the government was very crisis-conscious and on 31 May Lawless and several other young Irishmen were arrested. A letter was found in Lawless's rooms mentioning 'little Harry' and a zealous peace officer promptly arrested Grattan, who was taken to the Home Office and brought before the Home Secretary, the Duke of Portland. After an embarrassing interview for Portland, Grattan was released with apologies.[41]

Grattan did not return to Ireland. On 23 May a widespread insurrection broke out and County Wicklow was a seriously disturbed area, with the yeomanry (the conservatives in arms) apprehensively and aggressively striving to preserve order over a countryside where many of the inhabitants were sworn United Irishmen. The defenders of the established order viewed with suspicion critics of the government's emergency measures and Mrs Grattan was afraid that her property was in danger from extremists on both sides. In fact all that happened was that Tinnehinch, in the absence of the family, was searched for arms, a couple of horses were taken, and some trees were cut down by the military towards the close of the year. Mrs Grattan, anxious to keep her husband away from Ireland, shortly after the Maidstone trial came over with her children to North Wales, where Grattan joined her. They stayed for a while in the inn at Llanrwst, going for walks in country reminiscent of Wicklow, then moved to London, taking up residence at Twickenham, on an attractive and fashionable stretch of the Thames, where they stayed until the close of 1799 – Grattan paying two very short visits to Ireland.

Grattan was not in good health. Suffering badly from 'meagrims', he could not bear 'noise, or crowds or heat' and, hardest of all, he was unable to read. The doctor's remedies were 'air and amusement' and avoidance of political excitement. Grattan also visited with beneficial results the Isle of Wight for sea-bathing and boating, that is to say, sitting in a boat for hours with the wind blowing round him. Life was not devoid of pleasure. He saw Fox (who sent him a present of game which was 'extremely good') and other Whigs, he attended the opera regularly and he seems to have spent a good deal of time in bookshops. A diarist saw him in Wright's, the Piccadilly bookshop – 'a remarkably mean looking man – he was dressed in a blue coat and a spencer with half boots. I never saw a man in a respectable situation of life look less like a gentleman. Perceiving the eyes of the people turned upon him he soon quitted the shop.'

However, the diarist had to add that it was rumoured the Duke of Bedford was going to bring Grattan into Parliament.[42]

It is understandable if remarkable that during the critical months of 1798, one of the most spectacular periods in Irish history, the most distinguished Irish politician was absent and silent. Without a seat in Parliament, Grattan's occupation was gone, and if he had been in the House of Commons he would have found it difficult to speak with his usual confident vehemence. His feelings about the insurrection were strong and contradictory. Writing to Fox at the end of 1798 he characterized the insurrection as 'a revolt very criminal and very senseless, but deriving its cause from the government which was guilty not only of its own crimes but of the crimes of the people'.[43] Eighteen months later during the Union debates he went rather further, declaring that 'the great, originating and fundamental cause of the rebellion was the aversion of the ministry to the independence of the Irish parliament' – a simplistic view of the crisis which reflects his intense interest in constitutional questions and a reluctance to take radicalism very seriously.

Although he severely blamed, as might be expected, the Irish administration, Grattan would have no truck with rebellion. His feelings are revealed by his attitude to two acquaintances who were involved in revolutionary activities – William Dowdall and William Sampson. When Dowdall, the sometime Secretary of the Whig Club, solicited help on his release in 1802 from Fort George where he had been detained as a state prisoner, Grattan replied that unless Dowdall promised 'to keep himself out of all plots and confederacy' he considered it improper to give him pecuniary assistance or to recommend him as a commercial clerk (Dowdall ended his life as a captain in the French Army). Four years later, when Sampson, who with his family was travelling from Portugal to the United States, wrote to Grattan asking him to support his plea for permission to extend their stay in England, Grattan did not reply. Moreover, according to the indignant Mrs Sampson, he told a friend of the family not to call on Sampson, 'for it was treason to hold any correspondence with him'. About the same time Drennan noticed that Grattan, 'though civil to me when in a degree obliged to it by being my fellow traveller ... never showed the least desire of honouring me with a renewed acquaintance, though he has others with him often perhaps as little worthy of it'. (In Grattan's opinion Drennan was 'not a rebel but an enthusiast'.)[44] An orator who in his speeches frequently slipped into retrospect, Grattan rarely spoke of '98 in later years, and in the survey of recent Irish politics which he published in 1800 the insurrection is dealt with in one page while three and a half pages are devoted to the regency dispute.

In his absence from Ireland his reputation slumped. Government supporters who in the summer and autumn of 1798 had seen the constitution, their lives and their properties imperiled, intensely resented the parliamentary conduct of the Irish Whigs. Even charitable conservatives blamed them for trying to conciliate the uncompromising, for pedantically applying standards proper to normal conditions during a crisis which threatened the whole social order, and for their carping criticism of the forces defending law and order. The less charitable considered them radicals *manqué*, willing to wound but afraid to strike. To the more vehement administration supporters Grattan seemed the embodiment of Whig self-conscious moral and intellectual superiority and political irresponsibility. In June 1798 Patrick Duigenan published a bulky pamphlet which rapidly ran into a third edition, in which he accused Grattan, an ambitious, avaricious, disappointed and embittered man, of being 'a crypto-republican', 'a co-agent' of Wolfe Tone, whose aim was the separation of Ireland from Great Britain.[45] Grattan's response was that of an Irish gentleman. At the beginning of August he wrote to Duigenan, and, having described his pamphlet as 'a very gross, very unprovoked and very ludicrous performance', the work of a buffoon, informed him that for the next few days he was to be found at Kearns Hotel. Duigenan ignored the challenge. Either he disdained to meet a rebel, or did not want to risk his skin or thought it wrong to fight – William Wilberforce had recently condemned duelling as not only unreasonable but criminal, the consequence of 'an over-valuation of character'.[46]

Shortly after Grattan returned to London the reports of the parliamentary secret committees revealed that before the insurrection he had met and talked to leading United Irishmen. Irish conservatives were not in the mood to weigh judiciously the import of this; association was enough to suggest guilt and at the beginning of October the board of Trinity College considered whether Grattan's portrait should be removed from the Public Theatre. A short account of the discussion has been preserved:

> Dr Elrington [a strong conservative]: If I can see it will not be disrespectful to the crown, he being a privy councilor, I should vote for it.
> Dr Barret: Down
> Dr Browne [a Whig MP and a lawyer]: Doubts as to nature of evidence in the report, says crown seems to continue, we should not decide till they do – proposes to apply to him to explain his conduct first.
> Dr Hall [a future Provost]: Doubts if this could be done, thinks his intercourse with the rebels such as to make it improper to continue him.
> Dr Y[oung]: Down
> Dr Fitzgerald: Down
> Dr Kearney laments the question as to himself, Does not love to be juryman or executioner of an old friend.[47]

A few days later, Grattan's name having been erased from the Privy Council roll, the picture came down and was not seen again for many years. About the middle of October Grattan (along with the United Irishman Henry Jackson) was deprived of the Freedom of the City by the Dublin Corporation; he was expelled (together with four United Irishmen and a well-known Catholic agitator) from the Merchants Guild for having been concerned in bringing about 'the horrid rebellion'; streets named after him, it was reported, were going to be 'rebaptized' with the names of Nelson and Duncan; and it was rumoured that the Grand Jury might find a true bill against him.[48] The prevailing opinion of him in conservative circles was expressed by a newspaper poet:

> In a certain great house I haranged and I rowed
> While my squibs of rebellion ignited the crowd,
> The humbug I dealt in each florid oration
> Dwelt much on reform and emancipation.[49]

Grattan hit back. He published in an English liberal newspaper a long letter attacking the Guild of Merchants ('an inconsiderable gathering'), the City Corporation (which 'ever waited on the wink of power to praise or persecute') and the Board of Trinity College ('grave, orderly, regular, solid and most excellent clergymen' who had 'set an example of more than republican inconsistency'). He also prepared a detailed answer to the charges based on the Secret Committee's reports, but acting on the advice of Erskine, the Whig barrister, he decided not to publish it – 'Lest', he explained to Fox, 'it should appear abjuring a discomforted party in Ireland who had been driven into the measures they adopted by the great criminals of the country, the ministers'.[50] This was a chivalrous attitude. It also avoided provoking renewed attacks from indignant government supporters. Irish conservative hostility was balanced by English Whig goodwill. At a meeting of the Whig Club with Lord Holland in the chair, Grattan's health was proposed by Fox. Grattan, Fox declared, had devoted his life to maintaining constitutional principles and promoting the happiness of his country – 'he had never been concerned in disturbing its tranquillity and has never lent the sanction of his name to acts of violence and oppression'. The toast of 'Henry Grattan and the friends of liberty and moderation in Ireland' having been drunk, it was followed by 'A speedy and honourable peace' and 'Lord Nelson and the gallant tars of old England'. Grattan was greatly gratified and assured Fox, 'you were right in the opinion you have formed of my moderation'. He had thought of going to the meeting 'but was in doubt should I have gone what to say and therefore followed the rule of policy, when I was uncertain what was to do – to do nothing'.[51]

Grattan was attracted back into Irish parliamentary life by a political crisis of the first magnitude. The '98 insurrection convinced Pitt and his colleagues that a union of Great Britain and Ireland was the only solution for Ireland's problems, and at the opening of the session of 1799 the Irish Parliament was recommended in the Speech from the Throne to consider the possibility of a union which would consolidate into 'one firm and lasting fabric the strength, the power and the resources of the British empire'. By a narrow margin this proposal was quashed in the Commons, but Pitt persevered and it soon became obvious that the Union was going to be brought forward again in the next session and that the anti-Unionists would have to exert themselves to the utmost if they were to win the second round.

Grattan was determined 'to protect the constitution of which I was the parent',[52] and when at the close of 1799 one of the MPs for Wicklow died he agreed to stand for the borough. Its patron, William Tighe, was a strong anti-Unionist, and the writ having been moved on the day Parliament met Grattan was elected by midnight. The return was rushed to Dublin and at 8 a.m. on the morning of 16 January he entered the House towards the close of a long debate on an anti-Union amendment to the address – the anti-Unionists having spun out the discussion until he arrived.[53] Grattan began by asking the permission of the House to speak seated, his weakness and the slow enunciation for which he apologized lending weight to his words. He launched into a two-hour speech, 'a declamation in his old style',[54] according to a hostile critic, which was a vehement denunciation of the Union. After this speech, Grattan on emerging from the Parliament House was cheered to the echo by a vast crowd gathered in College Green and an attempt was made to chair him. He quickly retreated and later left the House by 'another avenue'.[55] Shortly afterwards he was the recipient of a less perilous tribute. A meeting of the citizens of Dublin thanked Foster, the Speaker, Beresford and Ogle, the City MPs and Grattan for their opposition to the Union. A great procession, 'Orangemen, opposition men, democrats, Catholics and Presbyterians; the omnium gatherum of the day', many wearing anti-Union ribbons and preceded by a band playing solemn music, marched through the streets to present the resolutions and the thanks of the meeting to the four MPs. But recent quarrels had not been altogether forgotten. Some common councilmen had already declared themselves against congratulating a man who had been deprived of the Freedom of the City, and it was said that when the procession approached Grattan's dwelling 'all loyal and respectable people filed off to a man'. Grattan addressed some 'firm and resolute' words to the procession and 'there was', Drennan wrote, 'a sort of huzza at his door but it seemed to my ear to be hollow and without much heart in it. The whole business was rather melancholy, perhaps adapted to the time'.[56]

A few weeks later Grattan was involved in an even more dramatic episode. During a debate on the principle of union, Corry, who had succeeded the anti-Unionist Parnell as Chancellor of the Exchequer, attacked Grattan for his address to the citizens of Dublin in 1797 and his contacts with the United Irishmen, implying that his behaviour bordered on treason. Corry, in the eighties, had been a keen parliamentary reformer and a severe critic of the administration. His political evolution could of course be attributed to growing maturity and an honest change of outlook. Grattan interpreted it differently. Corry, he said, had 'deserted the occupation of a lawyer for those of a parisite and panderer ... it was easier for a statesman of middling talents to sell his friends than for a lawyer of no talents to sell his clients'. But he abstained, he declared, from calling Corry a villain because it would be unparliamentary to do so. Corry promptly sent a challenge; they met and exchanged shots, Corry being wounded in the arm. Craddock, Corry's second, having said it would be regrettable if there was not 'some exchange of compliments', Grattan called on Corry and expressed his sympathy. Corry attended the House with his arm in a sling and Grattan, Cooke remarked, in 'this duelling country' gained 'some éclat'.[57]

In the session of 1800 Grattan was an heroic figure, the Father of Irish parliamentary independence, fighting *pro arcis et focis*. But though he was prominent amongst the anti-Unionists, publishing a pamphlet and making three set speeches (incidentally he seems to have played little part in the committee stages of the Union bills), he was less effective than might have been expected. He arrived a year late on the scene, and he may have been somewhat discouraged by the determination and conviction with which the Unionists pressed forward. Moreover, his dialectical powers were somewhat weakened by circumstances which he could not ignore. He was better at attack than defence, and in the Union debates he was compelled to justify the status quo. A committed advocate of Catholic emancipation, he found himself fighting shoulder to shoulder with anti-Unionist Protestant conservatives, so when he referred to the Catholic question he was on delicate ground. Then he was only too well aware that the Irish radicals had rejected by rebellion the constitution of 1782. Grattan of course asserted that it was the government's repressive measures that had provoked rebellion, but the implication that Irish radicalism developed intellectually only as a result of government pressure was unconvincing.

Grattan knew well that in debate attack is often the best form of defence and he spent much of his time in tearing Pitt's 'Jacobinism' to pieces. A union, Grattan pointed out, encouraged Jacobinism by contemptuously condemning the Irish ruling world. With only one hundred MPs in what 'the novel and barbaric phraseology of empire'[58] dubbed the imperial parliament, Ireland would be under-represented and over-taxed, the Irish contribution to common expenses being based on fallacious calculations. Absenteeism would be encouraged and Ireland would lose the power to protect, if necessary by retaliation, its industry and commerce against British competition and unfair practices. Pitt's optimistic forecasts of Irish economic development under the Union were dismissed by Grattan as 'a prophet's promissary note'.[59] Pitt's Irish speeches, which in spite of his undoubted abilities betrayed 'an ignorance that would disgrace an idiot',[60] illustrated perfectly, Grattan pointed out, how incompetent Westminster was to handle Irish questions. As for the Catholics, excluded from Parliament, they would remain an underprivileged section of the community. For Grattan the great weakness of Pitt's plan was that it provided merely for a merger of the two parliaments, not for 'an identification of the nations' (a phrase redolent of nineteenth-century nationalism). The obstacles to national 'identification' not abolished by Pitt's plan were, Grattan stated, Ireland's viceregal court, treasury and financial administration, 'with its distinct patronage and expense', and with its own system of tariffs and bounties. 'You are to be governed', he told the house of Commons, 'by distinct laws ... and by a distinct spirit and principle administrating those laws', so that it was not inconceivable that 'a military government as complete as in Russia' might be established in Ireland.[61] A Unionist could reply that the obstacles to a smooth working of the Union, which were mentioned by Grattan, could in time be removed (as some of them were). A few decades later Irish nationalists would be surprised at such minor matters being referred to when the national being, the right of the nation to have absolute control over its destinies, was at stake. But Grattan was a constitutional nationalist in the fullest sense of the term. For him the glorious constitution as settled in 1782 provided a sound and traditional structure, rooted in six centuries of history, through which the national will and spirit could express itself.

Parliament was the body where the whole intellect of the country might be collected and 'where the spirit of patriotism, liberty and ambition may all act under control of that intellect and under the check of publicity and observation'.[62] Then he referred with pride to what the Irish Parliament had accomplished since 1782. Much useful legislation had been enacted and there had been steady growth in Irish trade 'under the maternal wing of her own parliament'. At the same time 'the bond and connection of these islands through the medium of monarchy' had been preserved and Ireland had co-operated readily with Great Britain in defence of the Empire, though he had to admit that corrupt majorities in that parliament had often blocked good and backed bad measures. Grattan argued at immense length that 'the treaty' or 'adjustment' of 1782 was a final settlement of Anglo-Irish relations and he insisted that the Irish Parliament was not competent to transfer its powers to another legislature. In support of this opinion he cited Locke, Grotius, Burlamaqui and (a slight descent) the Whig Fathers Jekyll and Lechmere. Moreover, he asserted, it was consonant with 'the honest instincts of the human mind'. But he said nothing about the right of resistance and he seemed to admit that a long continuance of the Union would ultimately validate it. 'The principles of right and wrong so intermix in centuries of human dealing as to become as inseparable as light and shade.'[63]

VI

Return to Public Life

On 1 January 1801 a new century and a new epoch in Irish history began. For Grattan it seemed that the close of the eighteenth century had marked the end of his political career. The cause for which he had striven for twenty years, Irish parliamentary independence, was lost and the Irish Parliament itself had ceased to exist. Grattan's own constituency, Wicklow, was one of the boroughs disfranchised at the Union and he did not embark on the task of finding another seat. All that remained was a quiet, reflective life in rural seclusion.

But the sense of futility generated by an overwhelming defeat did not last for long. Grattan's resilience is reflected in an unexpected source, the Trinity College entrance book. When his elder son, James, entered in 1803 his father described himself with bitter defiance as 'ingenuous' (free born); but when his second son, Henry, entered a year later, Grattan used for himself the conventional and justifiable term 'armiger' (entitled to bear arms). However deep his loyalties and strong his memories might be, he was bound to be influenced by the prevalent current of opinion in post-Union Ireland. There was a widespread acceptance of the new political dispensation. The Union was after all not such a very revolutionary measure. Dublin businessmen, deprived of aristocratic custom, might talk in catastrophic terms. Their City, they declared, had dwindled from 'a scene of gaiety, splendour and elegance into the insignificance of a paltry, provincial town'.[1] But county politics continued on familiar lines, the administrative machine and the legal system were little altered, and some MPs who had steadfastly and eloquently fought the Union were soon thoroughly at home and articulate at Westminster. Those Irishmen who had a craving for peace and quiet and who tended to be content with the status quo, remembered with acute distaste the tumultuous and destructive days of '98. Although it could be argued that the existence of an independent Irish Parliament was not a contributory factor to the outbreak of insurrection and civil war, the last years of that Parliament were undoubtedly a time of bitter conflict and it was easy to confuse coincidence and causation. Finally, in the decade and a half following the Union the Empire was menaced by an incredibly powerful France led by a military genius, and Irishmen, with their eyes riveted on the conflict (and also on agricultural prices), had little time to spare for discussing a fresh, fundamental reconstruction of the parliamentary framework.

Grattan, though he looked back with pride to the great days of the Irish Parliament, did little or nothing to nourish the spirit of *revanche*. When in 1810 an anti-Union agitation, largely inspired by civic resentment, flared up in Dublin, and he was requested as MP for the city to present petitions against the Union to Parliament, his response, though sympathetic, was very cautious. He explained that he would support a demand for a repeal of the Union because he believed it to be consistent with the maintenance of the British connection and the preservation of harmony between the two countries. But, he emphasized, it would not be 'prudent or possible' to raise the question of repeal in Parliament unless it was backed by the nation.[2] And although he presented the petitions he did not initiate a debate on the question.

His instincts were sound. The agitation soon petered out, and when he did refer to the Union in debate he seems to have accepted it as being as permanent as anything could be in politics. One argument he employed when urging Catholic emancipation was that it had been understood that the Union would be accompanied by emancipation, the implication clearly being that if emancipation was granted, the contract between the two countries, embodied in the Union, would be fulfilled.[3] Again, when discussing Ireland's economic future, he implied that it was not undesirable that a united Parliament should be responsible for Ireland's welfare. When towards the close of his career he was asked on the hustings to state his attitude to the Union, his immediate reaction was to seek refuge in retrospect and then to advise his hearers to accept the status quo. 'I would ask', he said, 'whether any man, any servant of the people took a more zealous or a more active (I will not say able) part in opposing the dissolution of the parliamentary constitution of Ireland than I did? In a state of health too, which many would not have been able to contend with! But I should flatter and mislead my fellow citizens if I allowed them to believe that they were sending me into parliament to procure a repeal of the Act of Union. I cannot hold out any hope. It was urged in opposition to that dreadful enactment that it was final. To evils which are inevitable I submit. Shall I tell my fellow citizens that there is anything in my phisical or political life which would enable me to relieve you from that terrible affliction! I cannot so deceive them.'[4]

Grattan's first post-Union intervention in politics was at the general election of 1802. There were four candidates for Dublin: John Claudius Beresford and George Ogle, the sitting members, both strong Protestant conservatives who had opposed the Union; John La Touche, later a supporter of Catholic emancipation, who emphasized that 'his family had acquired great opulence and he trusted great respectability' by their attention to the commercial interests of Dublin; and Jonah Barrington, who cannot be easily labelled politically. Barrington, who was to provide for posterity an unforgettable if not altogether reliable picture of his times, was for contemporaries a thrusting legal careerist, who became involved in dubious financial dealings. A flowery and fluent debater, having steadily supported the government he was in 1797 appointed Admiralty Judge in Ireland. The following year he failed to secure the Solicitor-Generalship and strongly criticized Cornwallis's administration for displaying excessive leniency during the '98 Rebellion. In 1799 he was an outspoken opponent of the Union but at the beginning of 1800 he resigned his seat and desisted from opposition. At the close of the following year, being 'ill adapted to the permanent obscurity of an unpromising profession', he quietly intimated to the Chief Secretary that he was anxious to enter Parliament as a government supporter and hoped for assistance in obtaining a seat.[5] Nothing coming of this détente, six months later he stood for Dublin as a fervent admirer of Grattan and the Ponsonbys. He also promised that if he were elected he would promote trade union legislation which 'would make the journeyman more anxious to work without making him the slave of his master'. When the polling began his first tally was composed of Grattan, George Ponsonby and Curran – and on Grattan tendering his vote, John Giffard objected 'on the part of the freemen of Dublin', pointing out that Grattan had been disfranchised in 1798. After a brisk debate in which Grattan emphasized how pleased he was that the objection had not been lodged by Beresford and Ogle, the Sheriffs allowed his vote on the ground that his name had not been removed from the Freemen's Roll (presumably owing to an administrative error).[6] The result of the election was that Beresford and La Touche were returned, Ogle lost his seat and Barrington was at the bottom of the poll.[7] Though Grattan had not been very fortunate in his choice of a candidate, he had indicated to the Dublin electorate that he had not lost interest in politics; and when in 1804 Beresford resigned, the Corporation of Hosiers asked Grattan, whose 'rational but firm loyalty, patriotism and unrivalled talents' were needed in Parliament, to stand. He declined because he had not had time to take soundings in the constituency, and Robert Shaw, a banker and popular alderman who came forward supported by a number of guilds, was returned unopposed.[8]

Although Grattan was fully occupied, entertaining his friends, planting trees, supervising his children's education, strolling happily in the woods surrounding Tinnehinch and commanding the yeomanry corps which he raised from his Queen's County tenancy on the outbreak of war in 1803, he was clearly restless, consciously or unconsciously craving the joy of debate. Fortunately he had a very respectable reason for wishing to return to the political arena. An important question with which he was deeply concerned, Catholic emancipation, had been carried over from the Irish to the imperial Parliament. At the time of the Union it was a minor question in British politics. The disabilities imposed on religious dissenters in Britain were being gradually whittled away. Though the

English Catholics were still unenfranchised and excluded from public office and the legal profession, the onerous religious and economic disabilities which had oppressed them for centuries had been repealed and they could confidently look forward to securing further concessions in the near future. They formed a small, secluded and conservative community, very deferential when soliciting relief. It was difficult to see such a body as a danger to the Church or the established order. Indeed a staunch Church of England Tory would have found the political opinions and prejudices of many English Catholics remarkably reassuring.

But with the Union the question of Catholic emancipation took on a new dimension. The Irish Catholics were a large body, amounting to at least one fifth of the population of the United Kingdom. They had a vigorous leadership, predominantly middle-class, publicity-seeking and outspoken, which had gained considerable concessions by an aggressive, well-organized popular agitation. As a result, by the close of the eighteenth century only a few disabilities – exclusion from Parliament and a number of posts in the public service – injured and irked the Irish Catholics. The repeal of these surviving disabilities, intensely exasperating to the successful and ambitious, was for the Irish Catholic leadership the final objective. To those who were apprehensive about how the Irish Catholics would use political power, the remaining disabilities were the last line of defence. If Irish Catholics and their Protestant supporters felt that the opening of a new century should be marked by the removal of the last relics of an archaic and discredited penal system, there were Protestant conservatives who viewed with trepidation the prospect of a partnership in the United Kingdom with an Ireland politically transformed by complete emancipation.

So brilliant and impressive was the parliamentary debating talent arrayed in support of complete emancipation – Pitt, Fox, Canning, Castlereagh, Wellesley, Grenville, Grey, Windham, Brougham, Plunket, Grattan – that it is easy to underestimate the strength of the opposition. If the first-class brains were on the one side, on the other was a solid mass of peers and MPs who regarded further concessions to the Catholics with apprehension. Their spokesmen included three Prime Ministers, Addington, Liverpool and Perceval, all men of undoubted integrity and tenacity; Eldon, the quintessence of legal conservatism; his brother Sir William Scott, a great jurist; Charles Abbot, a keen administrative reformer and a respected Speaker of the House of Commons; Peel, a rising young man; and Henry Bankes, 'who took an active if not leading part in every debate of his time'. Outside Parliament, two well-known literary men, Southey and Wordsworth, were strongly opposed to emancipation and the dons of Oxford and Cambridge petitioned in support of the Protestant cause. In Parliament the opponents of emancipation deployed with conviction and confidence a wide range of arguments. To begin with, they called on the proponents of the measure to show a sense of proportion. Emancipation was a misleading term. The Catholics were not in a state of slavery. The privileges denied them were the right to sit in Parliament and to hold 'the principal situations of trust and power under the crown', the offices which might be regarded as constituting the government of the country. In short the Catholics were not asking for civil rights – these they already possessed – but were demanding political power. Was it expedient this demand should be met?

There were two reasons for returning a negative answer to this question. Catholics, members of a hierarchical church whose head was the bishop of Rome, were subject in spiritual matters to 'a foreign jurisdiction'; the spiritual sphere was surprisingly wide – for instance the decision on a matrimonial case could decide the disposition of property – and the Church of Rome claimed the right to fix its boundary. Secondly, one of the most essential features of the British constitution, 'our free and happy constitution', reflecting the 'practical wisdom of mankind, under which we enjoy liberty toleration, wealth, tranquility', was the partnership between Church and State.[9] But could Catholic legislators and office-holders be expected to protect an Anglican Established Church and defend its interests? Obviously the more loyal to their own faith they were the less they could be relied on to maintain the Established Church. The removal of the last Catholic disabilities would be followed by a vigorous assault on the Irish branch of the United Church of England and Ireland. The Irish Catholics would demand an abolition of tithe, the recognition of their ecclesiastical law and 'a splendid church establishment' for their clergy. If you intend to satisfy the Catholics by concession, Perceval told the House of Commons, 'you must establish the Catholic religion in Ireland'. It was also probable that the Catholics would very soon after emancipation be able to secure parliamentary support for their programme. The Irish Catholics, with leaders 'long accustomed to act in concert, brothers in debate, brothers in risk, and in perseverance', would easily capture most Irish constituencies. The Catholic priest, not the Protestant landlord, would dictate the choice of the Catholic voter, and moderate Catholic landowners who did not go along with their more aggressive co-religionists would be denounced as 'worse than Orangemen'. Once there was at Westminster a strong Irish Catholic party, it would find allies in 'every junto of republicans, every band of dissenters' and such a coalition would wield great power. Panic can sharpen perception, and the opponents of the Catholic cause were very conscious that the Irish Catholic Relief movement, a movement largely led by middle-class agitators who boasted that they had the backing of the masses, was a menacing manifestation of the democratic spirit which all over Europe was threatening the established order.[10]

From the moment the Union came into being Fox, the ardent defender of civil liberties during the war, was eager that his party should take up the Catholic cause. He was anxious to show the Irish Catholics that they should not think they would be driven to look to Bonaparte for relief, and as a party tactician he considered that the fight for Catholic emancipation would consolidate the opposition – 'it was', he wrote, 'the only question that can be started to make what can be called a cause against the Court'.[11] In fact their consistent advocacy of Catholic emancipation played an important part in holding the Whigs together during their long spell in the political wilderness which began six months after Fox's death, emancipation being their 'cloud by day and the pillar of fire by night'.[12] On the other hand their defiance of traditional anti-popery feeling was bound to damage the Whigs in some quarters.

By the close of 1803 Fox was sure that the time had come for 'the bringing on of the Irish question', and he wrote to Grattan and George Ponsonby for advice and support. Ponsonby, who, Grattan told Fox in confidence, 'loves his ease and his bed',[13] sent a brief, baffling reply. He wanted the question postponed for three months. 'What he means by this period', Fox wrote, 'I cannot guess.'[14] Ponsonby soon produced a simple explanation. He thought it injudicious to raise the question during the invasion season. If a debate on the Catholic question coincided with a French landing the opposition would be charged with lack of patriotism.[15] Grattan replied at much greater length. A system of government of which an essential feature was the maintenance of the Protestant ascendancy, he wrote, called for drastic reform, but in the short term it was important not to rock the boat. The Irish administration had benefited from 'the fatuity of the rebels and the despotism of Bonaparte', and in the immediate future it would be politic 'to bring forward the bad qualities of the enemy and keep in the background those of the government'. It would be very unfortunate if pro-French feeling was strengthened by the rejection of a Catholic relief bill, and Grattan was prepared to postpone Catholic relief when he considered what in recent years had been accomplished by 'the temperate exercise of the existing laws'. Indeed he went so far as to say that if Hardwicke had been Lord Lieutenant and Redesdale Lord Chancellor in 1798, the insurrection might have been averted. Grattan's long-term programme included Catholic emancipation ('for such I must call it'), the payment of the Catholic clergy, tithe reform and perhaps 'some little improvement regarding our church' (he probably had in mind a redistribution of ecclesiastical revenues and a strict enforcement of clerical residence). Above all there should be 'a cordial execution of the laws in favour of the Catholics'. They should receive official appointments and pressure should be applied to secure their admission to corporate bodies to which they were legally entitled to belong. Any government newspaper which 'wished to sustain a religious war' should be silenced and Catholics should be welcome at the Castle; 'the manners of the court as well as the measures' were of vital importance in creating a sense of unity. Grattan ended his long letter by declaring that he hoped for, although he feared he would not see, the victory of 'that executive and legislative philosophy that shall make the two countries one and that not merely from the dread of France or the apprehension of plunder from their own populace but from the love of one another – should such an event take place I shall have much joy and you much comfort in consciousness of being the principal cause'.[16]

In the light of the discouraging advice he received from Grattan and Ponsonby, Fox decided not to raise the Catholic question in the session of 1804, 'with more regret than I have ever felt upon any political subject in my life ... I am vexed, I owe very much vexed'. But towards the end of the year he was glad to hear the Irish Catholics were going to petition Parliament and he seems to have written to Grattan about the possibility of a Protestant petition or declaration in favour of the Catholics. Grattan replied that he would consult his friends in Dublin, though he was afraid the Protestants were 'cold and timid and yet if they considered how necessary for what remains of their liberty it has become to unite all members of the empire against a foreign power I think they should be active'. Emancipation, he added, was 'one of the few questions that makes me regret I am not in parliament'.[17] Liberal Protestant opinion did not express itself but the Catholics went ahead and early in the session of 1805 entrusted petitions for emancipation to Lord Grenville and Fox. With an important debate on the Catholic question impending, Lord Fitzwilliam offered to secure Grattan's return for Malton, a borough of which he was the patron. Charles Dundas, one of the sitting MPs, obligingly resigned; Grattan was elected in his place,[18] took his seat on 2 May and made his maiden speech at Westminster on 13 May, speaking in support of Fox's motion that the House should consider the Irish Catholic petition.

The debate had aroused considerable interest and by seven in the morning a large crowd had gathered outside the House of Commons. When the doors to the public galleries were opened 'the crush was truely dreadful',[19] and those who did manage to squeeze into the galleries had to wait for six hours before the debate on the Catholic Petition began about six in the evening with a splendid speech by Fox. For Grattan, who was not called until nearly midnight, it was a tense occasion. He had a great reputation; but as he himself had written referring to Flood, an oak cannot be transplanted at fifty (and Grattan was now sixty). He must too have had in mind Flood's unfortunate maiden speech at Westminster. When on December 1783 during the debate on Fox's East India Bill, Flood, fatigued by his journey from Ireland, rose to speak it was very late and the House was impatiently clamouring for a division. Nevertheless, 'in compliment to him ... as a speaker of great expectation', the noise died down. Flood's 'slow, sententious and measured' enunciation seemed to English MPs 'cold and stiff' and he began ineptly by explaining that though he knew nothing about the subject he felt that 'it was his parliamentary duty to say something'. He then, having lost the ear of the House, delivered in 'a barbarous brogue' a speech 'below mediocrity'. His 'debuté (to use a theatrical term)', General Burgoyne reported, was 'of the most discouraging kind',[20] though it must be added that it did not deter Flood from intervening effectively enough in later debates.

Grattan in May 1805 had two advantages over Flood. He knew his subject thoroughly and he was immediately preceded in the debate by Dr Patrick Duigenan, the self-appointed champion of Irish ultra-Protestantism. Duigenan, 'short, fat and stout' with a small wig perched on a large head, prolix, prejudiced and ponderous in debate, was easily caricatured by his opponents. But he was by no means a despicable adversary. From humble beginnings (it was rumoured that his father was a small farmer or schoolmaster) he had fought his way up the educational ladder. Having been elected a fellow of Trinity, he was called to the Irish Bar and in 1794 was appointed judge of the Prerogative Court. Twenty years earlier, when Hely-Hutchinson, a polished and arrogant man of the world, became Provost of Trinity, Duigenan attacked him in print with robust virulence, charging him inter alia with greed, vanity, ignorance and gross misuse of his powers as Provost. Duigenan may have been vulgar but he struck some shrewd blows, and Hely-Hutchinson was glad to be able to obtain for him a highly remunerated law professorship which could not be held in conjunction with a fellowship. From 1791 Duigenan, who sat in the Irish House of Commons as MP for Armagh and as an ultra-conservative, on more than one occasion crossed swords with Grattan, who in a violent outburst accused Duigenan of scorning 'everything that was classical, moderate or refined' and of preferring 'only the foul, the gross and the scandalous', 'the garbage his imagination could collect' and 'the flowers of the fish-market'.[21] In fact Duigenan's speeches smacked of the lecture room rather than Billingsgate. Roman Catholicism, he was convinced, was steeped in theological error and represented a serious menace to civilized society. Emancipation, he warned the House of

Commons, would release 'an inundation of impiety, democracy and bar-barity', and he endeavoured to prove his case by mobilizing with indis-criminate zeal a vast miscellany of evidence drawn from papal decrees, contemporary pamphlets, the statute book, Blackstone, Catholic theolo-gians and the missal.

Duigenan's oration, while inspiring to those that agreed with him, offered a wide front to counter-attack, and Grattan, who had armed him-self cap-à-pie by an intensive study of 'the Councils of Lateran and Con-stance',[22] summarized the speech 'as being composed of four parts, invective against Catholics in general, and invective against the present, past and future generations of Catholics, 'here the limits of creation interpose'. Having done his best 'to rescue the Catholics from his [Duigenan's] attacks and the Protestants from his defence', Grattan, with glow-ing fervour, urged that the cohering force in an Empire that comprised 'a very great proportion of the globe' should be civil and religious liberty.

Grattan's speech was a tremendous success. 'Not a smile', Lord Hol-land said, 'was raised at all Mr Grattan's contortions which are as won-derful as his eloquence.' According to Lord Byron, MPs fascinated by Grattan's 'harlequin delivery' did not know whether to cheer or laugh, until they saw Pitt, 'their thermometer' nodding approval, and then they burst into rapturous applause.[23] Later in the debate Pitt referred to Grat-tan's 'splendid eloquence' and privately he noted that Grattan spoke with less violence than might have been expected. This was perceptive. At the close of Grattan's career, Abbot, the Speaker, a shrewd if conventional man, pronounced that Grattan had been 'a wise and useful' member of the House – even though his eloquence was always fanatical and often ridiculous. After he heard the great speech of May 1805 Abbot made a careful assessment of Grattan's oratorical powers. Grattan, he wrote, was 'able and various in his topics; delivered in language quaint and epigram-matic, with occasional flashes of striking metaphors and in a manner dis-gusting, vain, conceited and affected. His eloquence fluent, sometimes rapid, with strained pauses and strange cadencies; his action, violent, throwing his body, head and arms into all sorts of absurd attitudes'.[24] Some years later a very different observer, an intelligent French traveller, attending the House of Commons during one of the Walchern debates, described how after three fairly young MPs had spoken with 'a sort of school-boy oratory', 'a veteran member arose next, old and toothless and speaking like a Jew, uncouthly and carelessly, but ardently, and with that seeming self-conviction which is among the very first requisites for eloquence. He stepped forward on the floor towards the table, and used animated gestures, a little á la françoise, or at least very different from the English mode of oratory; Mr Grattan is Irish.'[25]

But the most vivid if scarcely the most sympathetic account of Grattan in action is to be found in William Hazlitt's essay 'On the present state of parliamentary eloquence'. Hazlitt, an angry radical, surveying the House of Commons from a frustrating observation-post, the reporters' gallery, had an acrid opinion of all parliamentary politicians, Whig and Tory. When Grattan rose to make one of his motions on Catholic emancipation, Hazlitt wrote

you saw a little oddly compacted figure of a man, with a large head and features, – such as they give to pasteboard masks, or stick upon the shoulders of Punch in the puppet-show – rolling about like a Mandarin – sawing the air with his whole body from head to foot, sweeping the floor with a roll of parchment which he held in one hand, and throwing his legs and arms about like the branches of a tree tossed by the wind: every now and then striking the table with impatient vehemence, and in a sharp, slow, nasal, glutteral tone, drawling out with due emphasis and discretion, a set of little, smart, antithetical sentences – all ready cut and dry; polished and pointed; – that seemed as if they "would lengthen out in succession to the crack of doom". Alliterations were tacked to alliterations – inference was dove-tailed into inference – and the whole derived new brilliancy and piquancy from the contrast it presented to the uncouthness of the speaker, and the monotony of his delivery. His were compositions that would have done equally well to be said or sung. The rhyme was placed at the beginning instead of the end of each line; he sharpened the sense on the sound, and clenched an argument by corresponding letters of the alphabet. It must be confessed that there was something meretricious as well as alluring in this style. After the first surprise and startling effect is over, and the devoted champion of his country's causes goes on ringing the changes on "the Irish people and the Irish parliament", on "the guineas and the gallows" as the ultimate resources of the English Government – on "ministerial mismanagement and privileged profligacy" – we begin to feel there is nothing in these quaint and affected verbal coincidences more nearly allied to truth than false-hood; – there is a want of directness and simplicity in this warped and garbled style; and our attention is drawn off from the impor-tance of the subject by a shower of epigrammatical conceits and fanciful phraseology, in which the orator chuses to veil it. It is hardly enough to say in defence of this jingle of words (as well as of the overstrained hyperbolica; tone of declamation which accompanies it) that "it is the custom of Ireland".[26]

At the very beginning of Grattan's second session at Westminster, the death of Pitt was followed by the formation of a new ministry, the Min-istry of All the Talents, in which Whigs predominated. Grattan could have been Irish Chancellor of the Exchequer but he preferred to be an unofficial if influential supporter of the new government. Considering that with the Whigs in power it would have been scandalous for 'union-ists to be crammed and anti-unionists to starve', he pressed the claims of a few loyal Irish Whigs, not apparently with quite the energy the claimants felt their cases called for (the loaves-and-fishes aspect of poli-tics never appealed to him). In August 1806 he was readmitted to the Irish Privy Council and he attended 'a most splendid entertainment' given at Dublin Castle by the new Lord Lieutenant, the Duke of Bed-ford.[27] Bedford, according to his son Lord John Russell, regarded Grattan, the friend of Fox, as one of his three principal advisers (the other two being Elliot, the Chief Secretary, and George Ponsonby) and consulted him on the details of the Tithe Commutation Bill, which was to be one of the main planks in the government's Irish programme. It followed fairly closely the plan proposed by Grattan in the late eighties, but Bed-ford was anxious that it should be brought forward in the House of Com-mons by the Irish law officers, because if it were taken up by 'Sir John

Newport [the Irish Chancellor of the Exchequer] or Mr Grattan, a strong feeling of alarm would be excited in this country and a cry of "church in danger" would be heard from one end of the island to the other'.[28]

In the summer of 1806 Grattan supported in the House of Commons the government's bold scheme for raising additional men for the army by short-service enlistment. The scheme appealed to Grattan on both military and constitutional grounds. It would both make military service more attractive and identify the soldier and the civilian more closely with one another. Indeed he went so far as to assert that 'none was ever to be found, in the military character, by whom liberty had always been so highly prized, as by the old English soldier' and he took the opportunity of urging the importance of making 'an adequate provision to the soldiery after they had become unable to serve'. He concluded by warning the House against injudicious economy: 'Do not suffer yourselves to be drawn aside from the proper provisions for your security by financial calculations.'[29]

Naturally, then, when Grattan at the general election held at the close of 1806 decided 'not to set-up' for Wicklow but to stand for the City of Dublin, he was backed by the government. He came forward, he announced, at the wish of a number of his fellow citizens, on whose 'independent spirit' he relied. La Touche, defending his seat, stressed that he had opposed Pitt's administration and was a supporter of Catholic emancipation. Shaw claimed to be fighting for Dublin's independence. He implied in his Address that his two opponents, Grattan and La Touche, were supported by the government, and, anxious to conciliate moderate opinion, he denied that he had encouraged his supporters to wear Orange ribbons. A meeting of the Guild of Merchants was addressed by all three candidates, Grattan speaking with his customary energy. After the candidates withdrew Shaw was thanked for his services and Grattan was nominated by a well-known city liberal, Travers Hartley, as a candidate to be supported by the Guild. Jonah Barrington seconded. Giffard, speaking with 'some asperity', attacked Barrington for first brushing aside claims based on family reputation and then 'dwelling on Mr Grattan's pretension on that head'. After some wrangling the meeting adjourned without coming to a decision. But Grattan did secure the support of the Dublin publicans, who remembered his services to the brewery trade, and a letter signed 'a free hosier' called on the poorer freemen to defy their employers, who regarded them as 'mere machines' and vote for the man of the people, Henry Grattan. Grattan was returned at the head of the poll with 1675 votes, Shaw obtaining 1638 and La Touche 1522.[30] After the declaration of the result Grattan had the to submit to being chaired through the city and the 'liberties'. 'It was by no means a pleasant experience for him as it rained the whole day and he kept his hat off.'[31] La Touche petitioned against Shaw's return and a group of obscure citizens petitioned against Grattan, alleging that the government had excercised undue influence over those electors who were placemen or 'tradesmen or artificers or mechanics' who supplied government departments, and that revenue officers (disenfranchised by an act of 1803) and Catholics who had not produced their qualification certificates had been permitted to vote. Since the petition lapsed it is probable the allegations were exaggerated, though Grattan undoubtedly had the support of the Castle.

Grattan was so conscious of the benefits that a Whig administration could confer on Ireland that he was prepared to make considerable concessions to keep it in power. He endeavoured to persuade the Catholics not to embarrass a friendly government by petitioning in 1807 for complete emancipation. Although he approved of the government's intention to introduce in 1807 a bill improving the legal position of the Catholic army officer, when the King's reaction was that the cabinet should promise not to bring the Catholic question to his attention without his permission, Grattan hoped that the cabinet would accept the royal ultimatum rather than quit office. But Grenville and his colleagues preferred to resign and the installation of a Tory government was followed by a general election.[32]

Grattan braced himself to defend his Dublin seat, knowing that this time the influence of the Castle would be thrown into the scale against him. A number of potential candidates were mentioned but the previous election had shown that the interests represented by Grattan and Shaw were evenly balanced and the new Chief Secretary, Sir Arthur Wellesley, 'rich in saving common sense',[33] was anxious to keep Dublin politically quiet. So he decided not to attempt to win both Dublin seats. 'I think', he wrote, 'we should not succeed, we should put Shaw to great expense and possibly lose the election.' La Touche, whose petition had proved expensive both for himself and for Shaw, did not stand again for the city and at the nomination Grattan and Shaw were the only candidates proposed. They shook hands, 'the surrounding multitude applauding with shouts and huzzas', and each of them made a speech advocating harmony. Grattan exhorted the citizens, the inhabitants of the second city in the Empire and the first in Ireland, 'to love the Empire at large, love the land that supports you and love one another'.[34]

Grattan remained MP for Dublin until his death, he and Shaw being returned unopposed at the general elections of 1812, 1818 and 1820. Though Shaw was the more active constituency MP, being in close touch with Dublin municipal and business life, Grattan on occasion defended Dublin interests in the House of Commons. In 1813, when the Lord Mayor asked to be permitted to deliver a petition against Catholic emancipation at the Bar of the House (a privilege hitherto only possessed by the Sheriffs of London), Grattan, though he disapproved of the petition, moved that the Lord Mayor's request be granted. He was supported by Shaw and Castlereagh and the motion was passed unanimously (George Tiernay remarking that the citizens of Edinburgh were too prudent to send their chief magistrate 400 miles to present at a petition).[35]

On a more important issue, Grattan's breadth of view or lofty disregard of local opinion brought him into conflict with many of his constituents. In the aftermath of the Napoleonic Wars, there was throughout the British Isles a loud demand for a sharp reduction in taxation, expressed in Dublin by determined efforts to secure the abolition of the window tax. In the autumn of 1816 two Dublin parishes asked Grattan to support petitions in favour of the repeal of the tax. Replying to the parishioners of St Brigid's, Grattan assured them their petition would have his ardent support; simultaneously, when replying to the parishioners of St Michan's he wrote, 'I should be criminal if I flattered you with the hope (which I am sure you do not look to) of abolishing at this moment any of the capital resources of the state'. A liberal newspaper commented on these replies in a leader headed 'Grattan versus Grattan'. A year later, when a meeting comprising deputies from several Dublin parishes convened to fight the window tax asked Grattan to support its repeal, he replied that he would try to obtain 'every practical relief'. O'Connell, at a subsequent meeting of the parish deputies, said that this reply was 'equivocal' (though he did not fail to refer with great respect to 'the Father of Irish parliamentary independence'). The meeting dispatched a further letter to Grattan reiterating its request. Grattan replied at some length explaining that by 'practical relief' he meant 'such relief as was compatible with the necessary support of the empire and the substantial relief of the people'. Although he pronounced the window tax to be 'unequal and oppressive' he refused to pledge himself not to accept any relief short of its total repeal. His attitude annoyed some city politicians. He was strongly criticized for not obeying the instructions of his constituents, whose servant he was, and defended on the ground that 'no doubt age weakens the mind'. At the beginning of 1819 he informed the parish deputies that he would present and support their petition against the tax. It was, however, Shaw who in May took the lead in bringing the question before the House. At the close of an animated debate in which elaborate comparisons were made between the burden of taxation endured by Great Britain and Ireland respectively, Grattan in a low tone expressed himself hesitatingly. He did not want, he explained, 'to make an invidious contrast of the state of England and that of Ireland. Such a contrast might lead to a competition of strength between the two countries which ought always to be avoided and still more so after a marriage had taken place between them which it was in the interest of every loyal patriot to make as indissoluable as possible.' He then went on to give, parish by parish, the number of 'insolvent' (behind with their tax) houses in Dublin. When he then said he did not want to trouble the house further there were cries of 'hear, hear' and 'question', which suggested this may have been the occasion when Grattan near the close of his career, 'speaking in a style that betrayed the decline of the faculty of a once great man', on being interrupted 'paused and said in audible voice, "You are right Sir"' and sat down.[36]

It was the unpopularity he incurred over the window tax and the Corn Laws, together possibly with memories of his attitude on the Insurrection Act, that accounted for an unhappy occurrence at the general election of 1818. After the result had been declared, their supporters placed Grattan and Shaw in richly decorated chairs and started to parade them through the city. In Henry Street the procession was attacked by a violent mob, hurling stones. Shaw, 'seizing the readiest conveyance, made off'; Grattan, badly bruised on the forehead, took refuge in a house in Mary Street, besieged by the mob. Fortunately Charles Philips, a popular agitator, arrived on the scene. He made an adroit speech in which he referred to Grattan's past services and implied that the crowd had assembled to honour him. After this the mob dispersed. A great wave of sympathy with Grattan swept through respectable Dublin and the Corporation addressed him expressing their abhorrence of 'the gross and wicked assault' committed by the rabble. In his reply Grattan declared that 'the ancient city of Dublin' possessed 'a sober, serious sense of the value of liberty, with a love of order and a sense of the necessity of government'.[37]

VII

An Elder Statesman

The years following Grattan's election to the United Kingdom Parliament, tinged perhaps with regret but full and in some ways very enjoyable, had an elegiac quality. Creevy, a Westminster acquaintance, observed in 1809 that Grattan was 'a kind of stranger in a new country – he has no longer any object of ambition – seems to consider his day as past and to be perfectly satisfied with his lot'.[1] In the Irish Parliament Grattan had always been at full stretch, nervously alert to defend the rights of Ireland and Irishmen. At Westminster he could relax, intervening judiciously from time to time, and, at long intervals, exerting his full powers on a major occasion. As he aged and enjoyed his *otium cum dignitate* in a wider world than that of Dublin, he mellowed, was less prickly and suspicious, more generous and conciliatory.

Outside Parliament he had a varied and entertaining social life. When he came to England for the session he brought his family. They had naturally a base in London – in 1811 and 1812 a house in Waldeck Street, partly furnished, for fourteen guineas a week[2] – and they went for visits to Brighton, where they were entertained at the Pavilion ('Grattan is my friend,' the Regent effusively told one of Grattan's daughters), and to Eastbourne, where Grattan met Wilberforce and Sir Arthur Pigott, a barrister, gifted with a sense of proportion which 'enabled him to compress into a smaller compass than is usual with equity pleaders the merits of his case' and who was, as the *Gentleman's Magazine* put it, 'though ... what is called a Whig in politics, of most upright and unbending principles'.[3] Mrs Grattan was crippled by rheumatism, or arthritis, but had plenty of vitality (she survived her husband for eighteen years) and was kindly and capable. The domineering Lady Holland was afraid she was 'a bit of an evangelical' and in 1829 was scandalized to discover that she was not at all 'elated' by Catholic emancipation.[4] A solicitous father, Grattan worried over his children. James, his elder son, after graduating at Trinity became a partner in a Wexford bank. He soon resigned his partnership and in 1811 was commissioned as a light cavalry man, joining the 20th Dragoons, from which he exchanged into the 9th. Grattan was very keen that James should be professionally successful and exhorted him after he was commissioned to keep up his classics and get up early every morning, 'it contributes to a long life and to business'. Six months after James joined the army his family were distressed to hear that Richard Bushe, Grattan's nephew, had been wounded at Barossa. But Grattan consoled himself, as he told James, by reflecting that 'life is but secondary, no concern for your safety can affect my wishes for your credit'.[5] James attained the rank of captain, took part in the Walchern expedition (accompanied by his brother Henry, a civilian), served in Sicily and the Peninsula and retired in 1814 at the close of the war. Touring Europe in 1815, he arrived in Elba just in time to see Napoleon embarking for France. James as quickly as possible informed the British commissioner of Napoleon's departure and was entrusted with a dispatch giving the news to Castlereagh. He was publicly thanked by Castlereagh for his services and branded as an informer by French sympathizers in Ireland. After Waterloo James visited Paris and took a book out of Napoleon's library at Saint-Cloud 'by right of conquest'.[6]

When James was serving abroad, Grattan's younger son, Henry, was supposed to be reading for the bar. But his father mournfully wondered if Henry's undoubtedly extensive reading included much law (in a letter to his brother Henry exclaimed, 'Law books be damned').[7] Highly strung and intellectually effervescent, Henry was one of the first young Irishmen to react vigorously against the Union. Irish politics, he wrote to his brother, 'set me mad ... an Irishman of ambition dies in Ireland, he droops in England ... We have become a province drained of every particle of spirit ... By God the Irish mind is debased.' The Catholics were foolish, the Protestants petty tyrants, and Irishmen of his own world, he was afraid, 'do not belong to any country, half colonists, half indigent adventurers, men on garrison duty'.[8] His father listened to his spirited outpourings with tolerant amusement. Henry's politics, he remarked, 'are more violent than mine and he argues with too much acerbity but of that he will mend'; and when Henry was hoping to make his political debut at an anti-Union meeting in Dublin his father firmly advised him against doing so.[9]

Seeing his two daughters still unmarried in 1811 Grattan was 'very uneasy, however I must bear it'. A few years later Mary Ann, having lost what her brother Henry described as 'that little tierce manner which showed no more than a want of experience',[10] married John Blachford of Altadore, County Wicklow. Her sister Harriet remained for many years her mother's companion but in 1836 she married a middle-aged widower, the Rev. William Wake, a member of the Northamptonshire family which claimed descent from Hereward the Saxon hero. Grattan was also worried by another perennial problem – the cost of living in London. In 1805 horses, he complained, cost 'exactly double what I paid for them ten years ago', opera tickets had become outrageously dear and 'port has become claret in price and continues brandy in quality'.[11] The examples cited do not suggest penury, however, and the Grattan family's social life was not painfully constrained by financial considerations.

Grattan still insisted on periods of quiet reflection, quoting the maxim that a man should think more than he reads or talks.[12] But he had come to the conclusion that 'old men love society',[13] and in that English Whig world where politics, intellect, and fashion fused he found a milieu in which he was happily at home. It was a public-spirited, quick-witted, talkative, companionable society, tolerant and liberal, anxious to get rid of abuses but eschewing excessive enthusiasm. Contemptuous of Tory stupidity and radical silliness, the Whigs believed that the rational, independent individual should be allowed to enjoy life unharassed by the arbitrary power of the monarch or the mob. They also prided themselves on the range of their interests. They did not believe that devotion to the public weal justified a neglect of belles-lettres and that culture could be compartmentalized. The *Edinburgh Review*, founded three years before Grattan arrived at Westminster to expound Whig principles and their application to contemporary problems, published articles on poetry and politics, metaphysics, fiction, chemistry and international affairs. For Grattan and his friends the embodiment of modern Whiggery was Charles James Fox, the ardent and eloquent advocate of civil and religious liberty, a man of strong convictions and easygoing good humour, as happy in his library as in the House of Commons or the card-room of Brooks's. Comparing Fox and Pitt, Grattan gave full rein to Holland House prejudice. Pitt, he remarked, 'would be right for nineteen times for once Fox was right, but that once would be worth all the rest'.[14]

Grattan dined with Fitzwilliam in Grosvenor Square, at Spencer House, at Buckingham House (a reconciliation with its testy owner having been effected) and Devonshire House – the Duchess of Devonshire gave him an Italian translation of Horace's *Satires*. He visited at Connaught House (the Princess of Wales in 1816 sent him her love). He was a frequent guest of the great Whig hostess Mrs Crewe, with whom he had 'an affectionate and amiable intercourse', and of 'Conversation' Sharp, the wealthy businessman, essayist and Whig MP beside whom he usually sat in the House of Commons. Surprisingly, he seems on at least one occasion to have dined with William Godwin – Coleridge, a fellow guest, declaring 'that to sit at the same table as Grattan who would not think it a red letter day in the almanack of history'.[15] He met the elderly dramatist Cumberland at Tunbridge Wells, and he knew well Samuel Rogers, the poet, wit, and very hospitable host. Rogers Boswellized Grattan and with characteristic malice spoke of him as 'a sentimental harlequin'. Grattan formed an attachment to 'the Catalani', Maria Catalani, the great opera singer. A virtuous young woman, when she paid visits she was always accompanied by her husband, who claimed to be a ruined man of fortune but, rumour asserted, was in fact of humble origin. On one occasion when he and his wife were dining with the Grattan family, he 'eat and drank so much that he got the gripes and frightened all the ladies'.[16]

Fragments of Grattan's conversation survive, enough to show its tone and trend. Mackintosh and Brougham, visiting Holland House, listened with delight to Grattan talking about the great men he had met in his youth, particularly Lord Chatham, 'whose breathing thoughts and burning words ... it was impossible for such a man as Grattan not to prefer to the eloquence of argument and business which has succeeded'.[17] On another evening at Holland House, Grattan reduced the whole party to helpless laughter by giving them 'in his own inimitable grotesque, forcible and theatrical manner', the 'characters of some Irishmen who had flourished at the end of the last century'. Clare, he said, could be intimidated, 'though he had fought, and fought well too'. Bellomont, his old antagonist, he compared to 'a black bull, always butting', and, he added, 'Bellomont's wig was dirtier than Curran's hair.[18] (Curran when talking to his English friends mimicked Grattan bowing to the very ground and thanking God that he had no peculiarities of gesture or appearance.)[19] At Mrs Crewe's, he unexpectedly defended Spencer Perceval, remarking 'he is a bigot in religion, which is to be disapproved, but there is a sincerity in what he does, and upon such a subject, and when that is the case, allowance is to be made'. He condemned far more severely Foster, the Irish Chancellor of the Exchequer, for being 'a bigot in politics'. On another occasion referring in conversation to Percival he emphasized that, if not a brilliant orator, he possessed parliamentary qualities of the greatest value. Perceval, he said, was 'not a ship of the line, but he carried many guns, is tight built and is out in all weathers'. More charitable than in the past, Grattan argued that it was hard for men in office to be sincere, as he knew from his own experience when his friends were in power.[20] Chatting with Rogers, who Boswellized him, Grattan said that 'to beauty we owe poetry, to poetry civilization, to civilization every art and science'; in a more melancholy mood he wondered 'if a man were to be offered life with foresight of all the evils that would attend it, would he not reject it?' Discussing literature, he placed Milton above Pope and Pope, 'as the more moral man', above Dryden; Cicero and Burke were better to read than to hear. Talking of the past he said he should like to meet Caesar, as he was much interested in his times, but not Cleopatra: 'her beauty would make me sad and she would tell me nothing but lies'. Turning to the present, he said he would sooner be shot than go up in a balloon.[21]

However much he enjoyed England, Grattan when there sighed for Ireland; yet, such is human nature, during a severe winter at Tinnehinch he and Mrs Grattan found 'rain, cloud and wistle of the winds ... no very agreeable substitute for the gay society of Brighton'.[22] But Tinnehinch was home. It had a beauty which after years of careful planting and planning had attained, he thought, perfection. It was where he had brought up his children and where he entertained relations and friends. He had for some years two long-term guests, William Preston and Francis Hardy. Preston, prolific in poetry and prose, wrote with immense self-assurance on German literature, Irish economics and the structure of the Ode. A Whig verging on radicalism, he exasperated Grattan in 1806 by sending him five long letters 'asking and asking for what he was eminently unfitted'. Soured by lack of recognition, Preston spoke slightingly of Grattan behind his back but apparently did not refuse his hospitality.[23] Hardy, a staunch Whig and an able speaker when he was prepared to exert himself, was a widely read man whose 'stream of wit and innocent pleasant' flowed from morning until late at night. He was very lazy. 'Our friend Hardy', Grattan wrote in 1805, 'is doing what he has been doing for many years, nothing, and he is declining in spirits from the force of no object and no occupation. I dispair of him.' As a result of ceaseless prodding Hardy at last in 1810 published his life of Charlemont. A critic in the *Edinburgh Review* was obliged to point out that it was confused and in parts ungrammatical, 'the animated and versatile talk of a man of genuine feeling' rather than 'the mature production of an author who had diligently corrected his MS'. But the reviewer bestowed an accolade which would have delighted Hardy: the work was 'the life of a gentleman written by a gentleman'.[24]

The happy world of Tinnehinch was described at some length by a young visitor, George Eden, who stayed there in September 1813. 'I am in', he wrote, 'I should think the most beautiful country in the world and with one of the pleasantest families I ever saw.' Mrs Grattan was 'a very pleasing woman'; the Miss Grattan who was at home, although not very handsome, was 'placid and natural'; and the family with a number of relations who were staying at the house formed, Eden said, 'one of the pleasantest and easiest societies I have ever witnessed'. Grattan himself was 'quite delightful, playful, talkative, full of anecdote and candid and charitable to all mankind. His conversation is particularly entertaining though perhaps a little too epigrammatic for good taste but his pointed metaphors flow so easily that they do not offend. His life is most completely domestic. His walks much confined to his flowing gardens and shruberies – he has a little levee of beggars at the door every morning and he comes in now and then and says "there is a boy that looks hungry" and goes off with a plate of toast and an egg. This perhaps multiplies his petitioners a little and in the same good natured way he lets everything, animals, trees etc overgrow the place – but as the characteristic is wildness this does not injure its appearance.'[25]

After the dismissal in 1807 of the Grenville ministry, which he had so strongly supported, Grattan usually acted with the Whig opposition, a party which included at one extreme the Grenvillites, cautiously conservative on most issues, and at the other the advanced Whigs, dubbed the Mountain. The Whigs were united only in their advocacy of religious liberty and their unmeasured contempt for the epigones who were in power. It is not easy to place Grattan in the spectrum of Whig opinion. On one occasion he was listed as one of the Mountain but he did not consistently vote with it and on some questions – the war and law and order in Ireland – he differed sharply from this small group of progressive Whigs. In short he was idiosyncratic and highly independent, but weighing his words and votes he may be regarded as being a slightly left-of-centre Whig. Significantly, at a dinner given in honour of Sir Francis Burdett, the reformer, the toast of 'the Irish M.P.s who have done their duty to their constituents' was coupled with the names of General Mathew and Christopher Hutchinson, both undoubtedly more advanced in their liberalism than Grattan.[26]

Grattan was of course quick to defend civil liberty. He spoke against Burdett being sent to the Tower, reminding the House of Commons that when it 'went to hunt in holes and corners for questions of privilege, they diminished their own dignity', and he voted with the minority which condemned the use of the military for crowd control outside Carleton House.[27] On the Regency question he spoke a couple of times in 1811, refurbishing old arguments against restrictions on the Regent. He was not a member of the very small minority which supported Burdett's sweeping scheme of parliamentary reform but in the following year he voted for Thomas Brand's much more moderate plan. He maintained his long-standing adherence to the cause of administrative reform, his zeal being tempered by good nature. When in March 1809 the time arrived for the House to pronounce on the Duke of York scandal, which had for months diverted the parliamentary and public mind from more important military issues, Grattan abstained from voting with the minority which wanted the House to condemn the Duke for condoning corruption. But he did vote against a ministerial resolution which would have implicitly cleared the Duke of all blame. In the same year, in the debate on a motion severely censoring Castlereagh for being willing to use a piece of East Indian patronage to facilitate a friend in obtaining a parliamentary seat, Grattan made an ambiguous speech. He stressed that Castlereagh's offence was a grave one, undermining the constitution 'by selling what was not to be sold and buying what was not to be bought', but he dwelt with obvious pleasure on the candid manner in which Castlereagh had admitted his part in the transaction and he pointed out that though Castlereagh 'had evaded a great principle of the constitution he had not evaded with a view to attack the constitution but with a view to accommodate a friend'. Light and shade were so skillfully blended in Grattan's speech that some of his hearers may well have concluded that while Castlereagh's conduct was open to criticism it was unnecessary to pass a formal vote of censure. At the end of the debate a motion of censure on Castlereagh was defeated, Grattan voting in the minority. Grattan's son Henry was infuriated by 'Castlereagh's shameful let off', and explained to a friend that 'Mr Grattan did not say so much in favour of Castlereagh as was said, he was mild and it would not have become him to triumph over a fallen foe'. A more closely concerned commentator, Castlereagh, characterized Grattan's speech as 'gentlemanlike'.[28] In the following year Grattan again spoke as an administrative reformer, criticizing what he regarded as over-liberal superannuation arrangements in the Irish Post Office; and he raised a laugh by suggesting that 'all the superannuated officers be brought to the bar in order that the house might see what a hale, young and vigorous corps they would comprise'.[29]

During Grattan's first ten years at Westminster the great overshad-owing issue was the war, how it should be conducted and what would be its outcome. Grattan was intensely concerned with both the progress of the war and the future of the Empire, and for some years after the fall of the Grenville administration the mistakes and mishaps of the govern-ment enabled him to combine fervent anti-French feeling with astringent criticism of the Tory ministers who were managing (or rather mismanag-ing) the war effort. When the seizure of the Danish fleet at Copenhagen in 1807 was being debated, Grattan, though not prepared to go along with a small group of Whigs who opposed the vote of thanks to the expe-ditionary force, was one of the much larger minority who supported George Ponsonby's demand that the ministers should produce evidence justifying their attack on a neutral state.

In 1810 (aided no doubt by the fact that many members must have been aware that one of his sons had served at Walchern) he attacked the government for launching the expedition too late to be of help to Austria and involving the army in 'the inglorious struggle with pestilence and plague'. The expedition, he said, had been placed under the command of 'a general who declared he had no plan and grave doubts; and of an admi-ral without doubts who declared he knew nothing of navigation and that some other person should command the fleet'. The expedition, in Grat-tan's opinion, afforded 'the most convincing illustration of the doctrine, that upon military objects, your best dependence is upon the advice and intelligence of military men'.[30] He twice with great vigour denounced the Orders in Council as violating the laws of nations and imperilling Anglo-American friendship. By issuing the Orders Great Britain descended from 'the grand elevation that was peculiarly her own' to join with France against the neutrals in 'a sort of wicked emulation of injustice'. 'No mea-sure', he emphatically declared, 'should be more studiously avoided by England, than that which threatened to deprive us of the affections of America' – 'our own America – our colonized America'. 'Let England,' he said, 'be to America what she ought to be, and America will be to Eng-land all that we could wish her.'[31]

Unlike some of his Whig friends he was exhilarated by Wellington's successes in Spain. 'A dawn of light has broken upon us,' he wrote in 1811 after Wellington had driven the French out of Portugal, 'the troops and officers have won much renown and it is hoped the empire will reap advantage.' In 1813 he was chosen as one of the 'managers' of a scheme to erect a Wellington monument in Dublin.[32] Nearly two years later Grattan made his most striking contribution to the long debate on the great French War. When, a few months after Napoleon's return from Elba, the House of Commons was asked to vote an address to the Regent supporting allied action against 'the common enemy', the Whig attitude was wait and see. Napoleon might have learned his lesson and back in the Tuileries after defeat and exile might be content to rule as a constitutional monarch of peaceable and liberal inclinations. Grattan, separating himself with regret from his old political friends (including George Ponsonby), supported the Address in a speech remarkable for its cogent argument and glittering, hard-cutting phraseology. He began by agreeing with the opponents of the Address in deploring the evils of war. But he added, 'I depreciate still more the double evil of a peace without securities, and a war without allies'. There was in Napoleon's character 'a sort of theatrical grandeur. He had been the greatest actor in the bloody tragedy of modern Europe. The fire of his genius had inflamed the world. He was a military hero to France and a public calamity to Europe.' Having overthrown the mild monarchy of Louis XVIII, who had granted France a constitution on British lines, Napoleon had in alliance with the Jacobins established a military dictatorship, aggressive and predatory – 'his armies live to fight and fight to live' – which was a standing threat to Europe. If Great Britain now hung back from joining the European alliance against Napoleon, she would only postpone war with France until compelled to fight alone. Britain, he reminded the House, had strong allies, the British navy had already saved Europe and Britain's resources were greater than those of all the other powers. He concluded by calling on the House to 'recollect that money was only one part of strength. The name and part that we have borne preclude us from taking a second place. When we cease to be the first, we must be the last, when we descend from our exalted rank we should become nothing.' The speech was punctuated by loud cheering, and though Grattan's intervention in the debate cannot be regarded as decisive – the government had the support of more than three quarters of the House – supporters of the government's war policy, including Wellington, whom Grattan referred to as an 'unsurpassed general', were very glad to have Grattan's moral and intellectual backing. An oblique tribute to the influence of the speech was afforded by a keen Whig who wrote, 'Grattan was no great thing – full of wit, fire and folly; more failures than success in this antithesis and his piety and religious cant was offensive'.[33] The speech, one of the last of Grattan's great set pieces, was not only an oratorical tour de force but also constituted an important part of his political legacy. In it he expressed deep-rooted convictions which he shared with many Irishmen – loyalty to the Empire, readiness to assume imperial responsibilities, pride in renowned feats of arms and confidence in Britain's imperial destiny.

Although Grattan took part in a number of debates on British and imperial questions, his special subject was Ireland; and on the major contemporary Irish issue, Catholic emancipation, he eloquently exerted himself session after session. Grattan was convinced that emancipation would make a fundamental change in Irish life. If the Protestants generously granted emancipation and the Catholics graciously accepted the boon, immense goodwill would be generated, and Grattan was always confident that, given goodwill, difficulties and differences would diminish or disappear. Nevertheless, he was not a one-subject man and before discussing his eventual parliamentary campaign for complete emancipation something should be said about his approach to other Irish problems. An agricultural protectionist who supported the Corn Law of 1815, pouring scorn on manufacturers whose aim was cheap food and high prices for their own products, Grattan foresaw a prosperous future for Ireland in a tariff-encircled British agricultural market. Ireland, he expected, would continue to take British manufactures in return for Irish grain and the two countries would be physically identified with each other – mutually dependent upon each other and mutually independent of the rest of the civilized globe.[34] He continued, as he had been for thirty years past, to be intensely concerned over taxation. Although he was sure that Ireland at the opening of the nineteenth century was advancing economically, he was afraid that the developing Irish economy was at the stage when taxation above a relatively low level might be highly detrimental. Ireland, he explained to the House of Commons, was economically speaking 'like a child' that must be 'carefully nursed. You must not lay too heavy a burthen on her, otherwise you will destroy her future strength.' In 1815 he protested vehemently and successfully against the proposal that the property tax (the income tax), a tax 'injurious to the sensations of Irishmen', should be extended to Ireland. Though the Irish gentry, he explained, were ready to maintain the Empire with their property and their blood, they were strongly opposed to an income tax.[35] Successive Irish Chancellors of the Exchequer shared Grattan's approach to Ireland's fiscal problems, preferring to run into debt rather than increase taxation, until in 1816, with the amalgamation of the Exchequers, Ireland's greatly swollen debt was absorbed into the national debt of the United Kingdom.

In 1810 he was responsible for a small contribution to penal reform: an insolvent debtors act which mitigated the rules governing imprisonment for debt. He continued to urge three major measures which he believed would effect immense improvements in Irish social conditions – tithe reform, educational reorganization, and the discouragement of spirit-drinking by increased spirit duties. He denounced the tithe system. His remedy was a commutation on the lines he had suggested in the eighties, which would have protected the interests of the Protestant clergy, whom he highly praised, reserving his invective for the tithe proctor, who oppressed the poor peasant and cheated the parson and who was not a gentleman.[36] Education he saw as a great panacea. On the secondary level, he was anxious to concentrate resources to obtain excellence, proposing that the endowments of the royal and diocesan schools be used to found a few 'great public schools'. He also was eager that there should be a primary school in every parish, 'bringing education to everyman's door'. In these schools English would be the medium of instruction and agriculture and horticulture would be taught as well as the three Rs. Grattan did not see that religious teaching in primary schools could present a problem. He proposed that the children should be taught undenominational Christianity and instructed in their four great duties – to God, to man, to the country and to the government.[37] On the three subjects which have just been mentioned Grattan's views met with a large measure of acceptance. Everyone was for education and against drunkenness, and even ardent defenders of the established Church were prepared to consider modifications of the tithe system. But there was an Irish issue on which Grattan took a strong, and very controversial stance: law and order. In 1806–7 there were again widespread agrarian disturbances in the south of Ireland and in July 1807 the new Chief Secretary, Arthur Wellesley, introduced an Insurrection Bill (prepared, he pointed out, by the Whig administration which had just left office) conferring extensive powers on the magistracy in proclaimed districts. Though an amendment limiting the duration of the bill to one year rather than three which he recommended was rejected, Grattan came out strongly in favour of the third reading of the bill. According to Romilly, the legal reformer, it was Grattan's arguments, or rather his assertions, or, to speak still more accurately, his authority, which persuaded many MPs who came down to vote against the bill to leave before the division. Romilly himself regarded the Insurrection Bill as 'little short of madness' and another MP, Francis Horner, the liberal economist, was shocked by Grattan's inconsistency in supporting a bill worthy of Charles II's Scottish Parliament. Grattan, however, was convinced that there was at this time in Ireland a French party which was encouraging an armed banditti to rise against law and social order, and he had no hesitation in declaring that 'when the common law of the land was by no means sufficient for the safety and security of the country ... strong measures must be resorted to' (a principle enunciated by the supporters of the Irish administration at the close of the eighteenth century). Nine years later, in 1816, in a speech which Castlereagh characterized as 'statesmanlike', Grattan again emphasized the importance of maintaining law and order in Ireland, 'a great part of a great empire', adding that he trusted that the government would act in such a way that 'the very criminal who suffered under the influence of the law should allow the excellence of the constitution under which he was punished'. Cobbett in his report of this debate, having reminded his readers that Grattan had supported the 1807 Insurrection Act, summed up his speech by saying he spoke 'partly on one side and partly on the other'.[38]

Important as the issues which have just been mentioned may have been, for Grattan, the Irish question was Catholic emancipation, a measure which, he was convinced, would contribute to both the peace and prosperity of Ireland and the strength of the Empire. His character and reputation made him an ideal parliamentary crusader for that cause. His name was inseparably associated with an heroic period in Irish parliamentary history. A rhetorician whose fire and wit enlivened debate, he was clearly in earnest and transparently sincere; and the gentlemanly good manners with which he expounded what he obviously believed to be an irresistible case accorded well with what MPs considered to be the best traditions of the House of Commons.

The great speech of May 1805 was the first of eight major speeches on Catholic emancipation which Grattan delivered between then and 1819. Naturally they varied in effectiveness and inevitably were repetitive, though Grattan displayed considerable virtuosity in re-deploying well-worn arguments and in combating boredom by scintillating turns of phrase. He did not dwell at great length on abstract principles. This would scarcely have been a rewarding exercise in the House of Commons. He took for granted that he and his fellow MPs believed in civil and religious liberty. What, he asked the House, had raised England 'to such eminence in the world as that on which she now stands, but this inherent spirit of liberty? Did not Hampden think that a naked freeman was a nobler object than a superb slave?' Other nations, he pointed out to the House, 'in arts which accomplish and grace mankind, excelled you; they danced, they sung'. But England had taken the lead in liberating the human mind: 'the stating courageous truths; the breaking political or metaphysical chains; that was the robust accomplishment of your country'. It was a tragic inconsistency for a country with such an intellectual heritage to impose by law a religion upon a people and not to admit in the case of the Catholic that 'every man has a right of perfect domination over his own thoughts'. Nevertheless, Grattan was prepared to make considerable concessions to pragmatism. He conceded that a state might have 'to limit the political capacity' of some of its citizens if their religious opinions bred disaffection. However, continuing to be pragmatic, he believed he could prove that by the beginning of the nineteenth century there was no good reason why Irish and British Catholics should be excluded from the rights and privileges enjoyed by their fellow subjects.[39]

To the allegation that there were Catholic doctrines – that faith need not be kept with heretics and that the Pope could absolve subjects from their allegiance – which rendered Catholics a danger to civil society, Grattan replied that these doctrines had been repeatedly disavowed by competent Catholic theologians. As for obedience which Catholics owed to the Pope, it could never, he contended, conflict with their allegiance to the Crown. The former could be demanded only in spiritual matters; and the term spiritual, he insisted, was interpreted by modern Catholics in a narrow sense. To take concrete instances, marriage was regarded as a civil contract and excommunication did not carry temporal penalties – in any event if a Catholic considered himself injured in his material concerns by excommunication he could sue for damages. As for the Pope, an 'unhappy old man' dragged to Paris, he was simply 'a sort of president or chairman, in whose name the business of the Catholic church is conducted'. So much for the dreaded power of the papacy.[40] He had a latitudinarian impatience with many of the issues in dispute between the Churches. 'I avoid', he said, 'the dungeon of the theologian, the madhouse of casuistry, the noisy tribe of the sectarians' (he would not, of course, have shown the same airy disregard of constitutional niceties). He believed that the differences between Catholic and Protestant had been intensified by 'bigotry and fanatical zeal' and that a glance at the world showed how little these differences now affected political life. For years during the great French War which began in 1793 Great Britain had been in alliance with Catholic powers, and when peace returned to Europe in 1815 the Catholic Church, Grattan insisted, was one of the principal supports of social order. Both Catholics and Protestants, Grattan explained to the House of Commons in 1819, their former hostilities forgotten, 'are now in a state of mutual defence, each preferring its own establishment, but both concurring to defend the principle of government against the anarchist who should depose the king and the principles of Christianity against the infidel who would depose the Almighty'.[41]

Turning to history, that great arsenal of argument, Grattan emphasized that 'the historian is in the case of Ireland, generally speaking, peculiarly bad authority'. In his opinion, Irish historians, intent on 'private advantage', had devoted themselves to flattering biased partisan readers. The whole story, until Ireland became a nation a generation back, was a melancholy record of conflict and oppression – 'Whenever sects wage their war of persecution against each other, they will proceed to the last extremes of hostility. Theirs is no ordinary or generous warfare' – and he begged his countrymen not to 'go back to the battle of the Boyne'. In Ireland 'oblivion is patriotism'. Nevertheless, on occasion he himself plunged into history, producing an interpretation of events strikingly different to the ultra-Protestant version. A knowledge of medieval history, he pointed out, demonstrated that England's constitutional liberties had been largely won by Catholics. 'What,' Grattan declaimed, 'the authors of Magna Carta enemies to liberty!' The Rebellion of 1641 was not caused by religion but by 'the loss of the graces', the extermination of the Ulster population and by the bigotry and foreign education of the Roman Catholic priesthood. The Catholics had opposed William III in defence of those liberties which had been won in England by the Revolution, and the insurrection of 1798 was far from being a popish rising with tens of thousands of Protestants 'enrolled in rebellion'.[42]

Grattan not only refuted and ridiculed the reasoning behind the disabilities. He dwelt on the damage they were inflicting on Ireland, Anglo-Irish relations and the Empire. They bred bitterness, 'hatred and hostility', they were 'a staminal weakness' accentuating all the ills afflicting Ireland. They deprived the Empire of the full, wholehearted services of a fifth of its population, though Grattan did not fail to emphasize that Catholic loyalty remained to a remarkable extent unimpaired; witness the thousands of Catholics in the army and navy. To Grattan, 'These islands' were 'the ark in the French deluge – in it the living creatures, not yet swallowed up by France, are assembled and you propose, by your penal code, to make them drown one another'. The disabilities were 'a death-doing policy', and if their 'great renowned empire' was ruined its epitaph would be 'England died because she taxed America and disqualified Ireland'. On the other hand, complete emancipation would produce an identification of interests between Catholic and Protestant, would 'unite all in defence and support of privilege which all equally enjoyed' and put an end to 'whatever alienation towards this country [England] that may exist in the minds of the Irish Catholics'. Grattan was confident that the Protestants had nothing to fear from emancipation. The Irish Catholics were not fanatics and did not desire to see their Church dominant in British or Irish life. 'Protection not power', he declared, 'is the request of the Catholics.' 'The great population of the empire, the great property of the empire', he explained, 'is Protestant. This ascendancy the Protestants have a right to possess.' He made the point, too, that since the majority of Irish MPs were returned by the landed interest, after emancipation it was impossible there would be more than thirty Catholics in the House of Commons. In three respects Grattan was undoubtedly an optimist. He thought the penal disabilities would soon be swept away; he was sure that once they were gone there would not be any other obstacle to the development in Ireland of a happy consensus (what he called 'a cordiality of cooperation'); and with the rapid decline in religious animosities which would follow emancipation 'the causes of all the other evils of Ireland would be removed without difficulty'. 'I would recommend', he said, 'to all classes of British subjects, the spirit of concord and mutual charity. Banish from your breasts that fatal principle of exclusion and we may then indeed say, esto perpetua.'[43]

But though he battled for emancipation with skill and unflagging force, he had remarkably little contact with Irish Catholicism. Living in Ireland he must have met a fair number of Catholics at least casually. Occasionally he went to a public dinner at which Catholics were present in force. For instance in 1804 he was entertained at a dinner by the Catholics of County Kilkenny. The other guests were the High Sheriff, the Lord Mayor of the city and the officers of the garrison (one of the toasts being 'Our numerous illustrous admirals and generals'). 'Every one of the company', it was reported, 'loved one another and the good fellows of all religions stuck to the bottle until three in the morning' (the principal guest had probably left earlier). In 1811 he was a steward at a dinner given in London by the Friends of Religious Liberty for the Irish Catholic Delegates. In the following year he spoke at a dinner in Dublin given by the Catholics to the Whig Bishop of Norwich, his speech, in the opinion of an extreme nationalist, being 'as cautious, short and flimsy as usual since he became a British MP'.[44] He also once (and apparently only once) met at a private dinner party his successor as a national leader, Daniel

O'Connell. When O'Connell, as he himself put it, 'was beginning to be talked about', Grattan arranged for one of the O'Conor Don family to invite them to dinner together. Grattan's conversation, O'Connell recalled, 'contained much humour of a dry and theoretical kind and he never relaxed a muscle while his hearers were convulsed with laughter' – which suggests that while he contributed to the gaiety of the evening Grattan avoided an intimate exchange of ideas.[45] Naturally he did not attend the Catholic Committee or Board and his correspondence with the Catholic leadership, if effusive – full of gratitude on their side and goodwill on his – was distant and formal. He readily presented their petitions but made no attempt to share their deliberations. He did not travel much in Ireland; his family circle, including his uncle the Bishop and his brother-in-law the Vicar of Tuam, and all his old friends, were Protestants; and when in later years he made a number of new friends they tended to be broad-minded English Whigs.

Macaulay, referring to Burke's Indian speeches, said they showed that 'India and its inhabitants were not to him, as to most people, mere names and abstractions but a real country and a real people'. In contrast, from Grattan's speeches little can be learned about contemporary Irish Catholicism, its social composition, its religious and intellectual life, its political attitudes. In these orations the Irish Catholics appear typecast, the wronged victims of oppression and the potential beneficiaries of relief, not as members of a vigorous, evolving community, with a complexity of social, economic and geographic divisions, and with a distinctive outlook, moulded by harsh history and influenced by contemporary currents. Rarely in Grattan's emancipation speeches is there a memorable phrase encapsulating an illuminating insight into the life of the large community for whose rights he was striving. Grattan, needless to say, could have replied that Burke, with all his knowledge and perception, had often failed to hold his audience and that he himself was not giving a course of lectures on denominational sociology but trying to persuade MPs to go into the right lobby.

Grattan's lack of rapport with Catholic opinion was strikingly illustrated when the Catholic cause advanced to the point when the conditions on which full relief might be granted began to be discussed. In

every European country the Catholic Church, regarded as being a poten-
tially dangerous competitor with the State, was subject to restraints. Usually the government insisted on making or approving episcopal
appointments and on supervising relations between the local hierarchy
and Rome, sanctioning the publication of papal bulls and briefs. Zealous
churchmen might deplore these infringements on the ecclesiastical
imperium, but the Curia acquiesced and there were Catholic laymen
(including Bourbons and Habsburgs) who were determined to keep the
ecclesiastical power within what they conceived to be rightful and reasonable limits.

In Ireland during the eighteenth century the Catholic Church,
unprivileged and unendowed, was completely independent of the State.
But at the time of the Union Pitt and Castlereagh contemplated combining Catholic emancipation with a Crown veto on episcopal appointments and state stipends for the Catholic clergy – measures which, it was
hoped, would neutralize Catholic hostility to the State and, with the
Presbyterians already receiving a state subsidy, perhaps create a triple
Crown and Church alliance. In 1808 when Grattan and Lord Grenville
were about to ask Parliament to consider petitions from the Irish
Catholic Committee, John Milner, the Vicar Apostolic of the Western
District, a prolix and pugnacious controversialist who enjoyed playing a
part in high politics and who was acting as English agent for the Irish
hierarchy, had a talk with George Ponsonby, who had become the Whig
leader in the House of Commons. It being mentioned that the Irish bishops had been willing in 1799 to accept a Crown veto on episcopal
appointments, Milner expressed the opinion that they might still be prepared to do so. He also, he afterwards asserted, emphasized that he was
not empowered to commit the Irish hierarchy and would not have time
to obtain their views before the petitions were debated.[46] People's memory of a conversation is frequently like the curate's egg, excellent in parts
(participants being particularly impressed by what accords with their
own views). Milner later dwelt on how guarded he had been; Ponsonby
concluded that the Catholic bishops would almost certainly accept the
veto; and Grattan, when asking the House to consider the Irish
Catholics' petition, stated that the Catholics had authorized him to say

that the Crown might exercise a veto over episcopal appointments. 'The two churches', he declared 'will be as one, and the king at the head'.[47] The suggestion of a veto caused a furore in Ireland. There were those Catholics who thought emancipation worth a veto (not necessarily a bad thing in itself), and there were those who were determined that the Irish Catholic Church, a great cohesive force in the lives of its adherents who had stood by it through harsh times, would not fall under the control of Downing Street or Dublin Castle. The Irish Catholic bishops found an adroit formula: it was inexpedient to change the method of episcopal appointments. Expediency, Troy, the Catholic Archbishop of Dublin, explained to Newport, a leading Irish Whig, 'was regulated by variable circumstances'; and Troy, Milner and Moylan, the Catholic Bishop of Cork, when dining at Tinnehinch, assured Grattan that the bishops would have preferred to say nothing on the veto issue but felt 'it was absolutely necessary to resolve something to satisfy the laity'. Grattan simply expressed the hope that the Catholics would remain united. It need scarcely be said that Ponsonby and Grattan, politically embarrassed by the strength of anti-veto feeling, decided to have no further dealing with Milner, who had implied they were 'shameless liars'.[48]

Two years later in 1810, when supporting a Catholic petition in the House of Commons, Grattan implied that the Irish Catholics were ready to accept 'domestic nomination' – that is to say the appointment of their bishops by the cathedral chapters or by the Irish hierarchy. This, he contended, would act as a check upon a foreign, even perhaps a French, appointment of Irish bishops. As a result he was attacked at a meeting of the Catholic Committee by Purcell O'Gorman, who argued that Grattan, 'the idol of my boyish days', should have 'proceeded on a positive and special communication from the committee and not upon the untenable ground of hearsay'. O'Connell immediately intervened as a peacemaker. They must not, he said, forget what Grattan had done for Ireland and that he was 'the Man destined by Providence to sound the trumpet which shall awake her to a glorious Resurrection'.[49] In the following year Grattan had a minor clash with the Catholic activists. In May 1811, when a bill permitting the transfer of Irish militia units to Great Britain was under consideration, a Dublin Catholic meeting agreed to request the House of Commons to insert a clause guaranteeing the right of the Catholic militiamen to the exercise of their religion. Grattan refused to present their petition because it contained a phrase suggesting that a bill was 'a step to root out the Catholic religion'. However, when the bill was being debated he stressed that the religious freedom of the Catholic soldier must be guaranteed.[50]

For some years the question of the terms on which emancipation would be granted remained an academic one. After the defeat of 1808 the Irish Catholics were so discouraged that they did not petition in 1809, and in the three following sessions Grattan failed to persuade the House of Commons to consider the Catholics' claims, but the divisions on his motions show a slight growth in support and towards the close of the session of 1812 Canning, who Grattan pronounced to be 'sincere, brilliant and profound'[51] (there would have been universal agreement on at least the second adjective) carried a motion pledging the House to consider the Catholic question early in the next session. In the debate on Canning's motion Grattan offered the opponents of emancipation a dignified mode of retreat. Time, he pointed out, was 'an essential ingredient in the contest of opinions ... what at one time might appear most chimical, might at another be considered not only possible but politic ... what might have been temerity in one session became wisdom in the other'. Circumstances, he thought, now 'all tended to indicate a wish on the part of the people of England to shake hands with the people of Ireland', and he urged the government 'not to demand any securities but what were necessary and just'. Grattan had grounds for believing that the Irish Catholics would in that case acquiesce – after perhaps some ebullient talk. During the session a deputation from the Catholic Committee had been in London and had met Grattan, Grey and Grenville. Most of the delegates accepted that emancipation must be accompanied by 'an arrangement respecting their bishops' – a policy which it was said was favoured by almost all the Irish Catholic gentry and the bishops themselves – though 'the Dublin orators are hostile to it and keep them all in awe'.[52]

In March 1813 Grattan achieved his greatest parliamentary victory since 1782. His motion that the House should go into committee to consider the laws relating to His Majesty's Roman Catholic subjects was carried by 264 to 224. Grattan's speech on this occasion, if comparatively

speaking low-key, was admirably calculated to gain goodwill in the House
– as well as obviously reflecting his genuine feelings. He began by emphasizing that emancipation for the Catholic must be accompanied by security for the Protestant, speaking of his 'respect and love' for the
Protestant petitioners against Catholic emancipation, mistaken as they
were. He gratified his audience by reminding them that they constituted
not a partisan assembly but an imperial senate able to bring a comprehensive understanding to bear on great issues. He assured the House that
the Catholics were simply seeking to enjoy the full benefits of the British
constitution and he prophesied that emancipation would put an end to
the long conflict between the two islands, uniting all their habitants into
one people.

In March the House of Commons after a long debate resolved that a
Catholic Relief Bill should be prepared by a committee which included
Grattan, Plunket, Ponsonby, Newport Parnell and Maurice Fitzgerald
from Ireland; two distinguished party leaders, Canning and Samuel
Whitbread; and two well-known crusading MPs, Wilberforce and
Romilly. On 30 April Grattan presented a draft bill approved by this committee to the House. It provided that Catholics on taking a prescribed
oath would be eligible for Parliament, for civil and military offices and for
membership of corporate bodies – with relatively few exceptions. For
instance a Catholic could not be Lord Chancellor of England or Ireland
because of the ecclesiastical patronage attached to these offices. The
oath was a lengthy one (amounting to about 700 words); it comprised an
oath of allegiance, a promise to maintain the Protestant succession and
the rights of the Established Churches, a denial that the Pope possessed
any temporal power or jurisdiction in the United Kingdom and had the
right to dispense subjects from their allegiance, and a disavowal of the
opinions that heretics could be persecuted and that an immoral action
could be excused on the grounds it was for the good of the Church. In
addition all Catholic priests were to take an oath binding them not to
elect any person as a bishop whom they did not believe to be of unim-
peachable loyalty. After Grattan had introduced the bill, Canning suggested a number of additional clauses embodying a complex scheme for
imposing a Crown veto on episcopal appointments.

Two commissioners were to be appointed, for Great Britain and Ireland respectively, each composed of Catholic ecclesiastics and Catholic laymen of social standing and substance, within Great Britain a Secretary of State and in Ireland the Chief Secretary. The names of persons selected for Catholic bishoprics were to be submitted to these commissions and, if approved, confirmed by the Crown. Grattan explained that the drafting committee had not included Canning's clauses in the bill because it was not sure that they would prove acceptable to the Catholics. He himself, he said, approved of Canning's scheme. He had already said that he would accept any reasonable securities 'not trenching on the Catholic religion'; he was not 'that fool' who would 'sacrifice emancipation to a punctilo'. Later in the session, when Catholic hostility to the veto arrangements incorporated in the bill was manifesting itself, he declared that the Catholic clergy who opposed Canning's scheme were 'enemies to themselves and to the Catholic community'.[53]

By the middle of May 1813 with the Relief Bill in committee it seemed there was 'nothing for Mr Grattan now to do but march forward to his certain triumph'.[54] But on 24 May Abbot, the Speaker, moved the omission of the clause admitting Catholics to Parliament, and on this destructive amendment being carried by a very narrow majority (251 to 247), the bill was dropped. But a week later Grattan, long accustomed to defeat, gave notice that he would introduce a Catholic Relief Bill early in the following session.

The more aggressive Catholics, though disappointed by the postponement of emancipation, did not regret the loss of a bill that according to Milner, contained 'four or five different sets of galling restrictions so as to constitute a bill of pains and penalties rather than of relief', a bill worthy of Cecil or Robespierre.[55] The British Catholic Board sharply rebuked Milner for his attacks on the bill and thanked Grattan and the other MPs who had drafted the bill for their services. The Irish Catholic Board reacted differently. Though it thanked Grattan, it also by a large majority thanked the Irish Catholic bishops for refusing to accept a bill which, according to Daniel O'Connell, would have permitted 'English' interference in the affairs of the Irish Catholic Church.[56] A couple of weeks later the more politically irreverent Catholics, with O'Connell again well to the fore, impertinently flouted English respectability by holding a meeting of Dublin Catholics to vote an Address to 'an innocent female in a land of strangers', the Princess of Wales, congratulating her on her providential escape from a conspiracy endangering her life and honour. This outburst of noisy partisanship must have annoyed Grattan, who a year later was trying to smooth over the differences between the Prince and Princess of Wales, urging that the financial arrangements made for the Princess should not be regarded as a victory for the wife over the husband.[57]

Grattan was, according to his son, reluctant to agree that emancipation should be accompanied by securities. He tended to trust in goodwill and common sense rather than legal forms. But once he accepted the policy that emancipation should be combined with a measure of state control over the functioning of the Catholic ecclesiastical machinery in Ireland, he embraced it with force, fervour and growing conviction. It was for Parliament, rising above sectional and sectarian considerations, acting 'wisely, liberally, and rationally' and ignoring 'popular clamour', to settle the terms on which emancipation should be granted. Its duty was 'to serve not to satisfy' the Catholics, and as a guide to parliamentary action he drew attention to the fact that in all the great European countries there was 'a certain connexion between the clergy and the government, so as to preclude the danger of foreign influence'. In Ireland, he suggested that the Catholic Church should be incorporated with the State and its clergy paid by the government, so as to give the state an influence over that clergy.[58] An enlightened, generous-minded Irish Protestant, he found it hard to appreciate the significance of the theological objections to the securities and he was irritated by the hands-off-our-Church attitude of the Irish Catholic nationalists. Understandably, he was surprised, disconcerted and pained that the oppressed community which he was so anxious to help would not always accept gratefully and submissively the guidance of their experienced parliamentary advocates, listening instead to the vociferous, aggressive and politically radical elements in their leadership.

The more vigorous and assertive section of the Irish Catholic leadership, fervently nationalist, often radical in temper, deeply attached to their church, and suspicious of the Protestant English state, was bound to be exasperated by the way in which the Catholic cause was handled by peers and MPs who knew little about Catholicism and cared equally little about the niceties of Catholic doctrine and discipline. Moreover it was frustrating for men who were conscious of the growing strength of the Catholic community, highly articulate and dialectally skilled, to be compelled to rely on Grattan and other Protestant liberals to advocate their cause in Parliament. However, they were well aware that if emancipation was to be won they needed persuasive and respected parliamentary advocates. So at the end of October 1813, O'Connell, with the coming session in mind, proposed that the Catholic Board should entrust its petitions to Lord Donoughmore and Grattan. The Catholic Board agreed with this proposal and at the same time directed its secretary, Nicholas Mahon, to arrange for a consultation with Donoughmore and Grattan over a draft Relief Bill prepared by a group of lawyers. Grattan at first agreed to a meeting but Donoughmore, who had been following the Board's debates, concluded, not unreasonably, that he was going to be asked to commit himself to a cut-and-dried plan prepared by a body which claimed to represent the Catholics and which tended to imply that the Catholics were a separate section of the community negotiating with the State. Influenced by Donoughmore's attitude, Grattan refused to accept the draft bill or to take part in 'any proceedings like a dictation to parliament'.[60] The Board tried to soothe Donoughmore and Grattan by explaining that the draft bill was simply an attempt to indicate in concrete terms their wishes and expressing profound regret that Donoughmore and Grattan were constrained by their conceptions of 'parliamentary propriety' to say that they could not receive instructions from the Board. The Board then adopted an intelligent compromise. It decided to 'respectfully submit' to Donoughmore and Grattan suggestions which could be incorporated in a relief bill. Donoughmore replied that he would view the suggestions 'in no other light than the opinions of very respectable individuals'. Grattan, with what an indignant journalist called 'a coolness of insult', wrote that he would consider the suggestions and 'act according to my judgement'. The Board concluded the discussion by transmitting its petitions to Donoughmore and Grattan and resolving that in making the suggestions it was only exercising a legitimate right.[59]

Soon the Board was thoroughly dissatisfied with its parliamentary advocates. Though the petitions were presented no attempt was made to initiate a major debate on the Catholic question. The Board grew impatient and twice politely requested Donoughmore and Grattan 'to exert their great talents', a request backed by an aggregate Catholic meeting at the beginning of June. At this meeting Charles Phillips, a rising young man, eloquent barrister, novelist, romantic poet and coming politician who in his fifties was to subside into being a bankruptcy commissioner, was conspicuous. A fluent, flamboyant orator whose unrestrained rhetoric might not unfairly be characterized as Grattan vulgarized, Phillips sharply criticized his master, reminding Grattan of his famous apothegm that oak would not survive transplantation at fifty.[61] But in spite of prodding from Dublin Grattan abstained from raising the Catholic question during the session of 1814. He probably thought it would be a tactical error to thrust the issue on MPs preoccupied with the great events happening in Europe – the allied invasion of France, the fall of Napoleon and the Congress of Vienna.

While the Irish Catholics were waiting impatiently for Grattan to move into action the Roman Curia intervened briskly and decisively in their affairs. In the spring of 1814 Monsignor Quarantotti issued a prescript expressing approval of the Relief Bill of 1813 and reminding Catholics that it was 'the spirit of this holy and truely divine religion to favour established authority, to strengthen thrones and to make subjects obedient, loyal and devoted to their country'. The violent debate which ensued amongst Irish Catholics accentuated the divisions, temperamental and social as well as doctrinal, already existing in their ranks. The vetoists were encouraged. The anti-vetoists seized the opportunity to show themselves more Catholic than Rome by challenging Quarantotti's powers. O'Connell went further: seeing the veto as a threat to civil liberty, he boldly declared that he would as soon receive his politics from Constantinople as from Rome.[62]

Though the veto controversy was to cripple the Irish Catholics politically for years, they were unanimous in wanting to make a strong push for emancipation in the session of 1815. Towards the close of 1814 the

Catholics of Cork City and County, an energetic group, resolved to entrust their petitions to Donoughmore and Grattan if they agreed to accept the petitioners' instructions. Donoughmore (though an anti-vetoist) was not prepared to sacrifice his independence; Grattan was shocked by the suggestion, 'a proceeding new and extraordinary and of a tendency to create a supposition I could submit my conduct to the direction of any organ'. He took the same attitude when an aggregate meeting offered to entrust him with a petition on behalf of the Catholics of Ireland on the understanding that he would initiate a debate on emancipation: 'my attachment to the claims of the Catholics is known – my constancy on that subject is unquestioned'.[63]

Grattan's aloofness and confidence in his own judgement when it came to deciding on what terms emancipation should be granted and accepted aroused considerable irritation amongst his Irish Catholic clients. At a meeting of the Catholic Board in the middle of February, O'Connell, who had already complained of Grattan's 'inclination to make rhetorical concessions', attacked him severely for ignoring the Board and disregarding the instructions of his constituents. He concluded by declaring that since Grattan had begun to inhale the corrupt air of Westminster he had accomplished nothing worthy of his talents. Phillips, who was in glowing form, was bitterly indignant with Grattan. Referring to the 1813 Bill he exclaimed, 'I would as soon call an attorney's bill a relief bill'. Grattan, he declaimed, 'when the fury of his eloquence inflamed us to madness and the strait waist coat of his Relief Bill was near embracing us to death, jocularly recommended a little moderation'.[64]

Grattan conspicuously displayed his consistency, attachment to the Catholic cause, and detachment from Irish Catholic opinion when on 30 May 1815 Sir Henry Parnell, to whom the Catholics had entrusted their petition, asked the House to go into committee on the Catholic question. Grattan ardently supported the motion but made it clear that he would not agree to unconditional emancipation. His attitude commended itself to a section of the Irish Catholics, which, Grattan emphasized in the House of Commons, included many of 'the highest rank', who in 1816 entrusted him with a petition requesting emancipation 'under such circumstances as will render it satisfactory and unobjection-

able to all classes of men'.[65] At the same time another group, also desig-
nating themselves 'the Catholics of Ireland', entrusted a petition to Parnell asking for unqualified emancipation. With this second petition on
the table it is scarcely surprising that, after a short debate which did not
arouse great interest, Grattan's conciliatory motion that the House
should next session take the Catholic question into consideration was
rejected. Early in 1817 when the Irish Catholic leadership, with the anti-
vetoists predominant, adopted a petition requesting unconditional
emancipation, Grattan was unmoved. He wrote to the General Committee of the Catholics of Ireland saying that it should endeavour to win the
goodwill and affection of Parliament. O'Connell, commenting on the letter, retorted that Mr Grattan should realize that the opinion of the
Catholic people upon the subject of the veto 'remains and ever will
remain unchanged'.[66]

But Grattan was not to be diverted from his moderate and conciliatory policy, and when at the request of the group led by Lord Southwell,
which had produced the 1816 vetoist petition, he raised again the
Catholic question in the House of Commons on 9 May 1817, he emphasized Parliament's right to insist on securities. On this occasion, with 'a
particularly animated and happy'[67] second speech he managed to hold the
attention of an impatient House and his motion that a committee be
appointed to consider the Catholic disabilities, which was supported by
both Canning and Castlereagh, was lost by only 24 votes (245 to 221).
Mackintosh left the House at about three in the morning deeply
depressed by the result and at realizing he had seen 'poor Grattan's last
exhibition of his setting genius and of the gentle goodness which will
glow till the last spark of life shall be extinguished'.[68] Grattan was violently agitated and angered by his defeat. Writing to the Rev. William
Berwick, the Vicar of Leixlip, a keen Whig and a man of letters, he bitterly complained that 'the violence, the bigotry, the clamorous deafness
to argument proclaim the commons of Great Britain lost to all sense of
duty. We shall have no peace in our time, the union exists no longer.' Ireland, he feared, 'will be foolish if England is unjust'. The principal speakers against the motion, Peel and John Leslie Foster, 'ought not to have
the governing of the Isle of Man'. Peel was a green young secretary and

Foster, without heart or head, had a lying tongue. For good measure Grattan denounced Castlereagh for defending the suspension of the Habeas Corpus Act. But a few years later he referred in glowing terms to Peel, speaking of 'the brightness of his talents, the suavity of his manners, the excellence of his character'.[69]

During 1818 the Irish Catholics (perhaps taking to heart Donoughmore's advice not to go into battle until united and ready)[70] did not approach Parliament, but in 1819 the Catholics of a number of parishes scattered throughout Ireland petitioned and on 3 May Grattan moved that the House should go into committee to consider the Catholic disabilities. His speech was long and inaudible but powerful in print, and after the debate ended abruptly owing to several leading debaters reserving their fire until an opponent had spoken, his motion was defeated by only two votes (224 to 222). Though Grattan did not fail to reaffirm his adherence to the policy embodied in the abortive measure of 1813, he was thanked for his exertions by a Dublin Catholic Aggregate Meeting at which O'Connell played a prominent part.[71]

At the close of 1819 the Irish Catholic leadership – by now predominantly anti-vetoist – decided to petition Parliament in the coming session and was glad to know the Catholic cause would be advocated in the House of Commons by Grattan – in O'Connell's phrase, 'that old patriot who had given Ireland all she had and would have made her all she ought to be'.[72] In December three Dublin parishes pressed Grattan to present a Catholic petition and Grattan replied saying he would do so and expected to be successful. His confidence, he explained, was based not only on the merits of the case but on the admirable behaviour of the Catholics in a tense period (1819 had been the year of a violent reform agitation in England, Peterloo and the Six Acts). They had, he pointed out, repudiated with scorn the overtures of 'mischief, folly and infatuation' – a great reform meeting held in July in Smithfield, with 'Orator' Hunt in the chair, had called on the Irish Catholics struggling for emancipation to ally themselves with the radical reformers.[73]

In 1820 the death of George III in January and the ensuing general election postponed the opening of Parliament to the close of April. By then Grattan was definitely in bad health. Although from youth frail-looking, he had always had plenty of energy, fuelled by moral fervour, and in his seventy-third year he had delivered a long parliamentary speech. But from the autumn of 1819 he had intermittently difficulty in breathing and soon he began to suffer from dropsy, his legs swelling. Calmly he faced the inevitable and began deliberately to take leave of life. 'I have lived long enough,' he told his family, 'my friends are dead and I leave the world in a good time, but all your kindness makes me regret it.' In a wheel-chair he went for excursions in the grounds of Tinnehinch, gazing at the views he loved and lingering over the trees he had planted. His old friend Berwick, the Vicar of Leixlip, read prayers to him and administered the sacrament, and other friends of long standing, Plunket, Charles Bushe and Robert Day, visited him. 'Well,' Grattan said, 'I die like a gentleman with all my old and respected friends round me.'

But there was drama as well as dignity in his last days. Physically declining fast, he remained acutely aware of the political scene and there were two subjects on which he was anxious to speak in the House of Commons, Catholic emancipation and parliamentary reform – he wanted, by promoting a moderate Reform Bill, to cut the ground from under the radicals. In late April the medical men he consulted pronounced he might survive a journey to London if he went by slow stages and started soon (they passed sentence, Grattan remarked). After taking a rest early in May he came up to Dublin en route for London. An influential group of Catholic gentlemen who met in Essex Street, on hearing that he intended to travel to London for the purpose of advocating their cause, addressed him, expressing their profound gratitude and their concern for his health. Grattan having intimated in reply that he wished to meet a delegation from the group, six gentlemen, including O'Connell, visited him in St Stephen's Green. The meeting was affecting and short. Grattan, seated, huddled in a blanket, was unable to speak but he presented the group with a note he had already drafted, setting out in decisive terms his views on Catholic policy. The Irish Catholics should strive to maintain a perpetual connection with Great Britain, should keep clear of any movement aiming at universal suffrage and annual parliaments, and should accept emancipation on honourable terms. When the deputation returned to Essex Street, O'Connell, who must have been simmering with indignation, proposed the appointment of a committee to consider an answer to the note. But Shiel, more conservative in outlook, demurred. He argued that the note should be seen as 'a document intended more for posterity than the present generation and indeed in the light of a testamentary bequest of a great patriotic statesman', and O'Connell agreed to withdraw his motion.[74]

On 20 May Grattan sailed from Dublin in the Waterloo steam-packet for Liverpool, which he reached the next day. He then travelled by canal to within forty miles of London, completing the journey by carriage. He arrived at the house he had taken in Baker Street on 31 May determined to get down to the House of Commons – he must have had Chatham's last appearance in the Lords in mind. But he was too exhausted to leave his room. During the following days he saw a few callers, to whom he talked with some vigour, and sent messages of goodwill to Wellesley, the Duke of Norfolk and Castlereagh. On the evening of 4 June, surrounded by his family, he slowly lapsed into unconsciousness and died. On the morning of his death he had agreed with the wishes of a number of his friends, headed by the Duke of Sussex, that he should be buried in the Abbey, and on 16 June his funeral procession assembled in Parliament Street. The pallbearers were two members of the cabinet, Wellington and Harrowby, two Whigs, Norfolk and Holland, three Irish peers, Leinster, Donoughmore and Charlemont, and Leinster's brother, Lord Robert Fitzgerald. They were followed by a large number of peers and MPs, and when the coffin reached the Abbey it was placed in a grave beneath the monument to Grattan's early hero, Chatham. His grave was marked by a stone bearing the single world 'Grattan'.

Ireland also commemorated him. A few weeks after his death two of his friends, Robert Day and Maurice Fitzgerald, the Knights of Kerry, wrote to the press inviting subscriptions for 'a monument of national gratitude to Mr Grattan'.[75] Early in 1826 a statue by Chantrey was placed in the Royal Exchange, Dublin. It strongly expresses Grattan's energy, determination and warm humanity.

Epilogue

Grattan was to be the recipient of many tributes. Three statues – two in Dublin, one in London in St Stephen's Hall in the newly built Houses of Parliament – were erected in his honour. Contemporaries vied in praising him. Grattan, Sidney Smith remarked, believed that the noblest occupation of a man was to make other men happy and free.[1] Grattan's character, Mackintosh wrote, was 'marked by a peculiar benevolence not easily described'.[2] All Grattan's speeches, Coleridge declared, 'possessed that constant accompaniment of true genius, a certain moral bearing, a moral dignity. His love of liberty is $\dot{\alpha}\kappa\alpha\delta\eta\mu\rho\nu$, it has no snatch of the mob in it'.[3] Brougham pronounced that there was no man in politics who had so few faults of character as Grattan and that his eloquence, 'an unceasing flow of profound principles', was of the highest order, its only defect being 'an excess of epigram' (Brougham was, it has been hinted, always generous when assessing a man too old to be a rival).[4] Thomas Moore, a fervid Irish nationalist, very much happily at home in English Whig society, wrote that 'the eloquence of Grattan was the music of Freedom'. Eulogizing Grattan, he declaimed:

> What a union of all the affections and powers
> By which life is exalted, embellished, refined
> Was embraced in that spirit.

And he went on to refer to Grattan's victory in 1782 as

> The one lucid interval snatch'd from the gloom,
> And the madness of ages when filled with his soul,
> A nation o'er leap'd the dark bounds of her doom,
> And for one sacred instant, touch'd Liberty's goal.

Byron sang of

> Ever glorious Grattan the best of the good
> So simple in heart so sublime in the rest
> With all that Demosthenes wanted endued
> And his rival or victor in all he possessed.

And a more consciously aristocratic poet, Yeats, referred with admiration to Grattan, who spoke 'not for the mob that he scorned'.[5]

As this catena demonstrates, Grattan's admirers saw him as a superb artist in words, and a great moral and intellectual force rather than a conventional politician. His family, whose affection and reverence was unbounded, naturally were determined that he should be commemorated by a full biography and definitive edition of his speeches. Two years after his death, Henry Grattan, his younger son, published his father's speeches in four volumes, followed by a volume of his miscellaneous writings (pamphlets, public letters and literary fragments). This was not the first attempt to produce a collection of Grattan's speeches. In 1811 'Honest John Lawless', the Catholic agitator and publicist, published his *The speeches of the Right Honourable Henry Grattan*, vol. 1 (no further volumes appeared), based on 'mouldering newspapers and the widely extended surface of parliamentary debate' (apparently mainly the *Hibernian Magazine* and the *Parliamentary Register*), with a lengthy commentary. Henry Grattan the younger seems to have used newspapers as a basis for the earlier speeches as well as the *Parliamentary Register* and *Hansard*. In his preface he states that many of the speeches were 'revised and noted' by his father, and it has been pointed out that the Lawless and the Henry Grattan versions of some pre-1783 speeches differ, the latter versions being more polished and expressing opinions which Grattan held at the close of his career. For this a simple explanation has been advanced – that Grattan, in leisured and retrospective old age, revised his earlier speeches, improving their style and making skilful insertions which sacrificed reporting accuracy to consistency. On the other hand it should be taken into account that Grattan, although according to his son he seldom wrote out more than the heads of his argument, may at the outset of his parliamentary career, when his technique was developing, have written out important passages in full. Also, when consulted by his son he may have recalled some premeditated phrases which in the heat and haste of debate he had failed to use but wished posterity to appreciate.[6]

About the time he published his father's speeches Henry Grattan began to collect material for a biography, and in 1826 he contemplated entrusting its preparation to Thomas Moore, who had just published his successful life of Sheridan. Moore greatly admired Grattan, knew Ireland well, was in touch with political life through his many Whig friends, had a flair for collecting anecdotal material and wrote with ease and assurance. But he was disappointed by the memoranda which he was shown by Henry Grattan – 'almost all in his own handwriting, little of his father's ... Even the conversation of the father comes all darkened and diluted through the medium of the son's memory and taste'.[7] Moore in the end dropped the project and ultimately Henry Grattan tackled the task himself, producing a biography of his father in five volumes which appeared between 1839 and 1846. Filial affection, the younger Henry Grattan's principal qualification, unfortunately does not guarantee biographical expertise. Written in a style which managed to be both stilted and inflated, the *Life and Times* was a diffuse, badly proportioned work in which the account of Henry Grattan's career was frequently disrupted by the insertion of unwieldy chunks of general history. Politically vehement, and, as he himself put it, boiling with indignation at the ills inflicted on Ireland, he viewed his father's career as an unmitigated struggle of right against wrong and castigated his opponents not only for being politically mistaken but as steeped in moral obloquy. However, he deserves credit for printing a number of his father's letters and for preserving a considerable amount of family tradition and political anecdote.

Undistinguished as literature and with its impact diminished by its appearance over six years, the *Life and Times* aroused little comment, although later writers on the period were to quarry vigorously from its pages. Shortly before the appearance of its first volume a reassessment of Grattan appeared in the *Dublin University Magazine*, the organ of bold, intelligent, hard-hitting Irish Conservatism. Fervently Unionist and Protestant, the magazine was eager to become a focus for Irish intellectual life and to remind Irishmen of what the magazine regarded as their distinctive cultural heritage. In the middle thirties it began the publication of its 'gallery of illustrious Irishmen', Henry Grattan (sandwiched between Goldsmith and Berkeley) being second in the series. At the beginning of the article on Grattan it was stated that the authors of the series did not intend 'to mix in the strife of party', but it is hard to believe that the writer of the essay on Grattan, Samuel O'Sullivan, imagined himself to be completely detached from contemporary political controversy. At the outset he emphasized Grattan's integrity, industry and single-mindedness (which at times led him to attach undue importance to his objectives and to view 'this country as the centre round which British interests should revolve'). The essayist then expressed great admiration for Grattan's 'magical' oratory, quoting lavishly from his speeches, including the 1788 speech on tithes, 'glowing, impassionate, energetic and refined ... abounding in specious generalities'. But Grattan unfortunately was too inclined to theorize; and when he descended to the practical level he allowed his policy to be shaped by 'passion and sentiment'. His inability to grasp political realities was illustrated by his belief that after 1782 an independent country 'could be restrained within the bounds of moderation', and his lack of foresight was shown by his failure to perceive that from the early nineteenth century the Irish Catholics were becoming an ambitious political faction. Nothing, the essayist sadly added, 'leads us to believe that he set a due value upon the Christian religion'. The article concluded by stressing that at times Grattan was 'sublimely

apprehensive of truths which the mere dialectician could never arrive at'
and consequently was capable of breaking with his party when 'enlightened policy' required him to do so – for instance in 1807 over the Insurrection Act and in 1815 over the war. Indeed, 'had he lived to this our day
he would now be reckoned amongst the staunchest conservatives in the
empire'.[8]

Nationalists did not accept this interpretation of Grattan's outlook.
O'Connell, the outstanding nationalist leader in the years following Grattan's death, although he spoke of years between 1782 and 1798 as 'a halcyon period – an oasis in the desert of Irish history', rarely referred to
Grattan. They agreed on some issues but the hero of the Catholic masses
and the polished parliamentary orator belonged not only to different
generations but represented very different traditions. However, a highly
articulate section of O'Connell's supporters, the Young Irelanders, who
reluctantly accepted that O'Connell could on occasion be narrow and
vulgar, saw in Grattan a politician whom they could wholeheartedly
admire. Thomas Davis praised Grattan's zeal for liberty and for Ireland,
his 'divine protest' against religious ascendancy, his use of history – 'a
statesman's, not an antiquarian's'. Unfortunately he did not realize that
the consititution of 1782 could only be preserved by an armed force, the
Volunteers. No writer in the English language except Shakespeare, Davis
declared, possessed 'such a sublime and suggestive diction' as Grattan,
and his speeches 'the finest specimens of imaginative eloquence in the
English or any other language', were, Davis insisted, 'a fit handbook for
an Irishman', though he warned his readers that they must not attempt
to imitate Grattan's style.[9]

Davis did not examine closely Grattan's views on Anglo-Irish relations and Irish culture (on neither subject did they coincide with his
own). But one of Davis's literary collaborators, Daniel Owen Madden,
produced a long, carefully considered essay on Grattan, which he first
published in 1846, reprinting it in 1853 as a preface to Madden's edition
of Grattan's speeches. Madden, a contributor to the *Nation* and to London conservative newspapers, and the author of several works on contemporary history as well as a novel, *Wynville or clubs and coteries*, dealing
with the adventures of well-born youth in fashionable London, was fas-

223

cinated by Grattan as both a thinker and a man of action. He admired Grattan's 'vigour of will' and his physical courage – only too readily displayed. Grattan, 'the first great representative of Irish eloquence', not only invented a style to which 'the moral temperament' of his country responded, but by fusing oratorical energy with philosophical thinking he appealed to the 'higher tribunal of the thoughtful few'. 'If he was an Irish genius', Madden declared, 'he had given his mind a European education and amongst his contemporaries he ranked next to Burke, in knowledge of the speculative writers who have treated of Man in Society'.

To Grattan Irish liberty was 'a subject of sublime moral emotion'. He would have had Irish manners, Irish literature and Irish art, though in the political sphere he wanted Ireland to remain linked to Great Britain. Madden might have found it hard to prove that Grattan had been eager to encourage the development of a distinctive Irish culture. In any event he was sure Grattan's political ideals, 'the phantoms of a poetical fantasy kindled by a patriotic heart', differed sharply from the clear-cut policies of Tone and Castlereagh. Grattan's weakness as a politician, Madden argued, was that he was utterly mistaken on the nature of political power. He confounded fame with authority and celebrity with influence. The champion of Irish parliamentary independence, he ignored the composition of the House of Commons, and in the 1783–5 struggle over parliamentary reform between the Protestant aristocracy and the Protestant democracy he remained neutral. If he had joined the reformers or the government 'he would have clothed himself with that power which was denied him in his isolated position'. In short, Grattan's legacy was moral and intellectual, not a series of lessons in practical politics.

Another journalist strongly influenced by Young Ireland, Alexander Martin Sullivan, editor of the *Nation* and the *Weekly News*, was also fascinated by Grattan. Sullivan, warmhearted and emotional, a vivid writer and speaker, was a passionate nationalist, sitting in the House of Commons from 1874 as a Home Rule MP. He fervently advocated peace, goodwill and union amongst Irishmen, to be attained, he apparently assumed, by his opponents coming round to his own point of view. To Sullivan, Grattan, a man of genius, upright and tolerant, a Protestant patriot, was a public figure whom all Irishmen could admire; and Sullivan hoped that a study of Grattan's career and ideals would inevitably induce Irish Protestant Unionists to reconsider their attitude to Home Rule. In the early sixties he was presented with an opportunity for dramatically expressing his reverence for Grattan. In 1862, shortly after the Prince Consort's death there was a movement to erect a memorial to him in Dublin, and at the beginning of 1864 the Corporation was asked to grant a site in College Green between the statue of William III and the College for the memorial. Sullivan immediately informed the Corporation that a committee of gentlemen had been constituted with the object of erecting a statue to Grattan 'to stand at the threshold of the ancient state house'. His fellow-countrymen had granted him 'a territorial estate' worth £100,000; would the citizens of Dublin grudge him twenty square feet? After a sharp debate, in which it was pointed out that the suggestion that there should be a second Grattan statue in Dublin had only been made after the memorial to the Prince Consort had been proposed, the Corporation decided by 32 to 14 to grant the College Green site for the Prince's statue.

Sullivan and his supporters arranged for a protest meeting to be held in the Rotunda. The extreme nationalists attended in force, proclaimed their contempt for moderates, such as Sullivan, posing as patriots, and stormed the platform. A few days later Sullivan held another Rotunda meeting, with admission strictly controlled and the platform barricaded, which asked the Corporation to rescind its decision. The Corporation compromised by referring the question back to a committee. The supporters of the Prince Consort memorial were by now not very happy about the College Green site. Traffic was very congested in the Green; the base of the statue would, it was said, become 'a lounging place' for cabmen and news vendors and the statue itself could become a focal point for political demonstrations. Fortunately a suitable alternative site was available. The Council of the Royal Dublin Society were anxious that the memorial to a Prince so interested in industry and the arts should be placed on the lawn behind the Society's house in Kildare Street. The Queen approved the site and the Prince Consort memorial, one of Foley's finest compositions, was erected there, well protected from the patriotic vandalism which has destroyed several Dublin statues.[10]

The proposal for a Grattan statue having blocked the erection of a Prince Consort memorial in College Green, nothing more was heard of it for some years. But at the close of the sixties Sullivan revived the project. When in 1867 three Irishmen were executed for the murder of a policeman in Manchester, Sullivan, though as a constitutional nationalist he disapproved of the means and to some extent of the objectives of the Fenians, published articles in which he referred to 'the hidious act which blotted out the three Irish patriots'.[11] He was sentenced to six months' imprisonment for seditious libel; his friends presented him with three hundred pounds as a testimonial and this windfall he earmarked as the first subscription to a fund for erecting a Grattan statue, a project which he hoped would be supported by the Irish nation 'without discrimination of class, creed or party'.

The scheme secured widespread support, the committee including two liberal and two conservative MPs, the Lord Chancellor (a Conservative), two ex-Lord Chancellors (a liberal and a conservative) and an ex-Attorney General.[12] The statue, executed by Foley and placed in College Green, represented Grattan with 'sharp, stern features, lightened by passion', standing with his right arm extended in a grand oratorical gesture. When it was unveiled on 6 January 1876 by Lady Laura Grattan, Grattan's daughter-in-law, respectable Dublin was well represented on the platform and an enormous crowd filled the green. A few banners bearing the slogan 'Release the prisoners' (the Fenian prisoners) were a reminder of the strong, rough currents flowing under the surface of Irish constitutional politics, but they were scarcely noticed in the vast crowd. The speakers were Edward Gibson (later Lord Ashbourne), a Conservative, and three Home Rule MPs, Isaac Butt, Mitchel Henry and Sullivan. Controversy was sedulously avoided, the speakers dwelling on Grattan's eloquence, integrity and patriotism. For a moment it seemed as if Mitchel Henry, when he spoke of Grattan coming down from his sick-bed to the House of Commons to oppose the Union, was going to launch into contemporary politics. But 'so as not to mar the harmony of the day' he checked himself in time (ironically enough ten years later Henry was to vote against Gladstone's Home Rule Bill). In the evening Butt and Sullivan 'made up for the restraint' they had imposed on themselves at a 'Grattan

dinner' given by the Home Rule League, Sullivan declaring that earlier in
the day they had seen 'a prefiguration' of the restoration of the Irish Parliament.[13] All in all the proceedings illustrated very well the outlook of
the Irish Victorian upper and middle classes. They respected religious
toleration, oratorical prowess, political moderation and gentlemanliness
– an Irish lawyer with literary proclivities suggested that Grattan was a
political Colonel Newcome.[14]

Moreover, by the middle of the nineteenth century many Irishmen,
conscious they were living in a sober, serious, vigorous, industrious era,
began to look back nostalgically to the previous century as an age when
Irish society seemed to have been unusually buoyant, witty, convivial, and
occasionally entertainingly eccentric, with style in its bearing and its
buildings. Politics, the struggle against the Penal Laws, the Wild Geese,
the Volunteers, the parliamentary battles and crises, the Insurrection of
1798, were shot through with drama and the whole age closed with a
striking Götterdämmerung, the Union. This approach is vividly conveyed in a short essay by Charles Lever, who, with Jonah Barrington, was
largely responsible for creating the popular conception of the Irish eighteenth century. It is entitled, 'Be always ready with the pistol', an admo-
nition which Lever says was amongst the last words of Henry Grattan.
Though Lever is thankful that the bully and fire-eater have been driven
out of society and disavows any wish to revive the duel, he sighs for the
days when proven courage was deemed to be an essential part of a gentleman's nature. 'Rude as this chivalry was it reacted most favourably on
manners.' Bitterness rarely survived a 'meeting' and the good-fellowship
characteristic of the day sprang from the respect brave men had for one
another. Even a man such as Grattan, Lever points out, gentle and persuasive, with 'a high intellect' and 'the vigour and energy of a lion', was
ready to show that he was not deficient in 'whatever constitutes the
strength of an inferior order of men'.[15]

On a more serious level, as the great Home Rule controversy developed it seemed that eighteenth-century Ireland might afford some useful guidance in constitutional politics. Gladstone, when moving the
second reading of his first Home Rule Bill, quoted with respect Grattan,
the statesman who believed that imperial unity and diversity of legisla-

tion could be reconciled. (In reply Hartington pointed out that Grattan's parliament was 'a Protestant parliament in which the landlords were supreme' and that if Grattan had been present he would be one of the first to attack the bill.)[16] But though Grattan's parliament was frequently alluded to, Isaac Butt, the founder of the Home Rule movement, and Parnell (who unlike most Irish politicians rarely resorted to history) made it clear that they much preferred a federal solution to the 1782 settlement – Butt, both as a Unionist in the forties and as a Home Ruler thirty years later poured scorn on the adjustment of Anglo-Irish constitutional relations arrived at in 1782.

During the Home Rule debate two eminent Victorian historians, Froude and Lecky, trying to explain the Irish problem in the light of the past, devoted considerable attention to Grattan. Froude, who regarded Roman Catholicism as the enemy of liberty and progress and who was not an admirer of democracy, was a severe critic of Grattan and much of what he stood for, believing that those groups which were best fitted to rule should assume the responsibilities of government. He approved of a state paternalism which aimed at securing social justice and he emphatically asserted that property, especially landed property, had duties which outweighed its rights.[17] Naturally he was influenced by these presuppositions when in the early 1870s he tried to make a contribution to the solution of the Irish question by placing it in its historical perspective. Surveying the melancholy course of Irish history, he was driven to angry despair. The Celts were by nature anarchic. The Normans, who should have imposed law and order on the island, were either absorbed by the natives or adopted some of their worst habits. When in the sixteenth and seventeenth centuries England took the sensible course of building up a Protestant settlement through which Ireland could be governed, the fatal atmosphere of Ireland, in which common sense melted, helped to wreck the plan.[18] England's short-sighted, selfish commercial policy hindered the colony's economic development and infuriated the colonists, turning them during the eighteenth century into Irish nationalists. The Protestant ruling world neglected its duties. It did little to evangelize the Irish Catholic masses, it harassed its fellow-Protestants, the Ulster Presbyterians, and took full advantage of its politically privileged position to plunder the public. The Protestant landlords, intent on squeezing as much as possible out of their miserable tenancy, did little to improve their estates. Many were absentees; those who remained in Ireland were, generally speaking, idle, extravagant and reckless. In short, a ruling race degenerated into 'the politicians of 1782 and the heroes of the memoirs of Sir Jonah Barrington'. England, Froude concluded, should not have forced on Ireland 'a landed gentry of alien blood'. Rather she should have governed Ireland as she did India, giving Ireland 'firm, imperial, peremptory government'.[19]

Grattan, the hero and leader of Protestant Ireland, exemplified much of what Froude deplored. Admittedly Grattan was incorruptible – and so unique amongst Irish patriots – and he was a brilliant rhetorician. 'To bid Grattan to cease his oratory was to bid him to cease to be, for there was nothing else which he could do.' But Grattan misunderstood Ireland. Realizing that an Irish nationalism which excluded the bulk of the population was an absurdity, he thought of the Catholics as cowed, 'cringing before Protestant squires', full of docile affection and ready to respond to concession. In fact, according to Froude, the great bulk of the Catholics had one aspiration, separation from England. Incredibly, Grattan believed that out of the motley and discordant elements which formed the population of Ireland he could create a united, noble, self-reliant people, and that liberty, 'like the spell of an enchanter could form a legislature of pure and high-minded statesmen of the peers and MPs with whom he was familiar'.[20] Lack of comprehension meant wrongly directed effort. Instead of clamouring for independence and nourishing Irish vanity by his bombast, Grattan, Froude declared, should have tried to reform the Irish landed gentry, for instance by heavily penalizing absenteeism. But instilling a sense of duty into the eighteenth-century Irish landed world would have been work for a very Hercules' and Grattan had a very good reason for not embarking on this labour – the landed gentry provided 'the wildly disordered elements' which supported him in his campaign for 'renovating an Irish nationality'.[21]

Lecky's judicial tone, his dispassionate lucidity, contrasts strikingly with Froude's avowed and vehement partisanship, though Lecky too was keenly interested in politics and inevitably biased at times by political feeling. At the beginning of the sixties he made it clear in his *Leaders of Public Opinion in Ireland*, published in 1861 when he was twenty-three, that he regarded Grattan as the embodiment of the ideals he wished to see prevalent in Ireland. This work consisted of four studies of outstanding Irishmen – Swift, Flood, Grattan and O'Connell – and a long essay on clerical influences in Ireland. The aim of the work was twofold: to show how history had shaped present-day Ireland – 'A nation is always the creature of its past' – and to diagnose and suggest a cure for the Irish 'disease', which was manifesting itself in two forms – the intense aversion shown by the mass of the Irish people for everything English, and the sectarianism which bitterly divided Irish society.[22] Lecky, an intellectually fastidious young man, convinced of the profound importance of religion if hesitant in his beliefs, found the strident denominationalism which pervaded Irish life extremely distasteful. Irish Catholicism was strongly ultramontane, Irish Protestantism fervently evangelical. Every issue was liable to become impregnated by *odium theologicum*, polemics filled the press, the adherents of the contending faiths jostled one another in competition for power and place, and, while Irish Catholics displayed an unreasoning hostility to England, Irish Protestants were contemptuous of everything Irish. All this, Lecky thought, was largely due to the Union. The abolition of the Irish Parliament, on which the political life of the country centred, had left a vacuum which sectarianism had filled, and the long post-Union struggle over Catholic emancipation had stimulated religious rancour. The remedy, he believed, was the secularization of Irish politics.[23] The force which would accomplish this was Irish nationalism, uniting patriotic, public-spirited men in purely political activity. For the effectual expression of their feelings such men required a representative assembly. The imperial Parliament had failed to win the loyalty and affection of the bulk of the Irish people, so what was needed, Lecky implied rather than asserted, was an Irish legislative assembly. In what has just been said Lecky seems to be reiterating the creed professed by the United Irishmen and Young Irelanders. But he was not an orthodox Irish nationalist. Although he recognized the strength of nationalist feeling he considered that Ireland must remain closely connected with Great Britain. 'The two nations', he wrote, 'seem naturally designed for each other and each without the other is imperfect.' Fortunately, from the close of the seventeenth century, 'a few transcendent intellects' in Ireland had been striving to reconcile 'nationality with loyalty'; Swift and Flood had been pioneers in the endeavour and their labours had come to fruition with Grattan's victory in 1782.[24] Alas, with the Union Irish opinion, or at least the opinion of that great mass of the Irish people led by O'Connell, had become more narrow, sectarian and democratic. The last decades of the eighteenth century, the age of Irish parliamentary independence, was 'the one bright period there is in a history which is covered like the prophet's roll with lamentations'. It was the time when Grattan, eloquent, generous, profound, was striving to maintain both the rights of the Irish Parliament and the British connection and was making a sustained effort to unite Catholic and Protestant in a common patriotism. Lecky concluded his book by declaring that 'the mantle of Grattan is not destined to be for ever unclaimed'.[25]

Lecky's depressing assessment of contemporary Irish intellectual life was confirmed by the fate of his book. Brilliantly written, provocative but level-headed, combining historical awareness with incisive political comment, it 'fell absolutely dead', selling about thirty copies. After a long continental excursion Lecky settled in London and in 1865 published a major work, *The Rise and Influence of the Spirit of Rationalism in Europe*. He was, however, an Irish landlord and remained very interested in Irish affairs, which 'had so deeply coloured my ways of thinking',[26] and in 1871 when the Home Rule movement was gathering momentum and Gladstone was attempting for the first time to solve the Irish question, Lecky brought out a second and revised edition of *Leaders of Public Opinion*. He omitted the chapter on clerical influences, incorporating some of its contents elsewhere in the work, and he considerably enlarged the essay on Grattan, adding a long exposition of the 'scandalous methods employed to force through the Union'. The Union was, he pronounced 'not only a great crime but a great blunder'. Pitt's timing was bad – he was too precipitant. The Irish Parliament, bound to be reformed in the early nineteenth century, would have increasingly realized that it was in an intolerable position, with all imperial questions being 'necessarily' settled at Westminster. The inevitable result could have been a federal union, with the Irish Parliament accepting that it should be responsible only for local matters. Therefore Grattan's attitude in 1800 was the right one. Unfortunately, Lecky had to admit, by 1870, that a federal solution was not feasible. The lower orders in Ireland were permeated by 'a malignant type of disloyalty'; there was an unhappy schism between landlords and tenants and it was by no means certain that Irish opinion would be directed by men of property and intelligence who recognized the value of the British connection. Therefore, although he remained well aware of 'the evil consequences of disregarding the sentiment of nationality', Lecky insisted that 'the craving of Irish national feeling', for safety's sake, should be permitted to express itself only through a slow and cautious extension of the powers of local authorities such as the Poor Law guardians.[27]

By the time the great battle over the government of Ireland began in 1886, Lecky had become firmly opposed to Home Rule, which in his opinion was associated with agrarian robbery, intimidation and handing over the control of Irish affairs to those who could win the votes of an ignorant democracy. Campaigning as a Unionist, he was understandably irritated when his opponents quoted from *Leaders of Public Opinion* what he characterized as some of the worst specimens of his 'boyish rhetoric', and in 1903 he produced a new, much revised, edition of that work. The essay on Grattan was greatly expanded so that it became a judicious survey of Irish politics at the close of the eighteenth century, with loss of warmth and concentrated drive. Grattan's career was handled more critically. Lecky explains at length why the settlement of 1782 would have required supplementary legislation if it was to provide a permanent settlement for Anglo-Irish relations; Grattan's 1797 letter to the citizens of Dublin in which he vehemently denounced the British and Irish administrations, is declared to be 'one of his most questionable performances'; and to the account of Grattan's last days it was significantly added that 'he spoke with especial kindness of Castlereagh'. Lecky now drove home to his readers that for Grattan the Irish Parliament was not only the organ through which 'a strong, hearty national feeling' expressed itself but was also 'an instrument for keeping the government of Ireland in the hands of the Irish gentry', adding for good measure that 'the worst result of the Union has been that it has dragged Ireland into a plane of democracy for which it is utterly and manifestly unfit'.[28] Lecky was exasperated by the lack of historical sense shown by those controversialists who professed to see a close analogy between the eighteenth-century Irish Parliament and the proposed Home Rule Irish legislature, which he was sure would be dominated by disloyal men who hated the Empire and were contemptuous of 'the conditions on which the security of property must rest'. The nineteenth-century equivalent of the Irish Parliament in which Grattan had distinguished himself was the Church of Ireland General Synod.[29]

During the period when Home Rule was a major issue in British politics two lesser but highly competent historians, Robert Dunlop and Alfred Zimmern, published short, readable biographies of Grattan. Dunlop, who boldly stated that historically speaking 'Ireland is to me as ancient Egypt',[30] in 1889 brought out a straightforward account of Grattan's career. He greatly admired his character but regretted that in 1782 he had accepted a settlement which left the Irish executive under British control and that between 1783 and 1785 he had failed to support the cause of parliamentary reform. In 1902 Zimmern, a brilliant young Oxford graduate, published the essay on Grattan for which he had been awarded the Stanhope Prize. Zimmern found Grattan charming as a man but with serious weaknesses as a politician. He admired Grattan's integrity, generosity of spirit and (up to a point) his eloquence. His speeches, he pronounced, were well composed with a touch of philosophical imagination. But his intellect was not of the highest order (Zimmern was a Wykehamist) and he lacked the strong will and powerful personality of a great national leader. The settlement of 1782, which Grattan so ardently defended, had two obvious defects. The Irish executive was still dominated by Great Britain and the terms on which Great Britain and Ireland were to cooperate were not precisely formulated. The latter defect, Zimmern was convinced, reflected Grattan's failure to grasp the real significance of Irish nationalism. Undoubtedly there was in Ireland from the middle of the eighteenth century a strong and growing sense of nationhood. But this feeling did not necessarily express itself through the making of political demands. What Irishmen wanted at the beginning of the twentieth century was not, Zimmern argued, 'selfish power but opportunities for service, not the chief seats in a petty kingdom but fellowship in the society of imperial workers'. Ireland had much to gain and little to lose by a close association with Great Britain – an association which would not be incompatible with local self-government. It was a tragedy that Grattan believed and proclaimed that Ireland's national aspirations could only be met by complete, or almost complete, political independence. It was a policy which was bound to create tension between Ireland and Great Britain, and, paradoxically enough, Grattan could think it feasible only because he was both 'a thorough Irishman in sentiment' and 'a thorough Englishman in politics'.[31]

It is clear that Zimmern, when he was writing about Grattan, had already developed the ideas which were to influence him as a publicist during the ensuing half century. He respected, even admired, nationalism, a powerful and often beneficent force, binding men together in the pursuit of high ideals. But he did not believe that nationality and citizenship should necessarily coincide. Indeed, he considered the state which found room within its boundaries for all sorts or communities and nationalities preferable to the nation-state.[32] Englishmen, Scotsmen and Welshmen, although they prided themselves on their distinctive characteristics, happily shared the political life of the United Kingdom. And, had it not been for some unfortunate mistakes (for instance the Cromwellian Settlement), Irishmen, Zimmern sadly reflected, might also have done so. For Zimmern, far-flung associations of autonomous or semi-autonomous communities – the Athenian Empire, whose watchword was freedom, and the British Commonwealth, 'a partnership of many societies', all believing in political Liberty – were of inestimable value.[33] Grattan, proud to be a member of the British Empire, would probably have agreed with him.

But in Ireland from the beginning of the twentieth century, that section of nationalist opinion which fervently maintained that if Ireland was to preserve its culture, ideals and way of life, it must become a free and unfettered sovereign state, was gaining confidence and mustering support. With the collapse of the Home Rule movement and the lack of warm enthusiasm for the Commonwealth connection displayed even by supporters of the Free-State constitution of 1922, Grattan's stock was bound to fall. The founder of Sinn Féin, Arthur Griffith, dismissed him as an incompetent politician if a sincere patriot, a man whose favourite occupation was making eloquent speeches;[34] Pearse, understandably, did not include him amongst 'the moderns who have developed the conception of an Irish nation'; and de Valera, though he referred to Grattan as one of the most eloquent orators of his time, rather qualified the compliment by adding that Anglo-Irish literature was far less characteristic of the nation than that produced in the Irish language.[35] However, the year before the constitution of 1937 declared Ireland to be 'a sovereign, independent, democratic state', a writer in the republican tradition, Roger McHugh, published a compact, lively, fast-moving account of Grattan's career. Passing lightly over Grattan's loyalty to 'the English king' and not dwelling at much length on his conservatism, although admitting that he was decidedly not a separatist, MacHugh emphasized that Grattan had made an outstanding contribution to three great movements in Irish life: the agitation for Catholic emancipation, the constitutional movement for Home Rule and the Irish republican movement. To the first he gave 'political aim and direction'; to the second he supplied 'formulation and tradition'; and the crippling of his constitution of 1782 by 'forces which still operate in the north-east corner of Ireland' provided a republicanism with a powerful impetus. Both Parnell and Pearse, McHugh wrote, would have recognized Grattan as 'a man whose ways might not be theirs ... but whose work had become part of Ireland'.[36]

Three years after the appearance of McHugh's book, a representative of another school of Irish nationalism, Stephen Gwynn, published *Henry Grattan and his Times*, largely based on previously untapped newspaper and manuscript sources. Gwynn was an accomplished man of letters, a poet, a critic, a biographer and an essayist who wrote gracefully on travel, wine and mankind. Although his maternal grandfather was William Smith O'Brien, the gentlemanly rebel of 1848, most of his relations were Unionists – like Grattan he was of Church of Ireland clerical stock – and Gwynn himself took little interest in Irish politics until his late thirties. But in 1906 he was elected nationalist MP for Galway city, holding the seat until 1918 – 'a pleasantly diversifying experience for a literary man'.[37]

For Gwynn, Home Rule was not a *pis aller* or merely a stage in Ireland's advance to complete independence but a satisfactory solution of the Irish question. He had a profound affection for Ireland, 'sane and friendly, loving and lovable,'[38] but for many years he lived and worked happily in England. In 1919 he published one of the best Irish political biographies, *The Last Years of John Redmond*. It was the story of a political tragedy, the failure of a kindly and intelligent man, tolerant but with strong convictions, to impose what he regarded as a sensible solution on conflicting parties, Ulster Unionists and Sinn Féiners, who also had firmly fixed convictions. Twenty years later Gwynn produced another study of political failure, his perceptive life of Grattan. He dwelt on Grattan's sensitivity, on his superb advocacy of Irish parliamentary independence and on his long-sustained struggle for Catholic emancipation – Grattan being, Gwynn was quick to point out, 'attached more to national unity than to national distinctness'. Grattan expressed 'the poetry of politics', and 'the waves of emotion which he launched into atmosphere' had lasted for three or four generations. Surveying Grattan's career in the light of recent history, Gwynn was sure he would have been pleased to see Ireland again self-governing, even if divided. But he would regret that so far as the south was concerned 'the connection with the British crown has been deliberately loosened' and that over three quarters of the island the gentry were excluded from political life. In fact, Gwynn suggested, Grattan might have found himself more at home at Stormont rather than in Dáil Éireann. After all, the Parliament of Northern Ireland included a number of members whose ancestors had sat in the eighteenth-century Irish Parliament or been prominent in the Volunteer movement.

Grattan fascinated and baffled both posterity and his contemporaries. A man of integrity, intellect and charm, progressively minded with conservative loyalties, combining fervent rhetoric with moderate opinions, he was difficult to categorize politically. Outstanding as an orator in a highly oratorical age, aloof, independent and idiosyncratic, he was a conspicuous, admired and sometimes an influential actor on the parliamentary scene for forty-five years. It is easy to argue that in the short term at least, Grattan was a brilliant failure. A severe critic could emphasize how little he accomplished during his forty-five years in politics. His major achievement, the assertion of Irish legislative independence, was, after eighteen years, relegated to being a constitutional museum piece. The cause of which he was the outstanding parliamentary advocate, Catholic emancipation, did not triumph until some years after his death, and its success was associated with the emergence of tendencies in Irish life with which he would have been out of sympathy. His contributions to the statute book were few and ephemeral and he certainly was not an administrator. For only a few very short periods was he in close and constant touch with the administration of the day. Finally, most of his major interventions in debate, might be dismissed in Bosquet's phrase – 'c'est magnifique mais ne pas la guerre'.

However, on the credit side it should be taken into account that with his speeches widely reported and reprinted he must have contributed to the triumph of liberalism in the nineteenth century. For Englishmen, these speeches were splendid declamations, treating of issues – retrenchment, reform, religious and civil liberty and the reasonable claims of Ireland – which by the middle of the century seemed well on their way to being settled. Irish nationalists – repealers, federalists, Home Rulers – found Grattan inspiring and instructive. His denunciations of British politicians for mishandling Irish questions, his assertion of Ireland's claims and his belief in Ireland's future all accorded with nationalist orthodoxy. But when considering the views enunciated by Grattan on Anglo-Irish relations, it scarcely needs to be said that he was a hard-hitting parliamentary debater, who often expressed himself with a rhetorical excessive of emphasis; and his fundamental principles, as well as his temperament, set a boundary to his nationalism. He profoundly believed that Great Britain and Ireland shared common constitutional ideals and a common culture – he was soaked in English literature and greatly enjoyed sparkling and intellecually vigorous English society – and he envisaged both countries as tightly linked in an enduring political partnership at the centre of the Empire.

Notes

CHAPTER I

1. *Cal.S.P.Ire.*, *1509-73*, 125; *Cal.S.P.Com.*, *1533*, 82, 178, 266; *Cal.Carew MSS*, *1513-74*, 162.
2. J.B. Leslie, *Derry Clergy and Parishes* (1937).
3. H.B. Swanzy, 'Militia Commissions for the Country of Cavan', *Notes and Queries*, cxlvi, 465.
4. For the date of the marriage, see Langdale MSS, 39/4, 39/44.
5. *The History of Parliament: the House of Commons 1660-1690*, ed. B.D. Henning, iii (1983), 212.
6. *H.M.C. Ormonde MSS*, 14th report, pt 7, 356; *H.M.C. (Ormonde MSS)*, N.S., v, 223.
7. *Charge of the Rt Hon. Thomas Marlay ...* (1749); *Hibernian Magazine* (1771), 442-3; F.E. Ball, 'Some notes on the judges in Ireland in the year 1739', *J.R.S.A.I.*, xxxiv, 1-20.
8. Thrift Presentations, 1059.
9. H.M. Walker, *A History of the Northumberland Fusiliers* (1919), 123-30; *Irish Memorials Association Journal*, xii, 365-6.
10. *Freeman's Journal*, 10 Dec. 1771.
11. S. Rogers, *Recollections ...* (1856), 97-8.
12. J. Grattan, *A Letter to the Gentry, Clergy, Freemen and Freeholders of the City of Dublin* (1753); *Second Letter* (1758); *Pue's Occurrences*, 21 Feb., 11 Mar. 1758.
13. C. Lucas, *Seasonable Advice ...* (1760), 38-9.
14. Lord Broughton, *Recollections of a Long Life ...* (1909-11), i, 148.
15. The daughters were Ann, Elizabeth, Mary and Katherine (Reg. of Deeds 263/170308; Thrift Presentations, 1053, 1056; Langdale MSS 39/46).
16. W.B.W. Ball, *Ball Family Records* (1908), 156; *Hibernian Magazine* (1772), 328; H. Grattan, *Memoirs of the Life and Times of the Rt Hon. Henry Grattan*, i (1839), 42-4. (*Memoirs of the Life and Times* is henceforth cited as *Life*.)
17. A circular from the Senior Lecturer 'To the teachers of Latin and Greek through-

239

out Ireland' (TCD, Mun.V.27/2).

18. *Hibernian Magazine* (1771), 441.

19. *Ibid.* (1782), 422–3.

20. *Heads of a scheme for applying part of the increased rents of Erasmus Smith's lands to the use of college* (copy in N.L.I.).

21. T. Leland, *A Dissertation on the principles of human eloquence ... being the substance of lectures read in the oratory-school of Trinity College, Dublin* (1764), 32.

22. College Historical Society's Journal 1770-3, 206-16.

23. *Life*, i, 46, 47, 49.

24. *Ibid.*, i, 49, 148.

25. Thrift Presentations, 1056.

26. Langdale MSS, 39/44.

27. *Life*, i, 120.

28. *Ibid.*, i, 48-9, 51-2, 125, 138, 143.

29. *Ibid.*, i, 50.

30. *Ibid.*, i, 142-3, 147.

31. Broome was commissioned as a cornet in 5th Dragoons in 1762 and promoted to lieutenant in 1769.

32. Lord Lieutenant to Rochfort, 20 Sept. 1773; Rochfort to Lord Lieutenant, 20 Oct. 1773 (SPI, 63/440, 441).

33. *Life*, i, 142-3, 164-5, 247.

34. Wills, 834/1/284; N.L.I., MS 3716; Broome was a major in the County of Dublin Light Dragoons (*Hibernian Journal*, 29 Apr. 1782).

35. *Life*, i, 118, 139, 164.

36. S. Rogers, *Recollections*, 107-8; *Life*, i, 248-9.

37. *Ibid.*, i, 126.

38. *Gentleman's Magazine*, lxxxii, 193.

39. J. Almon, *Biographical Anecdotes* (1797), i, 16-17; *The Miscellaneous Works of Hugh Boyd*, ed. L.D. Campbell (1800), i, 10-23, 219-20; *Life*, i, 50-1, 115, 257.

40. *Life*, i, 123, 246-7.

41. *Ibid.*, i, 51, 53, 144, 247, 355.

42. *Ibid.*, i, 129, 144.

43. *Ibid.*, i, 127, 142, 166.

44. *Ibid.*, i, 237; H. Grattan, *Miscellaneous Works* (1822), 9-10.

45. J. Scott, *Common place book*, n.d., n.p., 51, 80, 97; *Life*, i, 143.

46. *Life*, i, 242, 260.

47. *Freeman's Journal*, 30 Oct. 1773; *Gentleman's Magazine*, lxi, 1164.

48. *Life*, i, 145, 160.

49. *Parliamentary Logick*, ed. E. Malone (1808), 15, 22, 32, 36, 37, 48; *The Works of Jeremy Bentham*, ed. J. Bowring, ii (1843), 383-7.

50. *Life*, i, 138.

51. *Horace Walpole's Correspondence*, ed. W.S. Lewis, xxxvii (1974), 46.

52. *Correspondence of William Pitt, Earl of Chatham*, ed. W.S. Taylor and J.H. Pringle, i (1838), 151-2.

53. *Speeches of the Rt Hon. Charles James Fox ...*, i (1815). Lord Erskine's remarks are quoted vii-ix.

54. *Irish Parl. Reg.*, x, 111.

CHAPTER II

1. Circumstances lend enchantment to a view. In 1811, with nearly forty years of achievement behind him, Grattan pronounced that the Bar formed 'the best society in Ireland', some of its members being 'able and talented', although their conversations tended to be confined to professional topics. For this of course the Union, which had narrowed their interests, was to be blamed (*Life*, v, 444).

2. *Life*, i, 254, 257-61; [J.R. Scott], *A View of the present state of Ireland ... to which is added sketches of the principal characters in the Irish House of Commons*, by Falkland (1789), 121-2.

3. *Life*, i, 115.

4. Langdale MSS, 39/5.

5. *HMC Charlemont MSS*, i, 7.

6. *Gentlemen's Magazine*, lxix, 813.

7. *HMC Charlemont MSS*, ii, 372; *The Irish Parliament 1775 ...*, ed. W. Hunt (1907), 9.

8. *Morning Herald*, 6 Mar. 1782.

9. *Irish Parl. Reg.*, iv, 238.

10. *Hibernian Journal*, 26 Sept. 1776.

11. H. Grattan to Fitzwilliam, 25 May [1795] (Fitzwilliam MSS, F. 29/56); *Freeman's Journal*, 22 Mar. 1792; *Irish Parl. Reg.*, vi, 39, 352, ix, 3, x, 34-41, xii, 277.

12. See D. Lamney, 'The growth of the "patriot opposition" in Ireland during the 1770s' in *Parliamentary History*, vii, 257-81; G. O'Brien, *Anglo-Irish politics in the age of Grattan and Pitt* (1987), 14.

13. *Hansard*, 1 series, xviii, 159.

14. C. Jenkinson to H. Flood, 27 Nov. 1775 (Add.MS 38306); Cavendish Debates, 5 Feb. 1778. The office-holder was Sir Hercules Langrishe.

15. *Gentleman's Magazine*, 1, 169.

16. *Irish Parl. Reg.*, x, 340.

17. S. Rogers, *Recollections*, 104.

18. *Hibernian Magazine* (1780), 409; *Morning Herald*, 6 Mar. 1782, *Drennan–McTier Letters*, ed. J. Agnew, i (1998), 356.

19. *The Irish Parliament 1775 ...*, ed. W. Hunt, 9.

20. *HMC*, Charlemont *MSS*, i, 71; *HMC*, 12 Report, Appendix ix.

21. *Gentlemen's Magazine*, lxxv, 678; *Life*, v, 465.

22. *Gentlemen's Magazine*, xxxvii, 505-7.

23. *Hibernian Journal*, 30 Feb. 1781.

24. *Ibid.*, 3 June 1778; see also *Irish Parl Reg.*, viii, 352.

25. *Hibernian Journal*, 30 Nov. 1781, 8 July 1782; Rosse Papers, PRONI Report C/15.

26. W.H. Curran, *The life of John Philpot Curran*, i (1819), 92.

27. *Hibernian Journal*, 18 Dec. 1775.

28. *Ibid.*, 14, 23 Feb. 1776.

29. *Ibid.*, 3 Apr., 19 July 1776.

30. Cavendish Debates, 5 Feb. 1778.

31. *Analecta Hibernica*, viii, 315-71; letters from Grattan to Forbes in N.L.I., MS 71013.

32. Conolly reported in Cavendish Debates, 21 Nov. 1777.

33. *Ibid.*, 5 Feb. 1778; *Hibernian Journal*, 17 Oct. 1777.

34. Cavendish Debates, 3, 6 Mar. 1778.

35. *Hibernian Journal*, 8 June 1778.

36. Cavendish Debates, 17 Nov. 1777, 5 June 1778.

37. *Ibid.*, 27 Mar. 1778.
38. *Ibid.*, 16 June 1778; *Hibernian Journal*, 17 June, 5 Aug. 1778.
39. Charlemont voted against the Bill (*Hibernian Journal*, 17 Aug. 1778).
40. Cavendish Debates, 8 Jan., 28 Mar. 1778.
41. *Ibid.*, 19 Nov. 1777.
42. *Public Advertiser*, 14 May 1782; *Life*, i, 383-9.
43. *Freeman's Journal*, 19 Oct. 1779.
44. *Hibernian Journal*, 19 Apr. 1780.
45. *Freeman's Journal*, 23 Dec. 1779.
46. *Hibernian Journal*, 18 Feb. 1780.
47. *The Complete Works of Benjamin Franklin* ..., ed. J. Bigelow, iv (1887), 2.
48. *Hibernian Journal*, 31 May 1780.
49. *Debates in the House of Commons of Ireland ... taken in Short Hand verbatim and litera-tum on Wednesday April 19, By a Gentleman*, 2nd edn (1780); *Hibernian Journal*, 31 May 1780.
50. Cavendish Debates, 24 May 1780.
51. *Hibernian Journal*, 10, 31 May 1780; Cavendish Debates, 8, 12, 16 Aug. 1780.
52. *Hibernian Journal*, 20 Aug. 1780.
53. Cavendish Debates, 17 May, 15 Aug. 1780.
54. *Ibid.*, 16 Aug. 1780; *D.E.P.*, 4 May, 22 Aug. 1780; *Hibernian Journal*, 4 Sept., 22 Aug. 1780.
55. 19 & 20 Geo. III, *c.* 30; Cavendish Debates, 1 June, 3 Aug. 1780; *Hibernian Journal*, 15, 17 May 1780, 19 Oct. 1785.
56. *D.E.P.*, 25 Apr. 1780, *Hibernian Journal*, 5, 14 May, 4 Sept. 1780.
57. *Hibernian Journal*, 14, 19 Mar., 2 May 1781.
58. *Ibid.*, 5 May, 27 June 1780; *D.E.P.*, 27 May 1780.
59. *Hibernian Journal*, 23 May, 11 July 1781.
60. Henry Grattan the younger, in his biography of his father, states that resolutions for the Convention were prepared by Charlemont, Flood and Grattan and that Grattan alone was responsible for the resolution favouring a relaxation of the penal laws which he gave to Francis Dobbs to take down to Dungannon. But Dobbs states that the resolution was drafted by Joseph Pollock, a well-known liberal (*Life*, ii, 204-6; F. Dobbs, *A History of Irish Affairs* ... [1782], 52).
61. *Irish Parl. Reg.*, i, 258-9.
62. *HMC* (*Carlisle MSS*), 556-7.
63. C.J. Fox to R. Fitzpatrick, 13 Apr. 1782 (Add. MS 47580).
64. *Hibernian Journal*, 15 April 1782; *Memorials and Correspondence of Charles James Fox*, ed. Lord John Russell, i (1853), 394-400.
65. *Irish Parl. Reg.*, I, 334-9; *Public Advertiser*, 26 Apr., 14 May 1782. The ringing and romantic phrase beginning 'Spirit of Swift, Spirit of Molyneux' and ending with the words 'Esto perpetua', which Grattan is supposed to have used amongst the open-ing sentences of his speech on 16 April, does not appear in contemporary reports. Either the reporters failed to grasp the words or Grattan, swept along fast by his own vehemence, forgot to use them. Less probably he coined the phrase after the event. The words first appear in print in the 1822 edition of Grattan's speeches.
66. *Morning Herald*, 29 Apr. 1782.
67. *Memorials and Correspondence of Fox*, i, 398; Rosse Papers, PRONI report, C/14/1-5.
68. *Journals of the Irish House of Commons* ..., x, 353.

69. *Memorials and Correspondence of Fox*, i, 404-9; *The Life of Charles Stanhope ..., 3rd Earl Stanhope*, ed. G.P. Gooch (1914), 49-50.

70. *Memorials and Correspondence of Fox*, i, 409-10. It may be added that two other members of Rockingham's administration agreed with Fox. Burke wanted 'a clear, solid' glorious Irish settlement; R.B. Sheridan urged that there should be 'a sort of convention' between the two countries, dealing with 'co-operation in great matters'. *Correspondence of Edmund Burke*, IV, 440, and *Letters of R.B. Sheridan*, ed. C. Price, i (1966), 139-40.

71. *Hibernian Journal*, 29 May 1782.

72. *Ibid.*, 31 May 1782.

73. *Ibid.*, 3 June 1782; *Freeman's Journal*, 3 June 1782.

74. J. Jebb to A. Dobbs, 27 Apr. 1782 (N.L.I., MS 2251).

75. T.C.D., Board Reg., 5 May 1782. The picture by Richard Hone cost 35 guineas (Ibid., 5 July, 1783).

76. Thomas Moore in 1825 when visiting Dublin mentioned to Gervais Bushe and Philip Crampton that he had heard that Grattan had provided in his will for twelve natural children. They both said that Grattan's gallantries amongst the cottagers in his neighbourhood were notorious and that he was not fastidious in the objects of his amours (*Journals of Thomas Moore*, ed. W.S. Dowden, i [1984], 866). An abstract of Grattan's will, signed 4 March 1818 and proved 28 Sept. 1820, names as beneficiaries only his wife, his sons Henry and James, and his daughter Mary Ann (Thrift Presentations, 1054). So the rumours recorded by Moore are best left to the obscurity of a footnote.

77. *Hibernian Journal*, 19 Apr. 1782.

78. *Ibid.*, 27 May 1782.

79. *Irish Parl. Reg.*, i, 376-81; *Hibernian Journal*, 31 May 1782.

80. *HMC Charlemont MSS*, i, 90.

81. *Freeman's Journal*, 15 Nov. 1798; *All the Talents in Ireland: a satirical poem* (1807); *Hibernian Journal*, 4 May 1785; *Freeman's Journal*, 21 Sept. 1785; *Irish Parl. Reg.*, ix, 155.

82. *Irish Parl. Reg.*, i, 399-40.

83. *Ibid.*, i, 454; *Memorials and Correspondence of Fox*, i, 404.

84. *Irish Parl. Reg.*, ix, 73-4.

85. *Ibid.*, i, 395, 408, 423, 425.

86. See Grattan to J. Barrington, 2 Mar. 1819 (Sir Jonah Barrington, *Historic Memoirs of Ireland* ... (1833), i, 147).

87. *Irish Parl. Reg.*, i, 416, 441; W. Beresford to W. Eden, 13 June 1782 (Add. MS 34418).

88. *Irish Parl. Reg.*, i, 466-7; Rosse Papers, PRONI Report, C/14/1-5; *Freeman's Journal*, 27 July 1782; E. Cooke to W. Eden, 27 July 1782 (Add. MS 34418).

89. *Irish Parl. Reg.*, ii, 166.

90. J. Jebb to —, 25 June 1782 (Add. MS 47582).

91. C. Sheridan to R. Fitzpatrick, 25 June 1782 (loc. cit.).

92. S. Rogers, *Recollections*, 101. Grattan left Ireland on 29 July and returned on 17 Oct. (*Hibernian Journal*, 2 Aug. 1782; *Freeman's Journal*, 19 Oct. 1782).

93. Portland to R. Fitzpatrick, 27 June 1782 (Add. MS 47582); according to Edward Cooke Grattan and Hussey Burgh were reluctant at this time to have close relations with Portland because of his connection with the Ponsonbys (E. Cooke to W. Eden, 2 May 1782, Add. MS 34418). But Cooke was in a waspish mood and in fact Burgh was appointed Chief Baron in July during Portland's Administration and the

Duke seems to have thought himself to be on good terms with Grattan.

94. *The Journal of the Hon. Edward Fox*, 1818-30, ed. Earl of Ilchester (1923), 33.

95. *Freeman's Journal*, 8 Aug., 21 Sept., 12, 14 Dec. 1782; *Hibernian Journal*, Nov. 1782.

96. *HMC Fortescue MSS*, i, 163.

97. *Ibid.*, i, 164, 166, 182, 191-3; *Memorials and Correspondence of Fox*, i, 148, 424-8; B. Yelverton to R. Fitzpatrick, 31 Dec. 1782 (Add. MS 47582).

98. *HMC Charlemont MSS*, i, 102-3.

99. Northington to W. Windham, Oct. 1783 (Add. MS 37873); Northington to Portland, 10 Sept. 1783 (Add. MS 38716); T. Pelham to W. Windham, 14 Sept. 1783 (Add. MS 37873); E. Cooke to W. Eden, 29 Oct. 1783 (Add. MS 34419); J. Fitzgibbon to W. Eden, 11 Oct. 1783 (Add. MS 34416); *HMC Charlemont MSS*, i, 104-5.

100. *Ibid.*, i, 105-6; Charlemont to A. Stewart, 8 June 1785 (PRONI, D/3167/I/13).

101. E. Cooke to W. Eden, 4 Sept. 1783 (Add. MS 34419).

102. *HMC Fortescue MSS*, i, 220.

103. Northington to W. Windham, 6 Oct. 1783 (Add. MS 37873).

104. [T.R. Scott], *A Review of the Principal Characters of the Irish House of Commons*, by Falkland (1789), 191.

105. W. Woodfall to W. Eden, 16 Aug. 1785 (Add. MS 34420), H. Flood to L. Parsons, 20 Feb., 9 Mar. 1789, L. Parsons to H. Flood, Apr. 1788 (Rosse Papers, PRONI Report, C/8/42,55,45).

106. Portland to Northington, 27 Oct. 1783 (Add. MS 33100).

107. Portland to Northington, 18 Sept. 1783 (Add. MS 33101).

108. Carlisle to Hillsborough, Nov. 1781 (Add. MS 34418, f.163v).

109. R. Fitzpatrick to C.J. Fox, 17 Apr. 1782 (Add. MS 37580).

110. *The Correspondence of Emily, Duchess of Leinster, 1731-1814*, ed. B. Fitzgerald, iii (1957), 401.

111. Grattan was with his uncle during his last illness and, to his own detriment, reminded him of numerous legacies he had intended to make (*The Marlay Letters, 1778-1820*, ed. R.W. Bond (1937), 63).

112. Langdale MSS, 39/8-9. Gervais Bushe, a relation, estimated that Grattan's income in his later years was £9,000 per annum and a debt of £50,000 borrowed to purchase, T. Moore, *Journals*, ed. W.S. Dowden, ii, 442.

113. S. Rogers, *Recollections*, 97, 104; Langdale MSS,39/6; H. Grattan to R. McCann [1810] (Langdale 39/3). *Diary of Joseph Farrington*, ed. V. Garlick and A. MacIntyre, iii (1979), 905. For a man with Grattan's income it was not difficult to indulge a taste for claret. About 1790 the price of claret in Dublin ranged from 22/9 to two guineas a dozen (*D.E.P.*, 25 Feb. 1790).

114. *The Miscellaneous Works of E. Cummins* (1808), Langdale 39/5, N.L.I. MS 3717, *Hibernian Journal*, 21 July 1783.

115. *HMC Charlemont MSS*, ii, 393.

116. Although her interests were centred on her home and family in 1783 she presented 'a superb and elegant' pair of colours to her husband's Volunteer Corps (*D.E.P.*, 5 Aug. 1783).

117. *HMC Rutland MSS*, iii, 337, 405, *Emily, Duchess of Leinster*, iii (1957), 401.

118. J. Carr, *The stranger in Ireland* ... (1806), 140-1; W. Drennan to Mrs McTier, 12 August 1796 (*Drennan–McTier Letters*, ii, 253). Grattan had a hermitage at Moyanna on his Queen's County estate (E. O'Leary and M. Lalor, *History of Queen's County*, i, 291-3).

CHAPTER III

1. T. Moore, *Life of R.B. Sheridan* (1825), i, 409-17. The commentator was Charles Sheridan.
2. Falkland, *A Review of the Principal Characters ...*, 187.
3. *Irish Parl. Reg.*, viii, 232.
4. *Ibid.*, xi, 193.
5. *Ibid.*, vi, 381, ix, 183, xii, 75, ix, 154, 254-7; Cavendish Debates, 3 Mar. 1789.
6. *The Times*, 27 Mar. 1797.
7. W. Eden to J. Blaquiere, [1782] (Add. MS 44118).
8. S. Rogers, *Recollections*, 110.
9. Cavendish Debates, 24 Feb. 1782; *Hansard*, 1 series, xxii, 732.
10. *D.E.P.*, 22 Mar. 1796; *Life*, v, 321-3.
11. *Life*, v, 277; C. O'Conor to T. Grenville, 26 Feb. 1815 (Add. MS 41858).
12. *Hansard*, 1 series, xi, 12-13; *Recollections of the table talk of Samuel Rogers*, ed. M. Bishop (1952), 124.
13. *Irish Parl. Reg.*, ix, 245.
14. *Ibid.*, vii, 379.
15. *Ibid.*, viii, 84.
16. *Ibid.*, xi, 45-8.
17. *Hibernian Journal*, 7 May 1784.
18. *Irish Parl. Reg.*, vii, 377.
19. *HMC Fortescue MSS*, i, 224.
20. H. Grattan to R. Fitzpatrick, 21 March 1785 (Add MS 47582).
21. T. Orde to W. Pitt, 12 Feb. 1785 (PRO/30/8/329).
22. *HMC Rutland MSS*, iii, 226, 233; *Irish Parl. Reg.*, v, 355, 369, 478.
23. *HMC Fortescue MSS*, i, 253; E. Cooke to W. Eden, 21 July 1785 (Add. MS 34420).
24. *Irish Parl. Reg.*, v, 350-5; Cavendish Debates, 12 Aug. 1785.
25. E. Cooke to W. Eden, 15 Sept. 1785; J. Fitzgibbon to W. Eden, 29 Aug. 1785 (Add. MS 34420).
26. *Irish Parl. Reg.*, vi, 350-1, xi, 242.
27. *Ibid.*, v, 246.
28. *Ibid.*, vi, 114, xi, 242, 269.
29. *Ibid.*, xv, 190-1.
30. H. Grattan to W. Forbes, [Aug.] 1782 (N.L.I. MS 71013).
31. *Irish Parl. Reg.*, iii, 84, v, 165.
32. *Ibid.*, iii, 85.
33. *Ibid.*, ii, 84, iv, 41-2, *Freeman's Journal*, 11 Oct. 1783.
34. *HMC Charlemont MSS*, i, 115; *Freeman's Journal*, 11 Oct. 1783.
35. *Irish Parl. Reg.*, xii, 13.
36. *Ibid.*, x, 58. Grattan even once remarked, 'I know a man may be an enemy to liberty and have many good private points about him, he may be an amiable, good humoured man' (Cavendish Debates, 24 May 1780).
37. *Irish Parl. Reg.*, vi, 120.
38. Rutland to Sidney, 17 Mar., 26 May 1784 (H.O.110/12).
39. *Irish Parl. Reg.*, x, 50, vi, 115, xi, 115, x, 150.
40. *Ibid.*, vi, 115-18.
41. C. Hamilton to H. Grattan, 20 June 1782 (Langdale MSS, 39/1).

42. *Life*, v, 277.
43. For an account of the disturbances in Munster see 'The Rightboy movement 1785-8' by J.S. Donnelly in *Studia Hibernica*, No. 17, 120-202.
44. *Irish Parl. Reg.*, vii, 359.
45. *Ibid.*, vii, 180, 200, 227.
46. *Ibid.*, viii, 214, 225.
47. *Ibid.*, viii, 225-6.
48. *Hibernian Journal*, 23 July 1783; *Speeches*, iii, 369.
49. *Irish Parl. Reg.*, viii, 65.
50. *Ibid.*, vii, 337.
51. *Ibid.*, vii, 338, viii, 209, 212.
52. From evidence carefully collected in two Kerry parishes it seems that Grattan when discussing tithe of potatoes in Kerry cited high rather than average figures (see M.J. Bric, 'Richard Townsend Herbert's "Information on the state of tithe in Kerry" in *Journal of the Kerry Archaeological and Historical Society*, No. 17, 89-97.
53. *Irish Parl. Reg.*, vii, 234.
54. *Ibid.*, viii, 215-18.
55. *Ibid.*, viii, 455.
56. *Ibid.*, viii, 224, 228.
57. *HMC Fortescue MSS*, i, 306; L. Parsons to H. Flood, [April] 1788 (Rosse Papers PRONI Report, C/8/45).
58. J. Nichols, *Illustrations of the Literary History of the Eighteenth Century*, vii (1848), 774.
59. *Irish Parl. Reg.*, viii, 231. For the Archbishop's views see 'Observations on Dean Erskine's plan ...' in H.O. 100/21.
60. *Irish Parl. Reg.*, viii, 199, 219, ix, 405, 452, vii, 359, viii, 231.
61. *Ibid.*, viii, 405; *Freeman's Journal*, 11 Nov. 1779.
62. *Irish Parl. Reg.*, xi, 35-6.
63. P. Lynch and J.E. Vaizey, *Guinness's Brewery in the Irish Economy 1759-1816* (1966), 58.
64. *Irish Parl. Reg.*, xii, 51.
65. *Ibid.*, xiii, 521-2.
66. *HMC Rutland MSS*, iii, 166; *Irish Parl. Reg.*, vi, 119, 306.
67. *D.E.P.*, 16 Dec. 1788, 17 Jan. 1789.
68. *Irish Parl. Reg.*, ix, 97.
69. F. Hardy to J. Forbes, 28 Feb. 1789 (N.L.I., MS 978).
70. *Irish Parl. Reg.*, x, 216, xii, 6.
71. *Gentleman's Magazine*, lxxvi, 1084, 1248, lxxxvii, pt 2, 83.
72. *Life*, iii, 191-6. Langdale MSS, 39/9; W. Wainwright to Fitzwilliam, 1, 3 Mar., 29 Oct. 1789 (Fitzwilliam MSS, F.89/107/112/218); H. Grattan to Fitzwilliam, 16 Dec. 1789, Aldborough to Bessborough (*Ibid.*, F.93/25,28).
73. L. Parsons to H. Flood, [*post* April] 1788 (Rosse Papers PRONI Report, C/8/45); H. Grattan to J. Forbes [early 1789] (N.L.I., MS 71013).
74. *Life and Letters of Lady Sarah Lennox* ..., ed. The Countess of Ilchester and Lord Stavordale (1901), ii, 76.
75. *Hibernian Journal*, 20 Feb. 1782.
76. *Irish Parl. Reg.*, vi, 340-50, 379, viii, 340-2, xi, 263-7, xii, 296.
77. *D.E.P.*, 30 Jan., 25 Feb. 1790, *Irish Parl. Reg.*, x, 315; F. Higgins to —, 13 Feb. 1797 (Rebellion Papers, 620/14); *Freeman's Journal*, 11 May 1790.
78. *Drennan–McTier letters*, i, 349; *Freeman's Journal*, 4 May 1790.

79. *Ibid.*
80. *Freeman's Journal*, 13, 15 May 1790.
81. *Cal. Ancient Records of Dublin*, ed. J.T. Gilbert and Lady Gilbert, xvii (1916), 216.
82. *Irish Parl. Reg.*, xi, 258, 304, 307-8, 312, xiii, 395.
83. *D.E.P.*, 2, 9, May 1797. Duigenan's Bill was based on measures for controlling building in London (4 Geo.III.c.14 and 6 Geo.III.c.37).
84. Strictly speaking two Dublin Police Bills were introduced in the session of 1795, Grattan's on 7 May and the Attorney General's on 8 May. It was the second of these which passed, but since it was on the lines of Grattan's it was probably for drafting reasons that it rather than Grattan's Bill was enacted.
85. *Proceedings of the Irish Parliament* (1793), iii, 94-9.
86. *The Times*, 24 Mar. 1808.

CHAPTER IV

1. *Irish Parl. Reg.*, xii, 169, xiii, 280.
2. H. Grattan, *An Answer to a pamphlet, entitled, The speech of the Earl of Clare* ... (1800).
3. *Correspondence of Edmund Burke*, vii, 46.
4. *The Writings of Theobald Wolfe Tone 1763-98*, ed. T.W. Moody, R.B. McDowell and C.J. Woods, i, 206, 226, 229-30, 257-9.
5. *The Creevey Papers* ..., ed. Sir Herbert Maxwell, ii (1903), 178; *Life*, iv, 70.
6. *The Creevey Papers*, ii, 178-9.
7. *Irish Parl. Reg.*, xii, 227, xiii, 283, 295.
8. *Irish Parl. Reg.*, xiii, 286, 356.
9. *Irish Parl. Reg.*, xii, 164, 172, xiii, 289-90, 294.
10. *Irish Parl. Reg.*, xii, 165, 169, xii, 296.
11. *Ibid.*, xii, 169-70, 240, 287.
12. *Ibid.*, xii, 228, xiii, 167.
13. *Irish Parl. Reg.*, xiii, 375; *D.E.P.*, 7 Feb. 1793; *N.S.*, 23 Feb. 1793.
14. *Irish Parl. Reg.*, xiii, 384-5; *Correspondence of Edmund Burke*, vii, 363-5.
15. Grattan's copy of the bill is endorsed 'against the principles of liberty' (T.C.D., MS 4232). *Correspondence of Edmund Burke*, viii, 365.
16. *Correspondence of Edmund Burke*, vii, 510.
17. *Freeman's Journal*, 23 Jan. 1794.
18. Parsons' Diary, 5 Feb. 1794 (Rosse Papers, F.19).
19. *Freeman's Journal*, 8 Feb. 1794; S. Douglas to E. Nepean, 5 Feb. 1794; E. Cooke to E. Nepean, 7 Feb. 1794 (H.O.100/52 and 100/51).
20. Parsons' Diary, 4, 5, 7 Feb. 1794 (Rosse Papers, PRONI Report, F.19).
21. S. Douglas to W. Pitt, 25 June 1794 (PRO 30/8/327), Parsons' Diary, 20 Feb. (Rosse Papers, PRONI Report, F19).
22. *Irish Parl. Reg.*, xiv, 80-3.
23. E. Cooke to E. Nepean, 7 Feb. 1794 (H.O.100/51).
24. S. Douglas to W. Pitt, 24 Aug., 16 Oct. 1794 (PRO 30/8/327); *Correspondence of Edmund Burke*, viii, (169), 20; W. Berwick to T. Percy, 17 Oct. 1794 (Add. MS 34756).
25. S. Douglas to H. Grattan, 30 Nov. 1794 (Langdale MSS 39/1); S. Douglas to G. Elliot, 6 July 1795 (Minto Papers).
26. Memorandum enclosed in W.B. Ponsonby to Fitzwilliam, 4 May 1795 (Fitzwilliam MSS, F.29a).

27. *HMC Carlisle MSS*, 712.
28. T. Elrington to Mrs Elrington, 21 Sept. 1794 (T.C.D., MUN P/1 series).
29. *Correspondence of Edmund Burke*, viii, 185.
30. Fitzwilliam to H. Grattan, 23 Aug. 1794; H. Grattan to Fitzwilliam, 31 Aug. 1794 (Fitzwilliam MSS, F.29).
31. W. O'Beirne to Portland, 23 Aug. 1794 (Fitzwilliam MSS, Northampton, 46).
32. T. Hussey to —, 16 Dec. 1794 (Fitzwilliam MSS, F.29).
33. *Correspondence of Edmund Burke*, viii, 19.
34. A. Browne to T. Elrington, 3 Nov. 1794 (T.C.D., MUN P/1 series).
35. *Correspondence of Edmund Burke*, viii, 65.
36. *Ibid.*, viii, 60-1.
37. Earl Stanhope, *Life of the Rt Hon. William Pitt*, ii (1861), 285-7; *Correspondence of Edmund Burke*, viii, 60-1; Portland to W. Windham, 19 Oct. 1794 (Add.MS 37845). It should be mentioned that Henry Grattan, Junior, in his biography of his father states that during this interview Pitt, referring to the Catholic question, said 'not to bring it forward as a government measure, but if government was pressed to agree to it' – words which Grattan committed to paper (*Life*, iv, 176-7). It is scarcely necessary to point out that this second-hand report was based on Grattan's memory of a conversation which took place during the October crisis in which the Catholic question did not loom large and that Pitt probably accepted that long-term Catholic emancipation was inevitable.
38. *Correspondence of Edmund Burke*, viii, 74-5.
39. Memorandum in Langdale MSS, 39/1.
40. Memorandum (Fitzwilliam MSS, F.29e, f.7).
41. *HMC Fortescue* iii, 38; Fitzwilliam MSS, F29.
42. Langdale MSS, 39/1.
43. Fitzgibbon to Westmorland, 25 Mar. 1795 (Fane Papers).
44. *Public Advertiser*, 12 Jan. 1795.
45. *The Correspondence of the Rt Hon. John Beresford*, ed. W. Beresford (1854), ii, 63-4.
46. *The Diaries of Sylvester Douglas*, ed. F. Buckley (1928), i, 144.
47. *Irish Parl. Reg.*, xv, 4-11; *D.E.P.*, 24 Jan., 5 Feb. 1795.
48. *D.E.P.*, 5 Feb. 1795.
49. *Irish Parl. Reg.*, xv, 167.
50. *D.E.P.*, 19 Feb. 1795.
51. Fitzwilliam to Portland, 12 Feb. 1795 (H.O.100/56); Fitzwilliam to the Abp of Armagh, 8 Feb. 1795 (Fitzwilliam MSS, F.4).
52. *D.E.P.*, 24 Jan., 5, 12, 15, 26 Feb. 1795 (*Correspondence of John Beresford*, ii, 71).
53. *Irish Parl. Reg.*, xvii, 169.
54. Portland to Fitzwilliam, 21 Feb. 1795 (Fitzwilliam MSS, F.31/34).
55. H. Grattan to Fitzwilliam, 2, 6 July 1795 (*Ibid.*, F.30/1).
56. *Correspondence of Edmund Burke*, viii, 150-1.
57. *D.E.P.*, 5 Mar. 1795.
58. *Ibid.*, 14, 26 Mar. 1795; *True Briton*, 23 Mar. 1795.
59. W. Windham to T. Pelham, 21 Apr. 1795 (Add.MS 33101); T. Pelham to Portland, 24 Apr. 1795 (Add.MS 33113); H. Grattan to Fitzwilliam, 28 Mar., 25 May 1795 (Fitzwilliam MSS, F.29/56).
60. Grattan to Fitzwilliam, 25 May 1795 (Fitzwilliam MSS F.29/56), *Irish Parl. Reg.*, xv, 332.
61. W. Drennan to Mrs McTier, 8 July, 29 Aug. 1795 (*Drennan–McTier Letters*, ii, 161,

175); E. Cooke to T. Pelham, 3 Sept. 1795 (Add. MS 33101); T. Pelham to E. Cooke, 10 Sept. 1795 (Rebellion Papers, 820/18A/5).

62. *D.E.P.*, 19 Dec. 1795; W. Drennan to Mrs McTier, 4 Jan. 1796 (*Drennan–McTier Letters*, ii, 198).

CHAPTER V

1. H. Grattan to Fitzwilliam, 25 Jan., 10 Dec. 1796 (Fitzwilliam MSS, F.30/63/78).
2. *D.E.P.*, 28 Mar. 1797.
3. H. Grattan to Fitzwilliam, 19 Apr. 1796 (Fitzwilliam MSS F.30/68).
4. W.B. Ponsonby to Fitzwilliam, 10 June 1796 (*Ibid.*, F.30/71).
5. *D.E.P.*, 23 Jan., 22 Oct. 1796.
6. *Ibid.*, 21, 23 Jan., 13 Oct. 1796.
7. *Ibid.*, 23 Jan. 1796; 21 Mar. 1797.
8. *Ibid.*, 3 Mar. 1796.
9. *Ibid.*, 2 Feb., 3 Mar. 1796. The Act referred to by the Attorney General was 15 & 16 Geo.III.c.21.
10. *Ibid.*, 25 Feb. 1797.
11. *D.E.P.*, 20 Oct. 1796.
12. *D.E.P.*, 15 Oct. 1796.
13. *D.E.P*, 15, 17, 24 Sept. 1796; *Freeman's Journal*, 31 Oct. 1796; J.W. to —, 31 Jan. [1797] (Rebellion Papers, 620/10/121).
14. *Freeman's Journal*, 14 Dec. 1796.
15. *Irish Parl. Reg.*, xvii, 72-80, 121-6.
16. *D.E.P.*, 1 Dec., 15 Nov. 1796, 18 May 1797.
17. H. Grattan to Fitzwilliam, 10 Nov. 1796 (Fitzwilliam MSS, F.30/74).
18. *D.E.P.*, 2 Feb. 1796.
19. *Ibid.*, 14 May, 9 June, 16 July 1796.
20. *Ibid.*, 18 Feb. 1796.
21. *Irish Parl. Reg.*, xvii, 399-402; *D.E.P*, 4 Mar. 1797.
22. A. O'Connor to C.J. Fox, 11 Oct. 1798 (Add MS 47569).
23. [W. Drennan], *A Letter to the Rt Hon. Charles James Fox*, 2nd ed. (1806), 19.
24. F. Higgins to —, 13 Feb. 1797 (Rebellion Papers, 620/14).
25. *Freeman's Journal*, 4 Mar. 1797, J.W. to —, 4 Mar. 1797 (Rebellion Papers, 620/10/121); F. Higgins to —, 5, 14 Mar. 1797 (*Ibid.*, 620/14).
26. *D.E.P.*, 8, 11, 13, 18 Apr. 1797; F. Higgins to —, 9, 10 Apr. 1797 (Rebellion Papers, 620/14).
27. The Address was published as a pamphlet in Dublin by at least three different publishers (one edition being sold at the low price of 3d) and in Belfast, Edinburgh and London.
28. *D.E.P* 20 July 1797.
29. *Freeman's Journal*, 28 Jan. 1792.
30. F Higgins to —, 16 Oct. 1796, 3 Feb., 11 July 1797 (Rebellion Papers 620/18/14). As early as the beginning of 1795 a conservative journalist hinted that Grattan was unwilling to accept office because he did not want to face his 'scorned, insulted and betrayed' Dublin Protestant constituents (*Freeman's Journal*, 24 Mar. 1795).
31. *D.E.P.*, 11 Oct. 1796, 27 July 1797.

32. *Ibid.*, 31 July, 8 Aug. 1797. On 22 July the Common Council by a large majority decided to support as candidates for the city Arthur Wolfe, the Attorney General, and Marcus Beresford. They were elected unopposed on 31 July (*Freeman's Journal*, 22 July 1797; *D.E.P.*, 1 August 1797).
33. *Ibid.*, 26 Oct. 1797; *Life*, iv, 321-3.
34. *D.E.P.*, 23, 25 Jan., 6 Feb. 1798; *Drennan–McTier letters*, ii (1999), 364.
35. *A Petition of the Whig Club to the King* (Dublin, 1798); W. Drennan to Mrs McTier, 7 May 1798 (*Drennan–McTier Letters*, ii, 398–9); C. Parsons to L. Parsons, 3 May 1798 (Rosse Papers, D/5/6).
36. *Drennan–McTier Letters*, ii (1999), 371, 375.
37. Bird's information is in Rebellion Papers (620/52/161).
38. *Press*, 6, 8, 17 Feb. 1798; F. Higgins to —, 30 Apr. 1797 (Rebellion papers, 620/14) (N.S., 23 Mar. 1795).
39. *Lords Journals Ireland*, viii, 158-9.
40. J.W. to —, 27 Apr. 1798 (Rebellion Papers, 620/10/121), *Drennan–McTier Letters*, ii (1999), 398-9.
41. *Freeman's Journal*, 5 June 1798; *The Journal of Elizabeth, Lady Holland*, ed. The Earl of Ilchester (1908), I, 191-2.
42. *Life*, iv, 381, 405, 438-44; H. Grattan to C.J. Fox, 20 Oct. [1798] (Add.MS 47569); Mrs Grattan to R. McCann [1799] (Langdale MSS, 39/3); *The Diary of Joseph Farington*, ed. C.Cave, K. Garlick, and A. MacIntyre, iii, (1978), 1108.
43. H. Grattan to C.J. Fox, 6 Dec. [1803] (Add.MS 47565).
44. H. Grattan to R. McCann, 6 Mar. 1802; *Life*, v, 232-3 (Rebellion Papers, 620/12/143); Mrs McTier to W. Drennan, 7 July 1806, *Drennan–McTier Letters*, iii (1999), 504; *Life*, v, 307.
45. The 1st edn was advertised in *Freeman's Journal*, 21 June 1798; the 3rd in *Saunder's Newsletter*, 11 Aug. 1798.
46. W. Wilberforce, *A Practical view of the prevailing religious systems of professed Christians in the higher and middle classes of this country contrasted with real Christianity* (1798), ch. vi, sec. 3.
47. T.C.D. MS 4958, *Freeman's Journal*, 9 Oct. 1798. A portrait of Grattan now hangs in the College Dining Hall. It was probably placed there in 1820 when it was decided to hang pictures in the Hall. For many years it was assumed that the portrait of Grattan by Robert Home which was taken down in 1798 had been destroyed and that the Dining Hall portrait was by N. Kenny, but in 1924 when the portraits in the Dining Hall were being cleaned the signature R. Home and the date 1783 became visible (T.C.D. Board Reg., vi, 276; Bursar's Papers; W.G. Strickland, *Dictionary of Irish Artists* ..., i (1913), 506, 577).
48. *Freeman's Journal*, 4, 16, 20 Oct. 1798; *Drennan–McTier Letters*, ii (1999), 416, 418.
49. *Freeman's Journal*, 4 Dec. 1798.
50. Grattan to C.J. Fox, 6 Dec. [1803] (Add.MS 47569).
51. *Morning Chronicle*, 5 Dec. 1798; Grattan to C.J. Fox, 6 Dec. [1798] (Add.MS 47569).
52. *Speeches*, ed. H. Grattan Jr, iii, 404.
53. *HMC Fortescue MSS*, vi, 105; *The Times*, 20 Jan. 1800; *Morning Chronicle*, 8 Feb. 1800. Since Grattan's election for Wicklow cost him £1200 it seems he felt obliged to pay this amount to Tighe (Langdale, MSS, 39/9).
54. *HMC Fortescue MSS*, vi, 105. The reporter was Edward Cooke.
55. *Morning Chronicle*, 8 Feb. 1800.

56. *Drennan–McTier Letters*, ii (1999), 562; *The Times*, 24 Jan. 1800; *Morning Chronicle*, 8 Feb. 1800.

57. *Freeman's Journal*, 26 Feb. 1800; *HMC Fortescue MSS*, vi, 150.

58. *Speeches*, iii, 365.

59. *Speeches*, iii, 324.

60. *Speeches*, iii, 365.

61. *Speeches*, iii, 362, 393, 416.

62. *Speeches*, iii, 417.

63. *Speeches*, iii, 391-2.

CHAPTER VI

1. *The Times*, 22 Sept. 1810.

2. *D.E.P.*, 11 Oct. 1810. Grattan's absence from a Dublin Repeal Meeting held at the Royal Exchange was noted in the press (*The Times*, 24 Sept. 1810).

3. *Hansard*, 1 series, xi, 559, xxii, 733-4, xl, 19-21, xxviii, 249.

4. *D.E.P.*, 2 July 1818.

5. J. Barrington to T. Pelham, 2 Nov. 1801 (Add.MS 33101), Statement by Mr Ramsden on his relations with Sir Jonah Barrington (Add.MS 40234, F.84).

6. Barrington in his *Personal Sketches of his Own Times*, i (1827), 183-91, describing this occasion, attributes to Grattan a strained philippic and to Giffard a coarse rejoinder. Neither is mentioned in contemporary press accounts.

7. *Freeman's Journal*, 22 July 1802; *D.E.P.*, 22 July 1802.

8. *Hibernian Journal*, 19, 30 March 1804.

9. *Hansard*, 1 series, iv, 677, 679, 691, 696, xvii, 183; *Journals of the House of Commons*, lx, 234.

10. *Hansard*, 1 series, iv, 681, 710, 754, 891, xi, 623, xvii, 187, xxii, 798, xxxvi, 329, 307.

11. *Memorials and Correspondence of Charles James Fox*, iii, 442.

12. Holland to T. Grenville, 3 Jan. 1810 (Add.MS 41858).

13. Grattan to C.J. Fox, 4 Dec. 1803 (Add.MS 47569).

14. Fox to Grey, 17 Dec. 1803 (Add.MS 47565).

15. G. Ponsonby to R. Fitzpatrick, 29 Jan. 1804 (Add.MS 47582).

16. H. Grattan to Fox, 6 Dec. [1803] (Add.MS 47569).

17. *Ibid.*, 4 Dec. [1804] (loc. cit.).

18. *The Times*, 12 Apr. 1805.

19. *Hibernian Journal*, 17 May 1805.

20. *Historical and Posthumous Memoirs of Sir N.W Wraxhall, 1772-1784*, ed. H.B. Wheatley, iii (1884), 185; J. Burgoyne to T. Pelham, 9 Dec. 1783 (Add.MS 33113); *Horace Walpole's Correspondence*, xiii (1948), 102.

21. *D.E.P.*, 4 May 1797.

22. *The Irish Catholic Petition of 1805*, ed. B. MacDermont (1992), 113.

23. *Byron, Letters and Journals*, ed. L.A. Marchard, ix (1979), 13, 17; *Lord Granville Leveson Gower, private correspondence*, ed. Castalia Countess Granville (1916), ii, 72.

24. *The Diary of Charles Abbot, Lord Colchester*, ed. Lord Colchester (1861), ii, 2-3, 118; *The Later Correspondence of George III*, ed. A. Aspinall, iv (1968), 328.

25. L. Simond, *Journal of a Tour and residence in Great Britain ...*, i (1815), 53.

26. *The Complete Works of William Hazlitt*, ed. P.P. Howe, xvii (1933), 11-12.

27. Hutchinson to Donoughmore, 4 Feb. 1806 (T.C.D., MS D/42/33); *Life*, v, 306; *Morning Chronicle*, 20 Nov. 1806.
28. Earl Russell, *Recollections, 1813-73* (1875), 31-2; *HMC Fortescue MSS*, ix, 61.
29. *Hansard*, 1 series, vii, 490-7.
30. H. Grattan to — Carroll, 26 Feb. 1806 (N.L.I., MS 2111); *Saunder's Newsletter*, 23 Oct., 5, 10 Nov. 1806; *Hibernian Journal*, 10, 12 Nov. 1806.
31. *The Times*, 24 Nov. 1806.
32. *Life*, v, 336, 344-5.
33. Tennyson, 'Ode on the death of the Duke of Wellington'; *The Civil Correspondence and Memoranda of Field Marshal Arthur the Duke of Wellington: Ireland 1807-9* (1860), 18.
34. *Freeman's Journal*, 16 May 1807; *D.E.P.*, 16 May 1807.
35. *House of Commons Journals*, lxii, 38; *Hansard*, 1 series, xxiv, 698-702.
36. *D.E.P.*, 3, 19 Oct., 7 Nov. 1816, 12 Jan. 1819; *Freeman's Journal*, 30 Dec. 1817; *The Times*, 6 May 1819; H.C. Robinson, *Diary* (3rd edn 1872), 328.
37. *The Times*, 4 July 1818; *Saunder's Newsletter*, 1, 4 July 1818; *Freeman's Journal*, 2 July 1818; *Grattan righted; in a letter from Tim O'Dougherty to his brother Terence ...* (1818); *Cal. of the Ancient Records of Dublin*, xvii (1916), 215.

CHAPTER VII

1. *Creevey Papers*, ed. H. Maxwell, i, 115.
2. Mrs Grattan to J. Grattan, 19 Jan. 1811 (N.L.I., MS 2111).
3. *Life*, v, 445; R.I. Wilberforce to S. Wilberforce, *Life of William Wilberforce*, iii (1838), 111, 231, iv, 260; *Gentleman's Magazine*, lxxix, 371-2.
4. *Letters of Lady Holland to her son, 1821-1845*, ed. Earl of Ilchester (1946), 103.
5. H. Grattan to J. Grattan, 28 Nov. 1810, 6 Apr., 7 Oct. 1811 (N.L.I., MS 2111); *Life*, v, 443.
6. N. Campell, *Napoleon at Fontainbleau and Elba* (1869), 337-8; W. Gregory to R. Peel, 20 Apr. 1815 (Add. MS 40234); *Hansard*, 1 series, xxx, 428; *Catalogue of the library of the Rt. Hon. Henry Grattan* (1888).
7. H. Grattan to J. Grattan, 6 Apr. 1811; H. Grattan Jr to J. Grattan, 31 Jan. 1812 (N.L.I. MS 2111).
8. H. Grattan to J. Grattan, 19 Aug. 1810, 31 Jan. 1812 (N.L.I. MS 2111).
9. H. Grattan to J. Grattan, 28 Nov. 1810, 7 Oct. 1811; H. Grattan Jr to J. Grattan, 19 Aug. 1810 (N.L.I. MS 2111). James Grattan sat as M.P. for County Wicklow, 1821-1841. A Whig, in 1841 he was admitted to the Irish privy council. His brother Henry, who became a repealer, sat for Dublin city, 1826-1830, and Meath, 1831-1852.
10. H. Grattan to J. Grattan, 7 Oct. 1811; H. Grattan Jr to J. Grattan, 19 Aug. 1810 (N.L.I. MS 2111).
11. *Life*, v, 265-6.
12. H. Grattan to J. Grattan, 3 May 1809 (N.L.I., MS 2111).
13. S. Rogers, *Recollections*, 93.
14. *Ibid.*, 110.
15. *Life*, v, 414; Broughton, *Recollections*, i, 148, ii, 51; *Catalogue of the Library of the Rt Hon. Henry Grattan* (1888); *Collected Letters of Samuel Taylor Coleridge*, ed. E.L. Griggs, iii (1959), 312; *Life*, v, 414.
16. Byron, *Letters and Journals*, ed. R.E. Prothero, v (1901), 430; H. Grattan to J. Grat-

tan, 3 May 1809 (N.L.I., MS 2111); *Farrington Diary*, viii (1982), 3163, xii (1983), 4422.
17. R.J. Mackintosh, *Memoirs of the Life of the Rt Hon. Sir James Mackintosh* (1835), ii, 353.
18. Broughton, *Recollections*, i, 146-8.
19. *Works of Lord Byron ...*, v (1901), 429-30.
20. *Farington Diary*, viii, 3093-4, Lord Holland, *Further Memoirs of the Whig Party* (1905), 133.
21. Rogers, *Recollections*, 93-111.
22. H. Grattan to J. Grattan, 28 June 1811 (N.L.I., MS 2111).
23. *Life*, v, 305; *Drennan–McTier Letters*, iii, (1999) 469.
24. *Life*, v, 278; *Edinburgh Review*, xix, 95-7.
25. G. Eden to Lady Auckland, 11, 17 Sept. 1813 (Add.MS 34418).
26. *Creevey Papers*, i, 216, 228; *The Times*, 1, 20 Aug. 1810, 11 May 1812.
27. *Hansard*, 1 series, xvi, 505, 543.
28. H. Grattan, Jr, to R. McCann, 3 May 1809 (N.L.I., MS 2111); *Later Correspondence of George III*, ed. A. Aspinall, v (1970), 263.
29. *The Times*, 23 Mar. 1810.
30. *Hansard*, xvi, 320-4, xii, 1202; *The Times*, 30 Mar. 1810.
31. *Hansard*, x, 1073-4, xii, 1199-1202.
32. H. Grattan to J. Grattan, 7 May 1811 (N.L.I., MS 2111); *The Times*, 29 July 1813.
33. *Hansard*, 1 series, xxxi, 418-30; *The Times*, 26 May 1815; *Creevey Papers*, i, 228.
34. *Hansard*, 1 series, xxix, 1055-9; *The Times*, 28 Feb. 1815.
35. *Hansard*, 1 series, vii, 49, xxx, 712, xxxviii, 261.
36. *Ibid.*, ix, 1205, xiv, 643-5, xxii, 244; *The Times*, 14 Apr. 1810.
37. *Fourteenth report of the commisioners of the board of education in Ireland*, 10, H.C. (21)J, 1812-13 (vi); *Hansard series* ix, 1205; *The Times*, 10 March 1812.
38. *Hansard*, 1 series, ix, 1203-4, xxxiv, 58-9; *The Times*, 27 Apr. 1816; *Weekly Political Register*, xxx, 554; *Memoirs of Sir Samuel Romilly* (1840), ii, 219-21; Francis Horner, *Memoirs and Correspondence* (1843), i, 408.
39. *Hansard*, 1 series, xx, 369-86, xl, 6-23, iv, 929.
40. *Ibid.*, iv, 929, xi, 555, xxii, 738-9, xl, 8-9, iv, 929.
41. *The Times*, 6 May 1808; *Hansard*, 1 series, xl, 10.
42. *Hansard*, 1 series, iv, 924, xx, 372, xvii, 30, iv, 924, xxxvi, 484.
43. *Ibid.*, xi, 550, 562, 569, iv, 924, xvii, 25, xxii, 744, 735, xxxiv, 660, xvii, 20, xxiv, 750, 751-2, xi, 569.
44. *Freeman's Journal*, 18 Oct. 1804; *The Times*, 3, 10 June 1811; *Irish Magazine*, May 1812.
45. *Personal recollections of the late Daniel O'Connell M.P.*, ed. W.J. O'N Daunt (1848), i, 138-9. About 1830 it was said that Grattan had remarked that O'Connell was 'a bad subject and a worse rebel' (T. Moore, *Journal*, ed. W.S. Dowden, vi (1987), 382).
46. *Six Letters on the subject of Dr Milner's explanation ...*, by A.B. (1809), xviii-xix.
47. *Hansard*, 1 series, xi, 556-7.
48. *HMC Fortescue MSS*, ix, 231-5; G. Ponsonby to Sir J. Newport, 11 Oct. 1808 (N.L.I., MS 796).
49. *D.E.P.*, 22 Dec. 1810.
50. *Proceedings of the Catholic Committee as taken from accredited papers* (1811); *Freeman's Journal*, 30 May, 10 June 1811; *Life*, v, 442.
51. *D.E.P.*, 22 Aug. 1811.
52. *D.E.P.*, 22 Aug. 1811; *Hansard*, 1 series, xxiii, 691-2; C. Butler to J. Weston, 9 May 1812 (Add.MS 25125).

53. *Hansard*, 1 series, xxiv, 1202, xxvi, 66, 354.

54. *Diary and correspondence of Charles Abbot*, ed. Lord Colchester (1861), ii, 447.

55. C. Husenbeth, *Life of the Rt Rev. John Milner* (1862), 233.

56. *D.E.P.*, 25, 29 May, 3 June 1813.

57. *The Times*, 21 June 1813, 24 June 1814.

58. *Hansard*, 1 series, xxxiv, 658, xxxvi, 438.

59. *D.E.P.*, 4, 16, 20, 23 Nov., 8 Dec. 1813.

60. *Ibid.*, 22 Feb., 26, 29 Mar. 1814.

61. *Ibid.*, 3 May, 2, 14, 18 June 1814.

62. *Freeman's Journal*, 9 May 1814.

63. *D.E.P.*, 8, 20 Sept. 1814, 8 Feb. 1815.

64. *Freeman's Journal*, 25 Jan., 18 Feb., 2 Mar. 1815.

65. *D.E.P.*, 26 May 1816.

66. *Freeman's Journal*, 5, 7 Mar. 1817.

67. *The Times*, 10 May 1817.

68. R.J. Mackintosh, *Memoirs of the Life of Sir James Mackintosh* (1835), ii, 342.

69. Grattan to W. Berwick, Sat. 24 [summer 1817] (PRONI T.415); *Hansard*, 1 series, xl, 19.

70. *Freeman's Journal*, 30 Apr. 1818.

71. *D.E.P.*, 3 July 1819.

72. *Ibid.*, 2 Mar. 1819.

73. *Ibid.*, 2 Mar., 25 July 1819, 1 Jan. 1820; *The Times*, 22 July 1819.

74. *Life*, v, 5, 39-54; *D.E.P.*, 4, 9, 16 May 1820; *The Times*, 26 May, 6, 17 June 1820.

75. *The Times*, *D.E.P.*; 10 June 1820.

EPILOGUE

1. Lady Holland, *A memoir of the Rev. Sydney Smith* (1835), i, 191-2.

2. R.J. Mackintosh, *Memoirs of Sir James Mackintosh* (1835), ii, 435.

3. *The collected letters of Samuel Taylor Coleridge*, ed. E.L. Griggs, iii (1959), 312.

4. Lord Brougham, *Historic sketches of statesmen*, i (1830), 260-8; *Journal of Henry Cockburn* (1874), i, 201.

5. *The poetical works of Lord Byron* (1921), 108; W.B. Yeats, *Autobiography* (1955), 420.

6. See 'The early speeches of Henry Grattan' in *Bulletin of the Institute of Historical Research*, xxx (19), 102-14.

7. T. Moore, *Journal and Correspondence*, v (1854), 30.

8. *Dublin University Magazine*, vii, 229-63.

9. Thomas Davis, *Essays literary and historical*, ed. D.J. O'Donaghue (1914), 21, 291-300.

10. *The Times*, 5, 25 Apr. 1864; *Irish Times*, 7 June 1872; *Freeman's Journal*, 16 Feb., 5 Apr. 1864.

11. *F.D.J.*, 17 Feb. 1868.

12. TCD, MS 1703.

13. *The Times*, 7, 8 Jan. 1876.

14. J.G. MacCarthy, *Henry Grattan*, 3rd ed. (1886), 31-2.

15. C. Lever, *Cornelius O'Dowd*, 3 ed. (1865), 160-9.

16. *Hansard*, 3 series, ccciv, 1045, 1248-50.

17. See J.A. Froude, *History of England*, i (1872), ch. 1.

18. J.A. Froude, *The English in Ireland* (1881), i, 569, ii, 205.

19. *Ibid.*, iii, 524, 546, 584.

20. *Ibid.*, ii, 198, 299-301, iii, 33.

21. *Ibid.*, ii, 357, 489.

22. W.E.H. Lecky, *Leaders of public opinion in Ireland* (1861), 114, 233, 273.

23. *Ibid.*, 42.

24. *Ibid.*, 2, 229, 296.

25. *Ibid.*, 152, 306.

26. E. Lecky, *A Memoir of the Rt Hon. W.E.H. Lecky* (1909), 76.

27. W.E.H. Lecky, *Leaders of public opinion in Ireland* (2nd edn 1871), xiv-xx, 194-6.

28. *Ibid.*, (3rd edn 1903), ii, xiii, 271, 303.

29. E. Lecky, *A Memoir*, 139.

30. Robert Dunlop, *Ireland from the earliest times to the present day* (1922), preface.

31. A. Zimmern, *Henry Grattan* (1902), 69-80.

32. A. Zimmern, *Nationality and Government* (1919), 32-86.

33. A. Zimmern, *From the British Empire to the British Commonwealth* (1941), 8.

34. A. Griffith, *The Resurrection of Hungary: a parallel for Ireland* (1904), 90.

35. M. Moynihan, ed. *The Speeches of E. de Valera* (1980), 232.

36. R.J. McHugh, *Henry Grattan* (1936), 195.

37. S. Gwynn, *Experiences of a Literary Man* (1926), 304.

38. *Ibid.*, 72.

Sources

MANUSCRIPT SOURCES

British Library

Auckland Papers Add.MSS 34418-20
Charles Butler's Letter Books Add.MSS 25128
Fox Papers Add.MSS 47565, 47569
Grenville Papers Add.MSS 41858
Holland House Papers Add.MSS 47580, 47582, 47585
Liverpool Papers 3Add.MSS 8306
Northington's Letter Book Add.MSS 38716
Peel Papers Add.MSS 40234
Percy Correspondence Add.MSS 34756
Pelham Papers 22100-2, 33113
Windham Papers Add.MSS 37873, 37845

Public Record Office (PRO)

Chatham Papers
Home Office Papers
State Papers, Ireland (S.P.63)

Sources

National Library of Ireland (NLI)

Forbes Letters
Letters of Henry Grattan (MS 2111)
Letters to A. Dobbs (MS 2251)
Grattan account books, 3715-7 (MSS 1816-18)
Letters of Sir John Newport (MS 796)

Irish National Archive

Fane Papers
Rebellion Papers
Thrift Abstracts and Prerogative Will Index
Thrift Presentations

Trinity College Dublin (TCD)

Bursar's Papers
Board register
College Historical Society's Journal 1770-73
Donoughmore Papers (Calendar)
Thomas Elrington's Board Notebook
Henry Grattan: notes for a speech [on the Convention Bill 1793] MUN.V.27/2.
Material relating to the erection of the Grattan statue in College Green (MS 1703)

Public Record Office of Northern Ireland (PRONI)

Berwick Letters

National Library of Scotland (NLS)

Minto Papers

Library of Congress

Cavendish Debates (reports of debates in the Irish House of Commons 1776-1789; see M.S. Jernegan, 'The Debates in the Irish House of Commons 1776-1789' [E.H.R., xxiv. 104-6]. A photostat of these reports is in the PRONI.) For a printed text of the debates see *The Cavendish Irish parliamentary diary*, ed. A.R. Black, 3 vols, Delavan and Westport, 1984-5.

Sources

Hull University Library

The Langdale MSS

Northampton County Record Office

Fitzwilliam MSS (Northampton)

Sheffield Public Library

Fitzwilliam MSS (The Wentworth Woodhouse Muniments)

Private Ownership

Rosse Papers (listed by PRONI)

PRINTED SOURCES

Henry Grattan's Writings and Speeches

Three letters signed Postumus and dated 30 Dec. 1769 and 9 and 20 Jan. 1770, and a
   letter signed Pericles, dated 14 Nov. 1772, are printed in *Baratariana: a select collection
   of fugitive political pieces*, 2nd edn, Dublin, 1773, 60-3, 64-9, 69-78, 336-42. The first
   two letters of Postumus and the letter signed Pericles appeared in the *Freeman's
   Journal*, 30 Dec. 1769, 9 Jan., 14 Nov. 1770.
*Observations on the Mutiny Bill; with some strictures on Lord Buckinghamshire's administra-
   tion in Ireland, Dublin, 1781.*
*The rights of Ireland asserted by Henry Grattan Esq. and the Address of the Honorable House
   of Commons with His Majesty's most gracious answer and the Duke of Portland's speech.* [A
   broadsheet with a portrait of Grattan, Dublin, 1782].
*An Address to the right Honourable Henry Grattan Esq ... By the Independent Dublin Volun-
   teers relative to simple repeal ... with Mr Grattan's answer ...*, London, 1782.
*A full report of the speech of the Right Hon. Henry Grattan in the House of Commons, on
   Thursday, 14 February 1788, in the debate on tithe.* Taken in shorthand by Mr Franklin,
   Dublin and London, 1788.
*Speech of the Rt Hon. Henry Grattan on the re-agitation on the subject of tithes, in the House of
   Commons, Friday, April 11, 1788,* Dublin, reprinted London, 1788.
'Epilogue to Comus', printed in *A Collection of poems, mostly original by several hands*, ed.
   Josuah Edkins, Dublin, 1789.
*Speech of the Right Hon. Henry Grattan, relative to tythe, in the House of Commons on Friday,
   May 8, 1789. To which is annexed a Bill to appoint commissioners for the purpose of enquiring
   into the state of tythes, &c. Also a manifesto of the parochial clergy of Munster, Dublin, 1789.*

Sources

Mr Grattan's speech in the House of Commons of Ireland, on Saturday, 26th March 1791, on the Responsibility Bill, Dublin, 1791.

Mr Grattan's speech in the House of Commons of Ireland on Thursday, 19th January 1792, on the Address to the King ..., Dublin, 1792.

Speech of the Right Hon. Henry Grattan in the House of Commons, Friday, 22 February 1793, on the Catholic Bill; also Mr Grattan's Reply to the Right Honorable the Speaker, February 27th, 1793. Dublin 1792.

A letter to the Right Honorable Henry Grattan on the state of the labouring poor in Ireland from the Rev. M. Sandys ... with Mr Grattan's answer. Dublin, 1796.

The Right Honorable Henry Grattan's celebrated Address to his fellow-citizens. Dublin, 1797, 2nd. edn Dublin, 1797. This edition was printed by Stockdale.

The Right Honorable Henry Grattan's celebrated Address to his Fellow-Citizens of Dublin. Dublin, 1797.

Mr Grattan's Address to his Fellow-Citizens. Corrected from the original copy. Dublin, 1797. Another edition priced 3d Dublin, 1797.

Genuine edition. Mr Grattan's Address to his Fellow-Citizens, 2nd edn Dublin 1797.

Mr Grattan to his Fellow-Citizens [of Dublin]. Edinburgh, 1797.

The Address of the Right Hon. Henry Grattan to his constituents ... on his retiring from the Parliament of Ireland ..., London, 1797.

The Address of the Right Honourable Henry Grattan to his Fellow-Citizens of Dublin with an epistle, said to be written by Mr Grattan to Dr Duigenan. To which is prefixed the Address of the Catholics of Dublin to Mr Grattan and his Answer. Likewise Dr Duigenan's Answer to Mr Grattan's Address. Dublin, 1798.

Mr Grattan's Observations on certain proceedings against him in Dublin: in a letter ... addressed to the Editor of the Courier. Dublin, 1798.

The speech of Henry Grattan Esq. on the subject of the legislative Union with Great Britain ..., Dublin, 1800.

The speech at length of the Honourable Henry Grattan in the Irish House of Commons against the Union with Great Britain. London, 1800.

An Answer to a pamphlet, entitled, The speech of the Earl of Clare on the subject of a Legislative Union between Great Britain and Ireland, Dublin and London, 1800.

Fifth edition with considerable additions: An answer to a pamphlet entitled The Speech of the Earl of Clare ... By Henry Grattan, Dublin, 1800.

Mr Grattan's celebrated speech on the motion of Mr Fox, in the House of Commons, on Tuesday, May 14, 1805, for the Irish Catholics, in reply to Dr Duigenan. Dublin, 1805.

Memoirs of Henry Grattan Esq., together with his speech in the Imperial Parliament on Monday, 13th May 1805 ... with a striking likeness of that celebrated senator, Dublin, 1805.

Genuine edition by authority. The speech of Mr Grattan in the House of Commons on the Catholic Question; with an appendix, also his speech on the Reform, 4th March 1794, Dublin, 1806.

Necessity for universal toleration, exemplified in the speeches on the Catholic Question in 1805 and 1808, by Mr Henry Grattan, M.P., Lord Hutchinson, K-B., the Earl of Moira, the Bishop of Norwich. 1808.

The speech of Mr Grattan on the Catholic Question; ... in the House of Commons, May 18th, 1810. London, 1810.

Mr Grattan's speech on the Catholic Petition on the 18th May, 1810, and his reply on the First of June. London, 1810.

Sketch of the speeches of the Earl of Donoughmore and the Duke of Sussex and the Marquis of

Wellesley in the House of Lords on 21 April 1812 ... with the speech of the Rt Hon. Henry Grattan in the House of Commons, 25 April 1812. Kilkenny, 1812.

The speech of the Right Hon. Henry Grattan for war on the debates of the Imperial Parliament on His Majesty's message, on 25 May 1815. Dublin, 1815.

Speeches with prefatory observations ... vol. I, Dublin, 1811.

The speeches of the Rt Hon. H. Grattan in the Irish and in the Imperial Parliament. Ed. by his son (H. Grattan), 4 vols, London, 1822.

Miscellaneous Works, London, 1822.

The Speeches of Henry Grattan ... with a commentary on his career and character. Ed. D.O. Madden, Dublin, 1853, 2nd edn, Dublin, 1854.

The beauties of Grattan consisting of selections from his Works, By Alfred Howard Esq., London, [1834?].

The beauties of the principal speeches of Henry Grattan M.P. with a memoir of his life, Dublin, 1846. In the National Library of Ireland series. The 'Memoir' is largely devoted to a violent exposition of the extreme nationalist viewpoint.

Parliamentary proceedings and debates and lists of MPs

Journals of the House of Commons of the United Kingdom.

Journals of the House of Lords [of Ireland]. From 10 Car.I.1634 to 40 Geo. III, 1800. 8 vols, Dublin, 1779-1800.

Journals of the House of Commons of the Kingdom of Ireland [18 May, 1613-2 Aug. 1800], 19 vols, Dublin, 1796-1800.

Parliamentary Register: or, History of the Proceedings and Debates of the House of Commons, 2nd edn, 17 vols, Dublin, 1784-1801.

Proceedings of the Parliament of Ireland, 3 vols, Dublin 1793.

The Parliamentary Debates, 1803-1820 (Hansard 1 series).

[Caldwell, Sir James] *Debates relative to the affairs of Ireland; in the years 1763 and 1764. Taken by a Military Officer*. 2 vols, London, 1766.

Debates in the House of Commons of Ireland ... Taken in Short Hand ... By a Gentleman, 2nd edn, Dublin, 1780.

Report of Debates in the House of Commons of Ireland, session 1796-7 ... to which are annexed Debates in the British Parliament upon Mr Fox's Motion touching the state of Ireland. Dublin, 1797.

Debates in the Irish House of Commons [on the subject of a Legislative Union between Great Britain and Ireland], Friday, February 14th, 1800, n.p., n.d.

A Report of the debate in the House of Commons of Ireland on Wednesday and Thursday 15th and 16th of January 1800. Dublin, 1800.

A Report of the debate in the House of Commons of Ireland on Wednesday and Thursday, 5th and 6th of February 1800 .... Dublin, 1800.

Bodkin, M., 'Notes on the Irish Parliament in 1773', *Proc. RIA*, xlviii, C, 145-225.

The Irish parliament 1775 from an official and contemporary manuscript, ed. W. Hunt, London, 1907.

Sayles, G.O., 'Contemporary sketches of the members of the Irish Parliament in 1782', *Proc. RIA*, lvi, C, 227-86.

Johnston, E.M., 'Members of the Irish parliament, 1784-7', *RIA*, lxxi, C. 139-254.

Sources

Biographies and biographical sketches of Henry Grattan

Davis, T. and Madden, D.O., *The Life of the Rt Hon. J.P. Curran by T. Davis ... And a Memoir of the life of the Rt Hon. H. Grattan by D.O. Madden ...*, Dublin, 1846.

Dunlop, R., *Life of Henry Grattan*, 1888.

Grattan, H., *Memoirs of the life and times of the Rt Hon. Henry Grattan*, 5 vols, 1839-46.

Gwynn, S.L., *Henry Grattan and his Times*, Dublin, 1939.

Jupp, P.J., 'Henry Grattan', in *The History of Parliament, The House of Commons 1790-1800*, iv, 6-8.

Lecky, W.E.H., *The Leaders of Public Opinion in Ireland 1861*, 2nd edn 1871, 3rd edn 1903.

MacCarthy, J.G., *Henry Grattan. A historical study*, 3rd edn, Dublin, 1886.

McHugh, R.J., *Henry Grattan*, Dublin, 1936.

Roxby, P.M., *Henry Grattan*, Oxford, 1902.

Zimmern, Sir A.E., *Henry Grattan*, Oxford, 1902.

Printed Collections of Documentary Material

Publications of the Historical Manuscripts Commission
Carlisle MSS
Charlemont MSS
Fortescue MSS
Ormonde MSS
Rutland MSS
P.V. Smith MSS

Beresford, John, *The Correspondence of the Rt Hon. John Beresford, Illustrative of the last thirty years of the Irish Parliament; selected from his original papers, and edited, with notes, by ... the Rt Hon. William Beresford*, 2 vols, 1854.

Broughton, Lord [John Cam Hobhouse], *Collections of a Long Life, By Lord Broughton ... with additional extracts from his private diaries, ed. by his daughter, Lady Dorchester*, 6 vols, 1909-11.

Burke, Edmund, *The Correspondence of Edmund Burke*, ed. T.W. Copeland, Camb. and Chicago, 10 vols, 1958-78.

Byron, *Letters and Journals*, ed. L.A. Marchard (12 vols, 1973-1982).

Colchester, Lord, *The Diary and Correspondence of Charles Abbot, Lord Colchester*, ed. by his son Charles, Lord Colchester, 1861.

Coleridge, S.T., *Collected Letters of Samuel Taylor Coleridge*, ed. E.L. Griggs, 6 vols, 1956-71.

Creevey Papers, *The Creevey Papers. A Selection from the Correspondence and Diaries of the late Thomas Creevey M.P. Born 1768 – Died 1838. Edited by the Rt Hon. Sir Herbert Maxwell, Bart ... with portraits*, 2 vols, London, 1903.

Douglas, S., *The Diaries of Sylvester Douglas, Lord Glenbervie*, ed F. Bickley, 2 vols, London, 1938.

The Drennan–McTier letters 1776-81, ed. J. Agnew, 3 vols, Dublin.

Dublin, *Calendar of Ancient Records of Dublin in the possession of the Municipal Corporation of that City*, ed. J.T. Gilbert and Lady Gilbert, 18 vols, Dublin, 1889-1922.

Farington, Joseph, *The Diary of Joseph Farington*, ed. C. Cave, K. Garlick and A. MacIntyre, Yale, 1978-83.

Sources

Fox, Charles James, *Memorials and Correspondence of Charles James Fox*, ed. Lord John Russell, 4 vols, London, 1853-7.

Fox, H.E., *Journal of the Rt Hon. Henry Edward Fox 1818-30*, ed. Earl of Ilchester, 1923.

Franklin, Benjamin, *The Complete Works of Benjamin Franklin including his private as well as official and scientific correspondence*, ed. J. Bigelow; 10 vols, New York and London, 1887-8.

George III, *The Later Correspondence of George III*, ed. A. Aspinall, 5 vols, Camb., 1962-70.

Hazlitt, William, *The Complete Works of William Hazlitt*, ed. P.P. Howe, 21 vols, 1930-4.

Holland, Lady, *The Journal of Elizabeth Lady Holland, 1791-1811*, ed. Earl of Ilchester, 2 vols, London, 1908.

Holland, Lady, *Letters of Lady Holland to her Son 1821-1845*, ed. Earl of Ilchester, London, 1946.

Leinster, Duchess of, *Correspondence of Emily, Duchess of Leinster 1731-1814*, ed. B. Fitzgerald, 3 vols, Dublin, 1949-57.

Lennox, Lady Sarah, *Life and Letters of Lady Sarah ...*, ed. The Countess of Ilchester and Lord Stavordale, London, 1901.

Leveson Gower, Lord G., *The Private Correspondence of Lord Granville Leveson Gower, 1st E. Granville, 1781-1821*, ed. Castalia Countess Granville, 2 vols, London, 1916.

Moore, T., *Journals*, ed. W.S. Dowden, 6 vols, Newark [N.J.], 1983–91.

O'Connell, D., *The Correspondence of Daniel O'Connell*, ed. M. O'Connell, 8 vols, Dublin, 1972-80.

Pitt, William, *Correspondence of William Pitt, Earl of Chatham*, ed. W.S. Taylor and J.H. Pringle, 4 vols, London, 1838-40.

Robinson, H.C., *Diary, Reminiscences, and Correspondence of H.C. Robinson ... Selected and edited by T. Saddler*, 2 vols, London, 2nd edn, 1872.

Scott, John, *Private Diary 1774-98*, n.d., privately printed.

Tone, T.W., *Writings ...*, ed. by T.W. Moody, R.B. McDowell and C.J. Woods, Oxford, 1998.

Walpole, Horace, *The Correspondence of Horace Walpole*, ed. C.S. Lewis, et al., 48 vols, London, 1937-83.

Wellington, Duke of, *The Civil Correspondence and Memoranda of Field Marshal Arthur Duke of Wellington, Ireland 1807-9*, London, 1860.

Contemporary Works

All the Talents in Ireland: a satirical poem (Dublin, 1807).

Almon, J., *Biographical Anecdotes*, 3 vols, London, 1797.

Barrington, Sir Jonah, *Historic Memoirs of Ireland ...*, 2nd edn, 2 vols, London, 1809-1833.

Barrington, Sir Jonah, *Personal Sketches of His Own Times*, 3 vols, London, 1827-32.

Bentham, Jeremy, *Works*, ed. J. Bowring, 11 vols, 1838-43.

Boyd, Hugh, *The Miscellaneous Works of Hugh Boyd ... with an account of his life and writings*, by Lawrence Douglas Campbell [with a portrait], 2 vols, London, 1800.

Catholic Committee, *Proceedings of the Catholic Committee as taken from accredited papers*, Dublin, 1811.

The Irish Catholic petition of 1805: the diary of Denys Scully, ed. B. MacDermot, Dublin, 1992.

Sources

The Irish Catholic question in Ireland and England 1798-1822: the papers of Denys Scully, ed. B. MacDermot, Dublin 1988.

Caulfeild, E. of Charlemont, *Memoirs of the political and private life of John Caulfeild, E. of Charlemont*, by F. Hardy, 1810.

[Clayton, R.], *Heads of a scheme for applying part of the increased rents of Erasmus Smith's lands to the use of the College*, nd., copy in N.L.I.

Campbell, Sir Neil, *Napoleon at Fontainbleu and Elba ...*, 1869.

Carr, Sir John, *The Stranger in Ireland ... in the year 1805*, London, 1806.

[Drennan, W.], *A Letter to the Rt Hon. Charles James Fox*, 2nd edn, Dublin, 1806.

Dobbs, F., *A History of Irish Affairs from the 12th of October 1779, to the 15th September, 1782*, Dublin, 1782.

Fox, Charles James, *The Speeches of the Rt Hon. Charles James Fox in the House of Commons*, 6 vols, London, 1815.

Grattan, J., *A Letter to the Gentry, Clergy, Freemen and Freeholders of the City of Dublin*, Dublin, 1753; *Second Letter*, Dublin, 1758.

[Grattan, J.], *Random Collections of the House of Commons*, 5th edn, 2 vols, 1837.

Grattan righted in a letter from Tim O'Dougherty to his brother Terence, Dublin, 1818.

Grattan, *The letters of Timoleon; and the answer thereto by an Irish whig ... on the late parliamentary conduct of the Rt Hon. Henry Grattan*, Kilkenny, 1807.

Hamilton, W.G., *Parliamentary Logick ...* [with a biographical preface by E. Malone], 1808.

Horner, Francis, *Memoirs and Correspondence*, 2 vols, London, 1843.

Leland, T., *A dissertation on the Principles of Human Eloquence*, 2nd edn, Dublin, 1765.

Lucas, C., *Seasonable Advice to the Electors of Members of Parliament at the ensuing General Election ...*, Dublin, 1760.

Mackintosh, Sir James, *Memoirs of the Life of the Rt Hon. Sir James Mackintosh*, ed. R.L. Mackintosh, 2 vols, 1835.

Marlay, T., *The Charge of the Rt Hon. T. Marlay Esq ... to the Grand Juries of Dublin ... 6 Nov. 1749*, Dublin, 1749.

Marlay Letters, 1778-1820, ed. R.W. Bond, 1937.

Milner, J., *Six Letters on the subject of Dr Milner's Explanation ... by A.B.*, 1809.

Nichols, J., *Illustrations of the Literary History of the Eighteenth Century ...*, 8 vols, London, 1817-58.

Pitt, William, *The Speeches of ... the Earl of Chatham ... with a biographical memoir...*, 1848.

Rogers, S., *Recollections of the Table Talk of Samuel Rogers* [ed. A. Dyce] *to which is added Porsoniana* [by W. Maltby], 1856.

Romilly, Sir Samuel, *Memoirs of the life of..., written by himself; with a selection from his correspondence; edited by his sons*, 3 vols, London, 1840.

[Scott, J.B.], *A view of the present state of Ireland ... to which is added sketches of the principal characters in the Irish House of Commons*, by Falkland, Dublin, 1789.

A Short Enquiry into the present alarming dearth of coals ... Dublin, 1800.

Simond, L., *Journal of a Tour and residence in Great Britain ...*, 2 vols, Edinburgh, 1815.

Whig Club, *A Petition of the Whig Club to the King*, Dublin, 1798.

Wilberforce, W., *A Practical view of the prevailing religious systems of professed Christians in the higher and middle classes of this country, contrasted with real Christianity*, London, 1798.

Wraxhall, Sir Nathaniel William, *Historical and Posthumous Memoirs of Sir N.W. Wraxhall, 1772-1784 ...*, ed. H.B Wheatley, 5 vols, London, 1884.

Sources

Newspapers and Magazines

Dublin Evening Mail
Dublin Evening Post [D.E.P.]
Dublin University Magazine
Edinburgh Review
Faulkner's Dublin Journal
Freeman's Journal
Gentleman's Magazine
Hibernian Journal
Irish Magazine
Irish Times
Morning Chronicle
Morning Herald
Northern Star
Notes and Queries
The Press
Public Advertiser
Pue's Occurrences
Saunder's Newsletter
The Times
True Briton
Weekly Political Register

SECONDARY WORKS

Ball, F.E., 'Some notes on the judges in Ireland in the year 1739', *J.R.S.A.I.*, xxxiv, 1-19.

Ball, F.E., *The Judges in Ireland*, 2 vols, 1927.

Ball, W.B.W., *The Ball family records*, York, 1908.

Bolton, G.C., *The passing of the Act of Union: a study in parliamentary politics*, Oxford, 1966.

Byron, Lord, *The Works, Letters and Journals of Lord Byron*, ed. Rowland E. Prothero, 6 vols, 1898-1901.

Catalogue of the Library of the Rt Hon. Henry Grattan, Dublin, 1888.

Davis, T., *Essays literary and historical*, ed. D.J. O'Donaghue, Dundalk, 1914.

Derry, J.W., *The Regency Crisis and the Whigs, 1788-9*, Cambridge, 1963.

Derry, J.W., *Politics in the age of Pitt, Fox and Liverpool*, London, 1990.

Duffy, Sir Charles Gavan, *My Life in Two Hemispheres*, 2 vols, 1898.

Ehrman, J., *The Younger Pitt*, 3 vols, London, 1969-96.

Froude, J.A., *History of England from the Fall of Wolsey to the defeat of the Armada*, 12 vols, London, 1872-5.

Froude, J.A., *The English in Ireland in the Eighteenth Century*, 3 vols, London, 1881.

[Grant, J.], *Random Collections of the House of Commons*, 5th edn, 2 vols, 1837.

Gwynn, S.L., *Experiences of a Literary Man*, London, 1926.

Hill, J. *From patriots to unionists: Dublin civic politics and Irish protestant patriotism, 1660-1840*, Oxford, 1997.

Johnston, E.M., *Great Britain and Ireland, 1760-1800*, Edinburgh, 1963.

Sources

Jupp, P., *Lord Grenville 1759-1834*, Oxford, 1985.

Jupp, P., 'Earl Temple's Viceroyalty and the question of remuneration, 1782-3', *I.H.S.*, xvii, 499-520.

Kavanagh, A.C., *John Fitzgibbon, Earl of Clare*, Dublin, 1997.

R. Koebner, 'The early speeches of Henry Grattan' in *Bull IHR*, xx, 102-14.

Kelly, J., *Henry Flood: patriots and politicians in eighteenth-century Ireland*, Dublin, 1998.

D. Lammey, 'The growth of the "Patriot opposition" in Ireland during the 1770s', in *Parliamentary History*, vii, 257-81.

Lecky, W.E.H., *A History of Ireland in the Eighteenth Century*, 5 vols, London, 1892.

Lecky, E., *Memoirs of the Rt Hon. W.E.H. Lecky*, 1909.

Leslie, J.B., *Derry Clergy and Parishes*, Enniskillen, 1937.

Leslie, J.B., *Armagh Clergy and Parishes ...*, Dundalk, 1911.

Lever, C.J., *Cornelius O'Dowd upon Men and Women*, 2 series, 1865.

Lynch, P. and Vaisey, J.E., *Guinness's Brewery in the Irish Economy 1759-1876*, Cambridge, 1966.

McCartney, D., 'Lecky's *Leaders of Public Opinion in Ireland*', *I.H.S.*, xiv, 119-41.

D. McCarthy, *W.E.H. Lecky*, Dublin, 1994.

W.S. McCormick, 'Vision and revision in the study of eighteenth-century Irish parliamentary rhetoric', in *Eighteenth-century Ireland*, ii, 149-66.

Malcomson, A., *John Foster: the politics of the Irish Ascendancy*, Oxford, 1978.

Milner, J., *Life of the Rt Rev. John Milner*, by F.C. Husenbeth, Dublin, 1862.

McDowell, R.B., 'The Fitzwilliam Episode', *I.HS.*, xvi, 115-30.

O'Brien, Gerard. 'The Grattan mystique', in *Eighteenth-Century Ireland*, i, 176-94.

G. O'Brien, *Anglo-Irish politics in the age of Grattan and Pitt*, 1987.

O'Connell, D. *Personal Recollections of the late Daniel O'Connell*, ed. W.J. O'N Daunt, 2 vols, 1848.

Pitt, Wm., *Life of the Rt Hon. William Pitt, Earl Stanhope*, by Philip Henry Stanhope, 5th Earl Stanhope, 4 vols, 1861-2.

Russell, Earl, *Recollections and Suggestions*, 1875.

Roberts, M., *The Whig Party, 1807-12*, London, 1939.

Stanhope, Earl, *The Life of Charles Stanhope, 3rd E. Stanhope*, ed. G.P. Gooch, 1914.

Strickland, W.G., *A Dictionary of Irish Artists...*, 2 vols, Dublin and London, 1913.

Smith, E.A., *Whig principles and party politics: Earl Fitzwilliam and the Whig Party 1748-1833*, Manchester, 1975.

Swanzy, H.B., 'Militia Commissions for the County of Cavan', *Notes and Queries*, cxlvi, 465.

Walker, H.M., *A History of the Northumberland Fusiliers*, London, 1919.

Wilkinson, D., 'The Fitzwilliam episode, 1795; a reinterpretation of the role of the duke of Portland', in *I.H.S.* xxix, 315-39.

Index

266

Index

Index